IMAGES
of America

KENTUCKY'S PACKHORSE LIBRARIANS

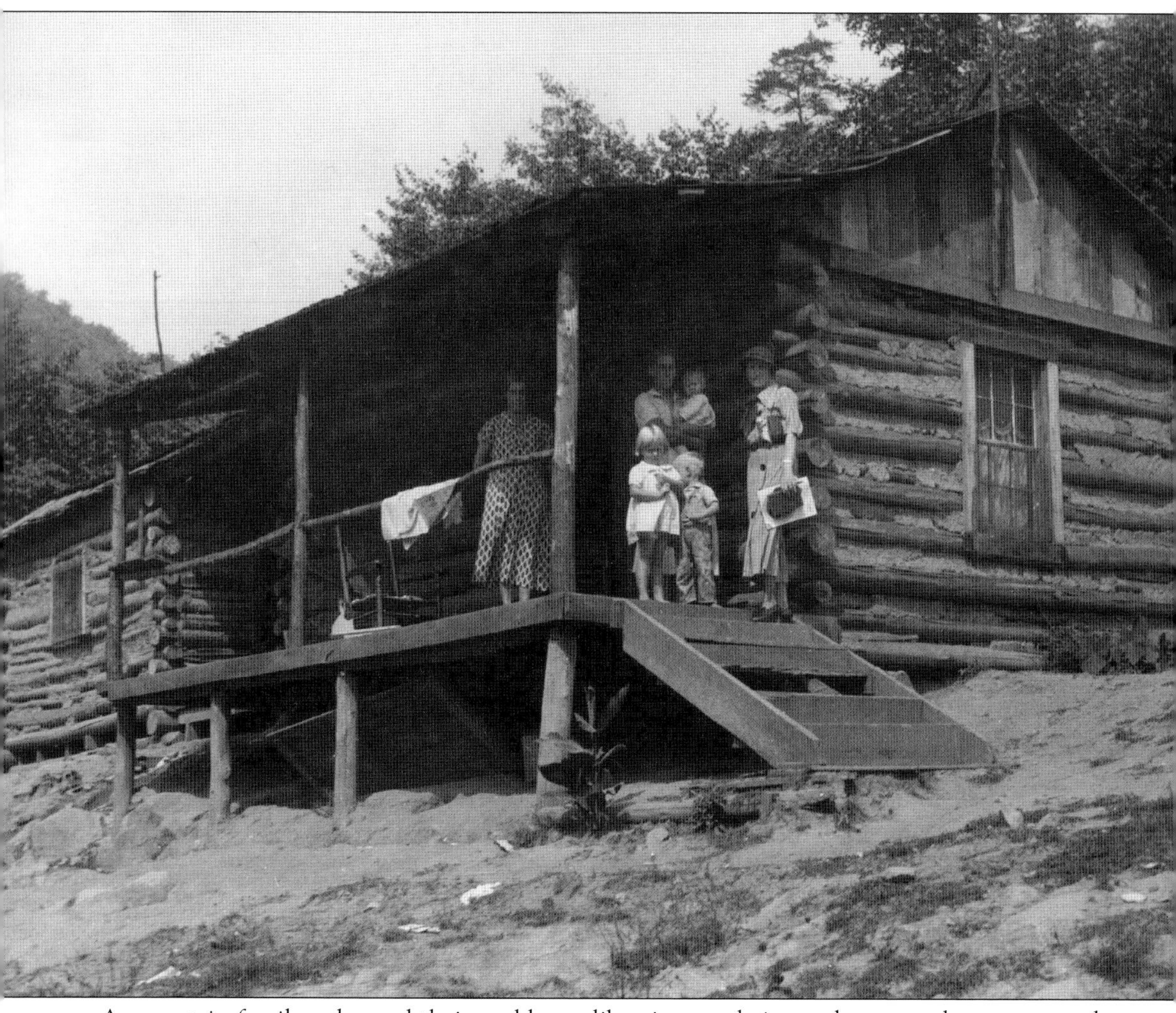

A mountain family welcomed their packhorse librarian on their porch to see what treasures she brought this visit. Packhorse librarians worked three to four days a week and traveled a different section of their route each day. Patrons could count on a delivery every two weeks. (Courtesy of WPA collection, Archives and Records Management Division, Kentucky Department for Libraries and Archives.)

On the Cover: Packhorse librarians delivered hope, one book at a time. Literature was not the only thing they brought to patrons. They taught reading lessons, read stories aloud, passed news on to others, and offered a friendly smile. (Courtesy of WPA collection, Archives and Records Management Division, Kentucky Department for Libraries and Archives.)

IMAGES
of America

KENTUCKY'S PACKHORSE LIBRARIANS

Nicki Jacobsmeyer

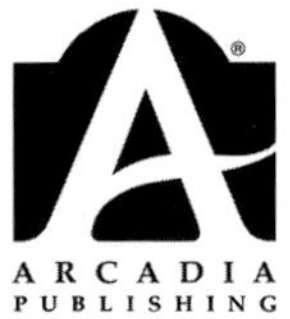

ISBN 978-1-4671-6218-0

Published by Arcadia Publishing
Charleston, South Carolina

Printed in the United States of America

Library of Congress Control Number: 2024944064

For all general information, please contact Arcadia Publishing:
Telephone 843-853-2070
Fax 843-853-0044
E-mail sales@arcadiapublishing.com

Visit us on the Internet at www.arcadiapublishing.com

To librarians everywhere–past, present, and future

Contents

Acknowledgments

While I strived to include as many historical facts and photographs as possible, the real experts are the many Kentuckians and scholars whose support and generosity made this book possible. A huge thank you to the following for sharing their time, knowledge, and photographs: Patty Reeves and the Johnson County Public Library; Robin Smith and Heath Reynolds of the Kentucky Department of Librarians and Archives; Sarah Insalaco of the Hindman Settlement School; Tim Binkley, Caitlyn Rahschulte, and Lori Myers-Steele of Berea College; Dieter C. Ullrich of Morehead State University; Kaira L. Tucker, Vanessa Coleman, and Carissa Miller of Louisville Public Library; Jeff Urbin and Kirsten Carter of Roosevelt Presidential Library and Museum; and to all the welcoming faces during my time in Kentucky while researching for this book. The passion for your home and community is evident in all you do.

I would like to thank Jason Vance and his talent for capturing the heart and soul of the packhorse librarians' scrapbooks through his photographs. Understanding the bond between horse and rider would not have been possible without the guidance and encouragement of horse trainer and friend Christine Watts-Wright. Thank you for taking a chance on me. To Wright Equestrian, thank you for welcoming me into your barn family and inspiring others. You all share the same grace and grit as the packhorse librarians.

Thank you to my devoted critique group, Jill Burkemper, Chris Schmidt, and Jess Townes, for encouraging me to persevere. To my fearless Way-Word Writers partners, Stephanie Bearce and Heather Cashman, I am grateful for your mentorship and friendship through this journey.

I would like to thank my editor, Caroline Vickerson, for her enthusiasm and guidance throughout this process. Thank you to my mother and sister who have always been my biggest cheerleaders. I also want to thank God for His matchless grace.

Last but not least, thank you to the three most important people in my life. To my sons, Andrew and Caleb, thank you for your laughter and support; they keep me going. To my husband and best friend, Ryan, thank you for holding my hand as I chase my dream.

INTRODUCTION

The state of Kentucky has always been rich in its history and traditions. If you follow the creek beds and mountain paths, you discover homes in the hollers of the beautiful Appalachian Mountains. It is here, in southeastern Kentucky, where the kinship and rural communities persevered through generations.

During the early 1900s, mountain folks worked hard in the coal mines, on the farms, and in their homes. Every member of the family had a job to do, and they relied on one another to do their part. Since they were self-reliant, they learned how to be resourceful and improve mountain living. The day left little time for leisure, which included books and reading. In the 1930s, illiteracy rates were as high as 35 percent and even higher in rural areas. Not knowing how to read was not for a lack of desire, but a lack of resources. Organizations strived to help improve those circumstances. The Kentucky Federation of Women's Club established in-home reading clubs, but they did not survive long due to the time needed to harvest and preserve crops. Traveling libraries began through Berea College Extension Library in Berea, Kentucky, which loaned out books in movable wooden cases and then with book wagons visiting homes in rural areas. Families traveled to the road in order to get their hands on the books. The Hindman Settlement School in Hindman, Kentucky, had a traveling library for the school, town, and surrounding area. In 1933, when the state's programs ended, books were not accessible to the counties.

The stock market crash in 1929 ushered in the Great Depression. People lost their money and jobs all across the country. Kentuckians felt the pressure as their main resource, coal mining, became unstable. Mines and factories closed down, leaving men without jobs. The Ohio River floods of 1930 and 1937 devastated farmlands across the state. Folks were hungry and homeless. They craved a solution. The solution came in the form of Pres. Franklin D. Roosevelt and the New Deal. Roosevelt's programs, like the Works Progress Administration (WPA), helped people find work and get out of the Depression. Harry Hopkins, a trusted representative to Roosevelt, supervised the WPA and other relief programs. Assisting Hopkins with the WPA was Ellen Woodward, a Mississippi state legislator. Also, First Lady Eleanor Roosevelt was always seeking to advance opportunities for women.

In 1935, the WPA Packhorse Library Project started and delivered hope on horseback. The packhorse librarians originated in Paintsville, Kentucky, by May Stafford. Other places attempted to replicate the programs but none as successfully as southeastern Kentucky. The librarians were local women, and a few men, who were familiar with the community and knew the rugged territory. They needed to have excellent equestrian skills, be resilient to endure the grueling conditions, and the ability to read was a huge advantage.

Packhorse librarians across southeastern Kentucky delivered books and reading materials to homes and schools in isolated, rural areas. Some children had never checked out a book until the book women. The librarians visited their central library to fill their saddlebags with up to 100 books and then mount up to start their book route. Reading materials included books, newspapers, magazines, and homemade scrapbooks. One of the most requested books was the Bible, along with instructive literature and books by Mark Twain, Charles Dickens, and Shakespeare. Newspaper comics like *Dick Tracy* and *Little Orphan Annie* were a hit because there was not any trace of the Great Depression, only laughter. Librarians attempted to find their patron's favorites and enjoyed their requests. Carriers visited mountain homes twice a month and not only delivered books, but gave reading lessons, brought and passed on news, and read stories aloud. Teachers and students welcomed the sight of their packhorse librarian arriving in the schoolyard. Since the schools could not afford many textbooks, they supplemented with loaned reading material, which helped with class lessons and learning. Unfortunately, not all children went to school. Some were needed at home to work the farm or a job to make money for the family. Others did not have enough clothes or shoes in the household, so they either could not attend at all or had to take turns.

The Packhorse Library Project thrived on donations from schools, churches, clubs, philanthropists, academics, and individuals. Donations included books, magazines, readers, recipe collections, quilt patterns, and religious works. Once books and reading materials became damaged or worn, librarians created scrapbooks. Materials like binders, file folders, wallpaper, and cardboard were reused to construct these keepsakes. The pages included the remaining pieces of books, magazines, newspapers, pamphlets, drawings, and stories. The scrapbooks had different themes, including recipes, quilts, mountain ballads, Kentucky history, religion, animals, local flora, fashion, stories, and more. Patrons felt proud donating a quilt pattern or recipe to be displayed in the book. It was a treat seeing new additions to the circulating scrapbooks, which captured the culture of the community. More than 2,000 scrapbooks were created and donated by librarians and patrons during the Packhorse Library Project.

Packhorse librarians cherished their books, patrons, and routes. However, challenges occurred in different ways. The bookwomen and their mounts took the shortest course in order to visit all the people on their book route. Sometimes this meant traversing rocky and dangerous terrain, which was taxing on the rider and mount. Since roads were impassable due to the mountain or weather conditions, the creek beds became their highways. Depending on the time of year, the creeks could get high or freeze, causing endless issues. Although most were overjoyed to see their carrier, some did not trust their motives or the diverse reading materials offered. Books around the house caused distractions from work and chores, and some preferred they did not exist. Those who read in the evening after their work was completed needed to refill the oil lamp more frequently, which cost money they did not have.

In 1943, the Packhorse Library Project ended when the WPA stopped funding. The wartime economy was putting Americans back to work, so the projects tapered off. Many packhorse librarians returned to their family farms or became schoolteachers. By the end of the project, nearly 1,000 packhorse librarians had served 105 million patrons in 48 Kentucky counties. Not until the 1950s did these remote, rural communities have access to bookmobiles. The Library Service Act of 1956 added more than five million reading materials to rural libraries and put 200 new bookmobiles on the road. In 2014, Kentucky public libraries had 75 bookmobiles, which was the largest in the nation. Literacy continues to be cultivated and nurtured. During the Great Depression, the packhorse librarians delivered hope and a brighter future to the people of Kentucky, which can still be seen today.

One

Early Literacy Endeavors

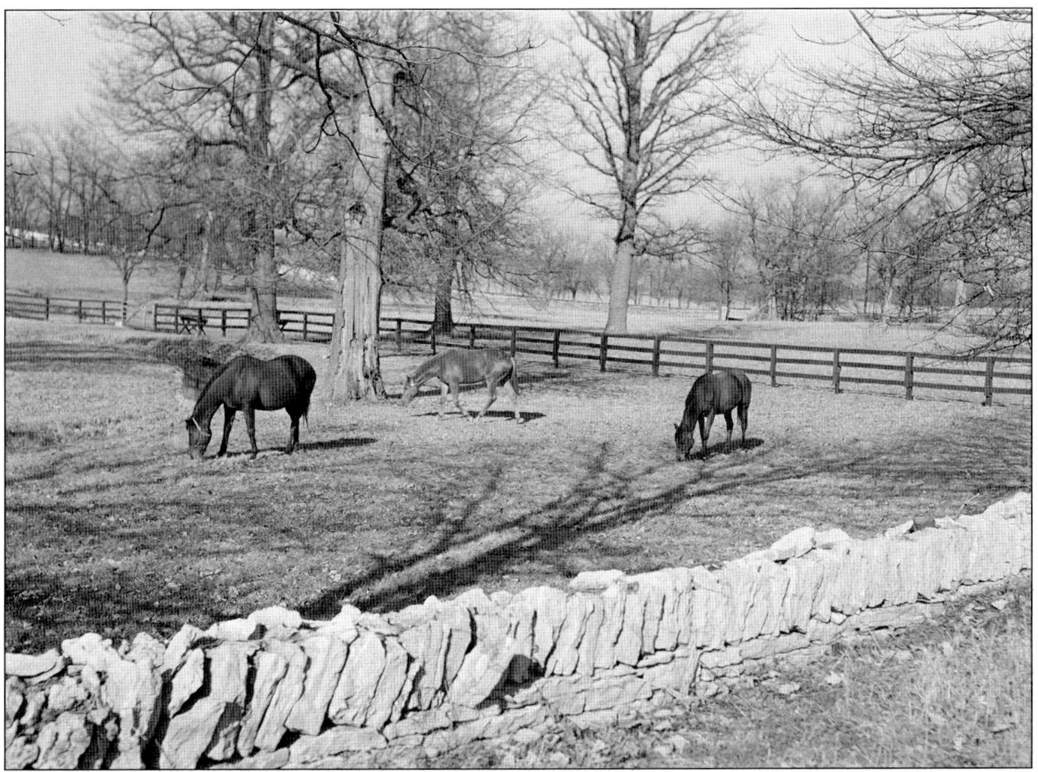

The Bluegrass State of Kentucky is not only known for horses, bourbon, and the lush bluish-purple pastures. Its rich cultural history and cherished traditions are reflected in the music, art, cuisine, and people. Kentuckians are proud of their home, offering a warm welcome and southern hospitality. (Courtesy of the Library of Congress.)

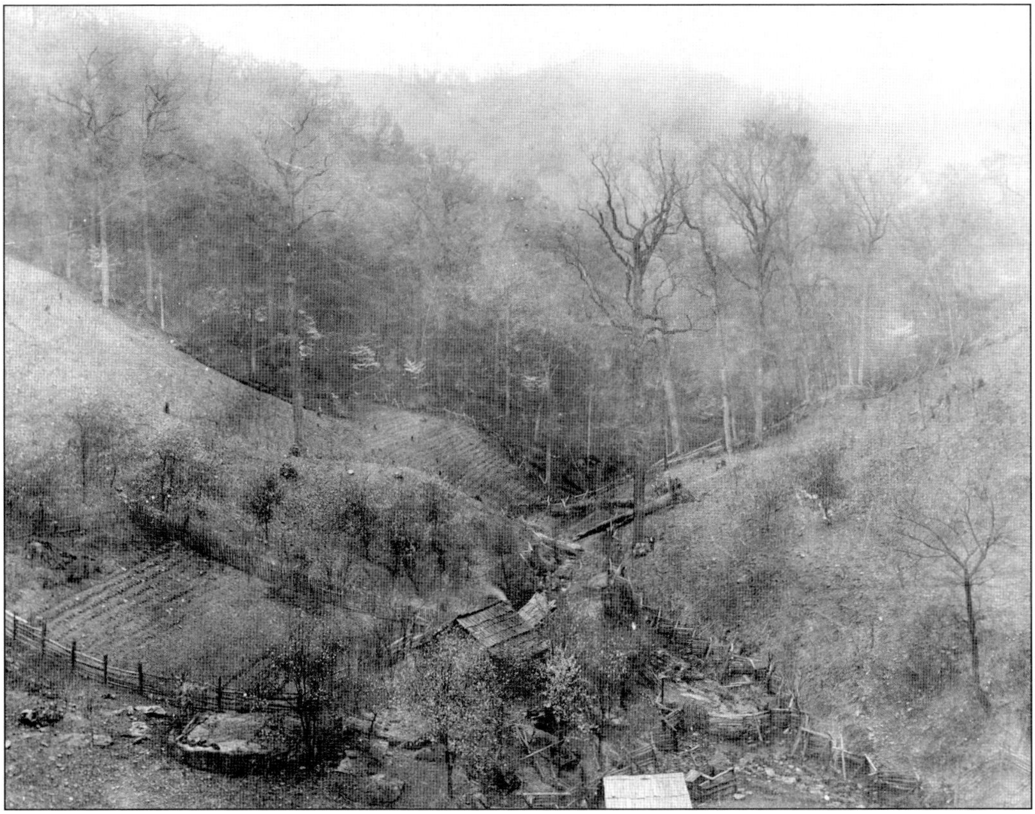

In the early years, people followed creek beds and mountain paths to their home in the hollows or "hollers" of Kentucky's Appalachian Mountains. A holler is a narrow, secluded valley between two mountains. The creek beds were the roads through these rural towns. Within these hills, families came together to form close-knit communities who were deeply connected to their roots. These communities have thrived for generations by passing down their traditions. In the past, their kinship wove a tapestry of perseverance and hope, which still continues today. (Above, courtesy of Mallie Cody Turner Collection [MS049-1993], Morehead State University Special Collections and Archives; below, courtesy of the Library of Congress.)

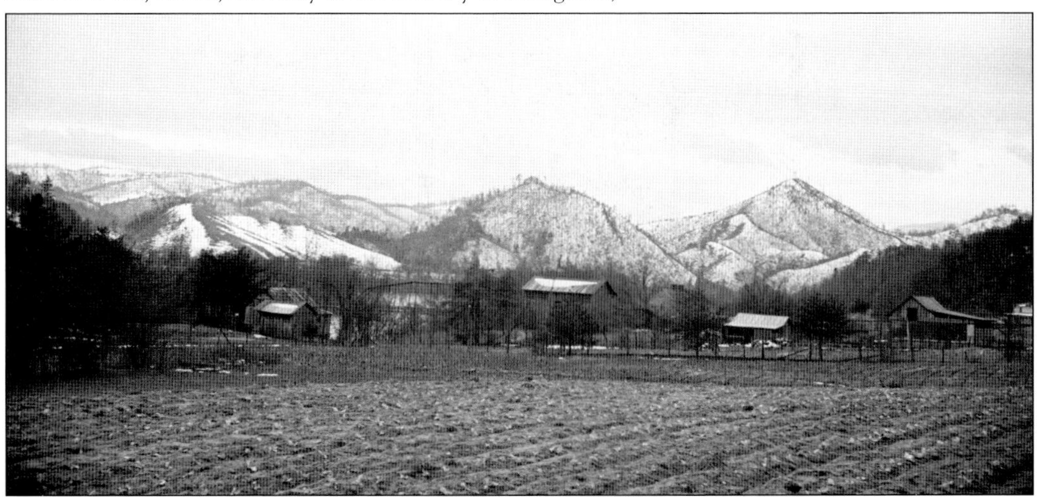

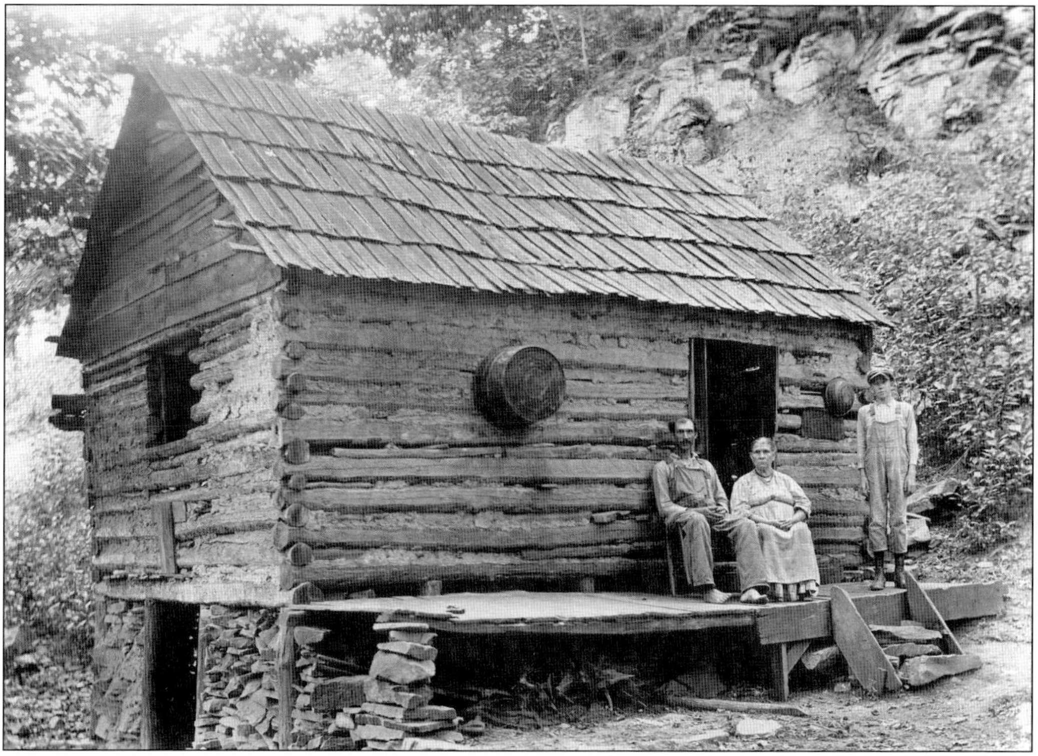

A rural family rested on the porch of their log home in the Cumberland Mountains, and the young and old shared a heartfelt moment. Rural people of Kentucky were self-reliant and diligent. Endless chores around the house combined with working on the farms, in mines, and in other jobs had folks working from sunup to sundown. Every member of the family, both young and old, participated in mountain living. Although breaks did not come often, they were precious. Since they did not have the luxury of time, learning had to have a practical benefit. People had to choose between learning how to survive and expanding their worldview. Longevity won, and a common view was that "all the world seemed foreign." (Both, courtesy of WPA collection, Archives and Records Management Division, Kentucky Department for Libraries and Archives.)

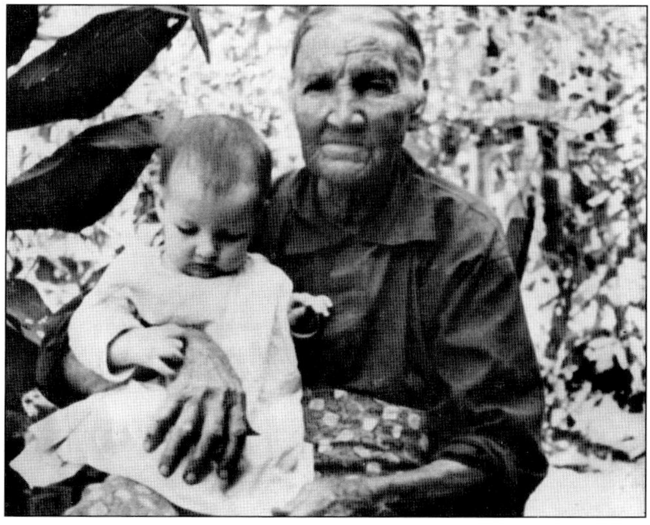

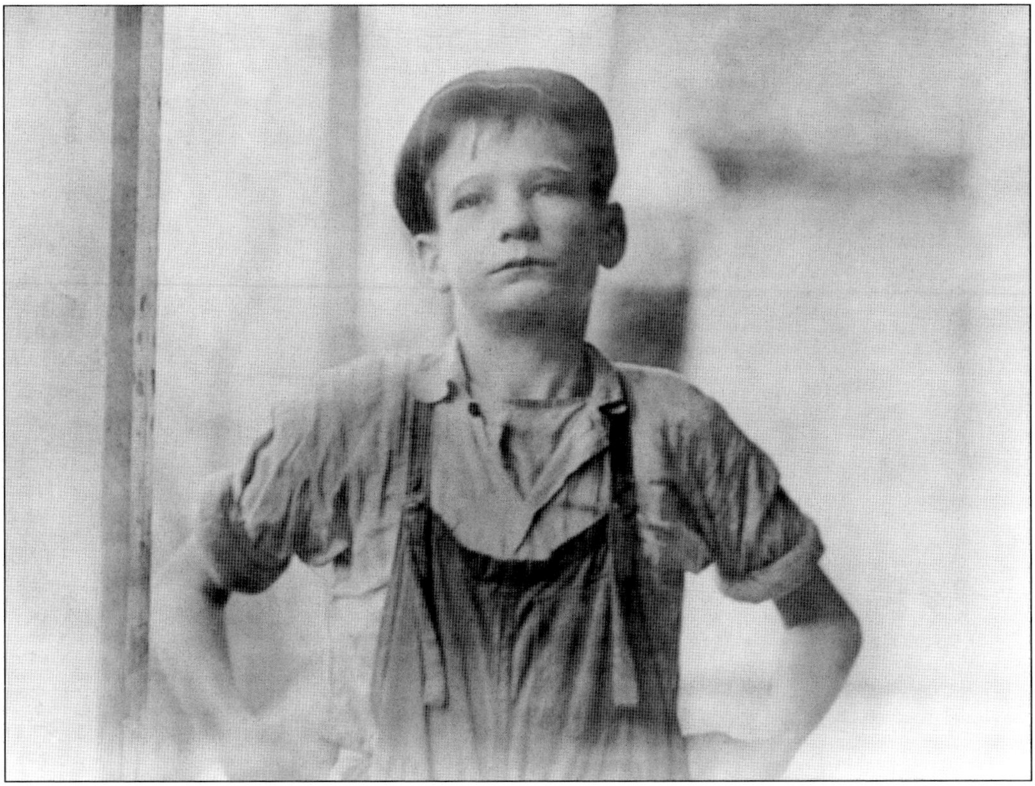

A 12-year-old boy cannot read and does not know the alphabet. "Yes, I want to learn but I can't when I work all the time." He had already been working in mills for seven years because his family needed the money. Some adults were illiterate also as they either never attended school or only for a short while. In 1930, illiteracy ranged from 19 to 31 percent. (Courtesy of the Library of Congress.)

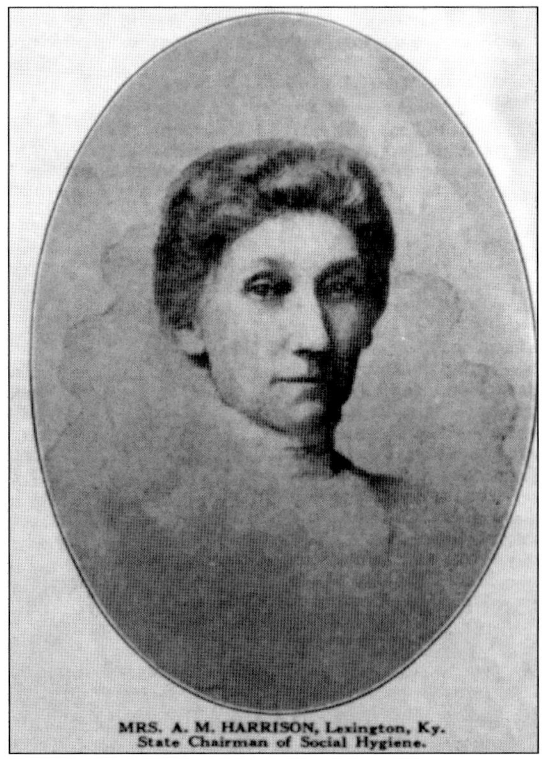

Ida Withers Harrison of Lexington, Kentucky, was named honorary president for life of the Kentucky Federation of Women's Clubs (FWC). As one of the early literacy efforts in June 1896, the Kentucky FWC established in-home reading clubs organized and led by the women of the household. (Courtesy of Wikimedia Commons.)

However, the women found with the planning and harvesting of crops and then the preserving and canning of food, they had little time to read. Unfortunately, most of the in-home reading clubs did not survive more than two years. In 1905, the Kentucky FWC's replacement program came in the form of traveling libraries. (Courtesy of the Library of Congress.)

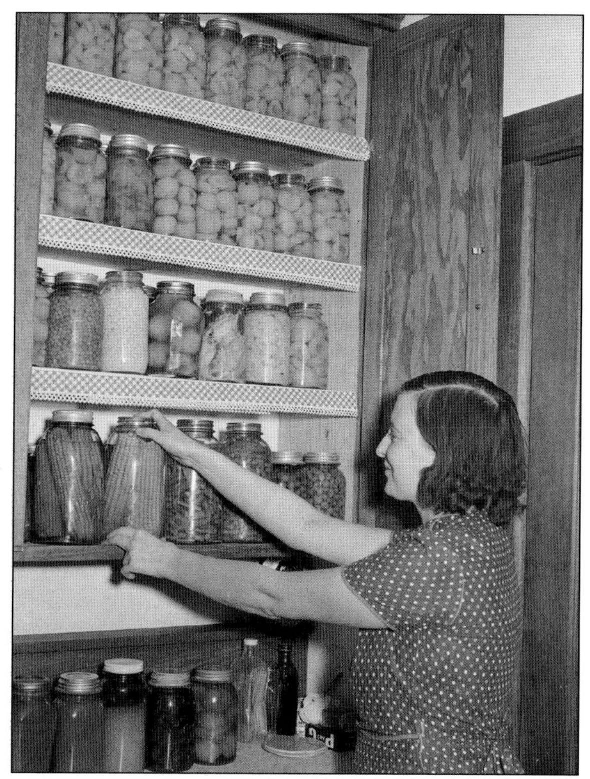

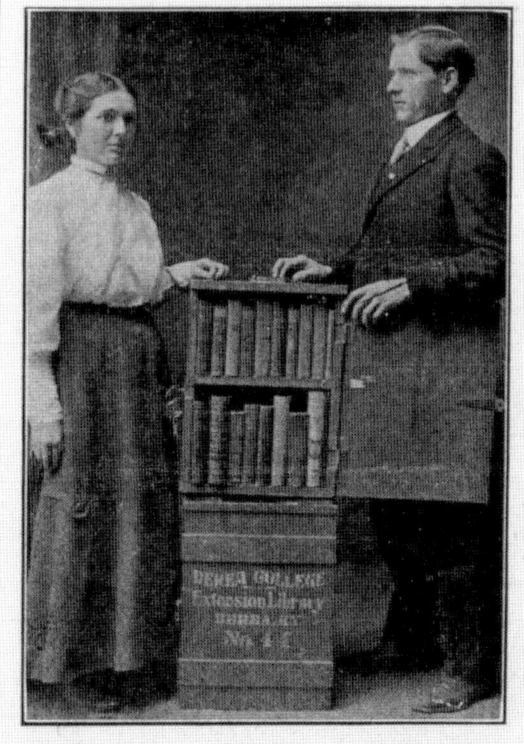

Around 1896, the Berea College Extension Library in Berea, Kentucky, sent out traveling libraries to loan out books, specifically for the mountain students. These traveling libraries were movable wooden cases containing 15–50 books and traveled by mule back, wagon, or train, whichever was most convenient for the borrower. (Courtesy of Berea College Special Collections and Archives.)

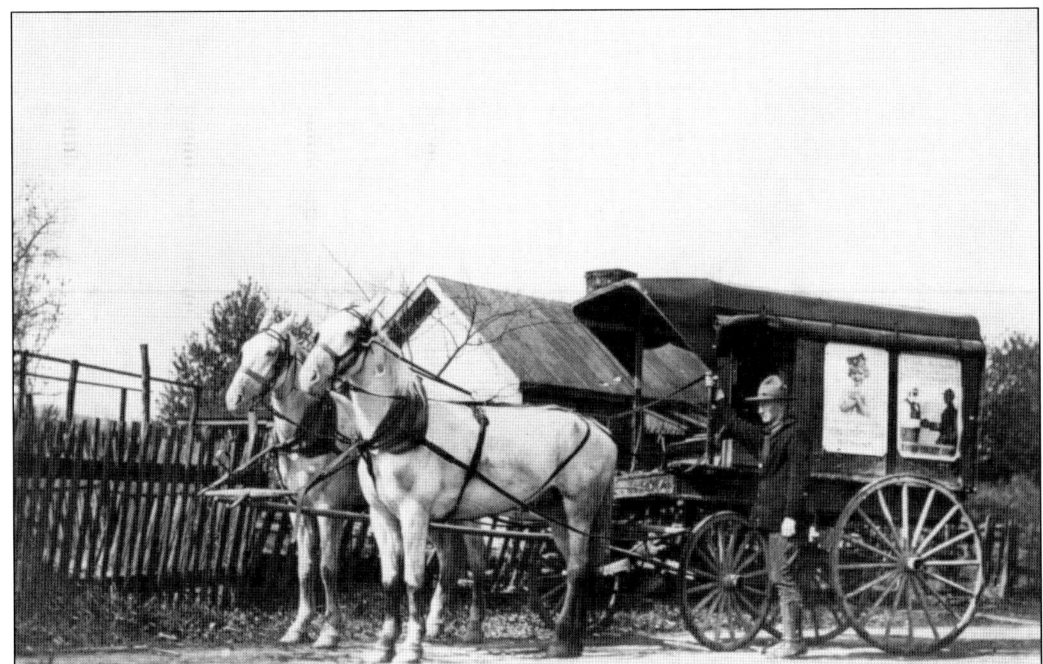

In the late 1910s and early 1920s, the Berea College Extension Library sent horse-drawn covered book wagons into rural mountain communities to bring them books. The college's book wagon, and eventually book cars, served the Appalachian region until the first Works Progress Administration (WPA) Packhorse Library was formed. (Courtesy of Berea College Special Collections and Archives.)

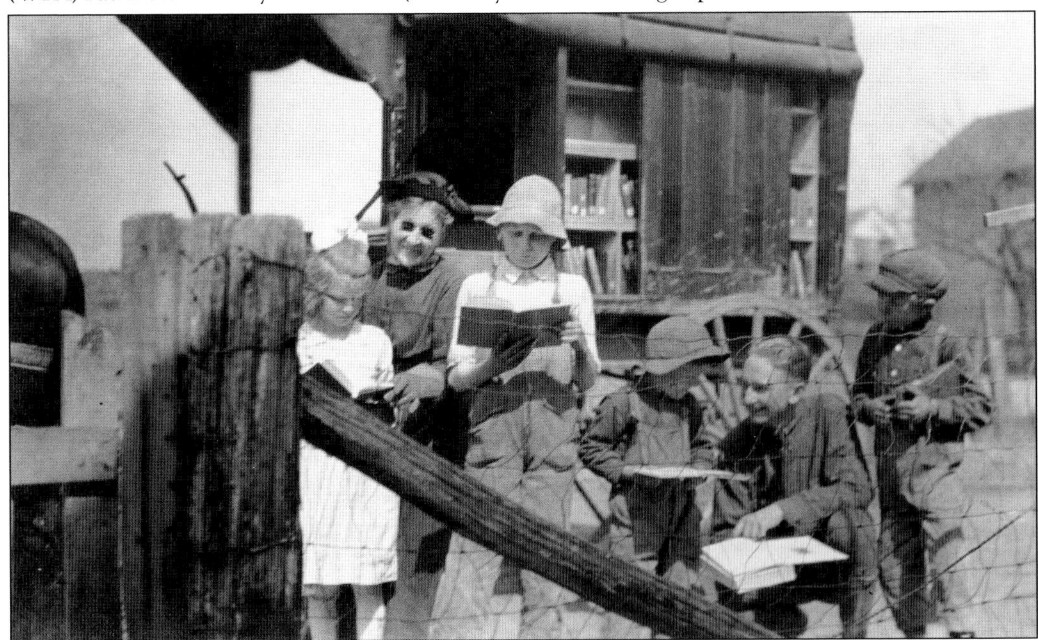

Children cherished the librarian's visit and thought the book wagon must be a relative of Santa Claus. One parent shared, "My little boy wants everything you've got about Daniel Boone. He is named after him." Another girl faithfully waited by the road for the book wagon regardless of the cold winds and brewing storm. (Courtesy of Berea College Special Collections and Archives.)

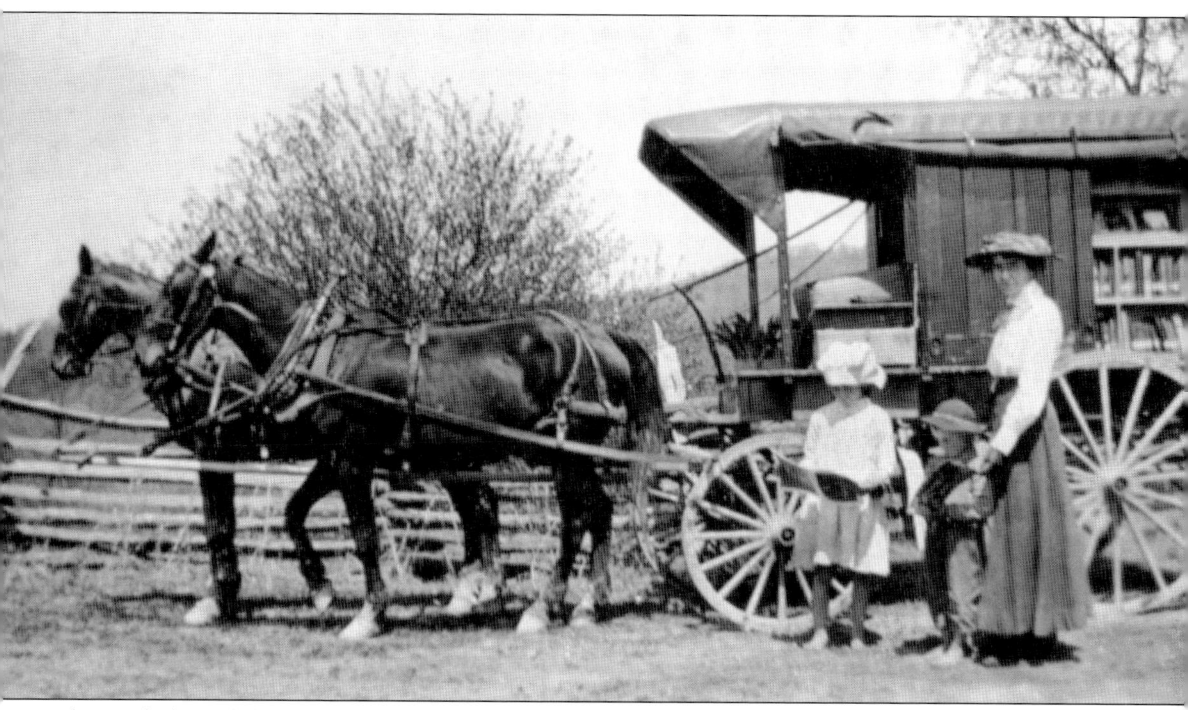

The Anderkim children decided which books to choose with the help of Mrs. Ridgeway, a Berea College Extension librarian during the college's first library program, c. 1915–1925. The Berea College book wagons had built-in shelves filled with books and were pulled by the college's farm horses, referred to as "beastes." Mules and ponies were also hired from various owners. This book wagon made its stop over the line where Rockcastle and Madison Counties meet in southeastern Kentucky. (Courtesy of Berea College Special Collections and Archives.)

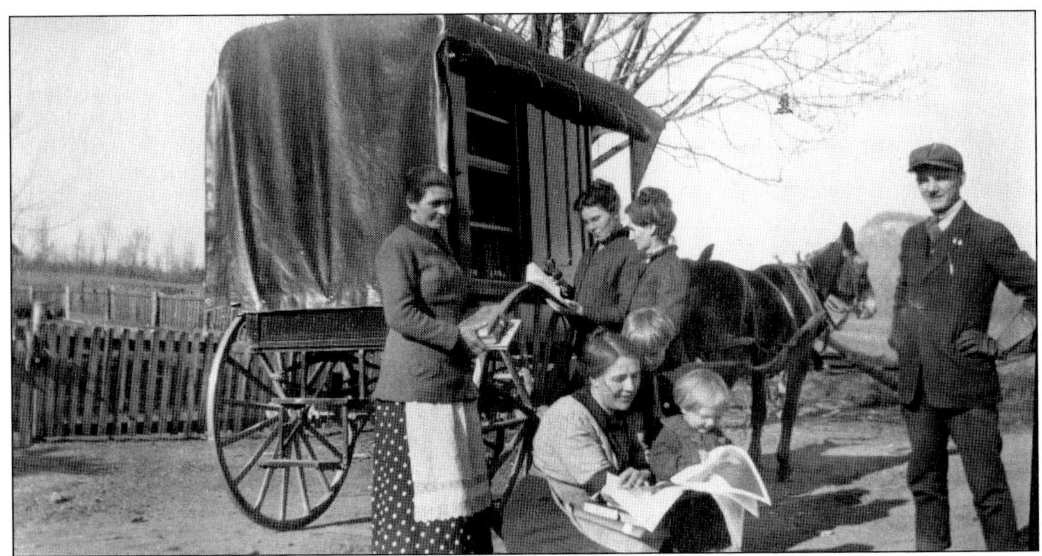

Hellen Ranson (center) was the fourth librarian hired in 1915 by Berea College in Berea, Kentucky. She gathered with neighbors on Big Hill Road and helped the women make book selections for themselves and their families while the student driver, Roy Bell (right), looked on. (Courtesy of Berea College Special Collections and Archives.)

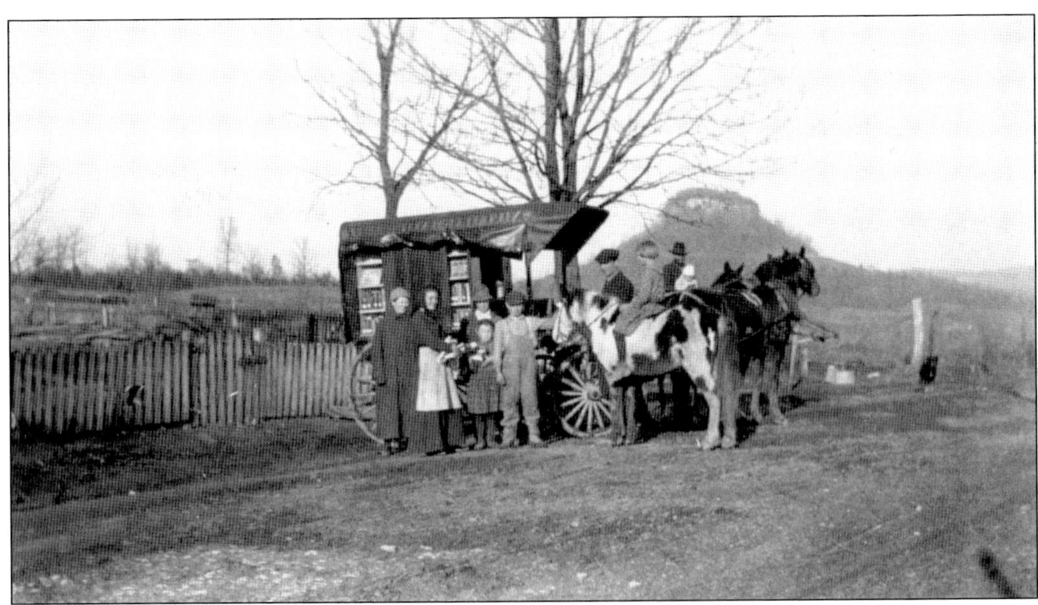

Four families met at the Berea College Extension Library book wagon, sometime between 1915 and 1925. People traveled up the hollows to meet the book wagon at their neighbor's house along the road. At one home, nine families were supplied books in a single stop. One woman shared her appreciation, "Your books help me to live better." (Courtesy of Berea College Special Collections and Archives.)

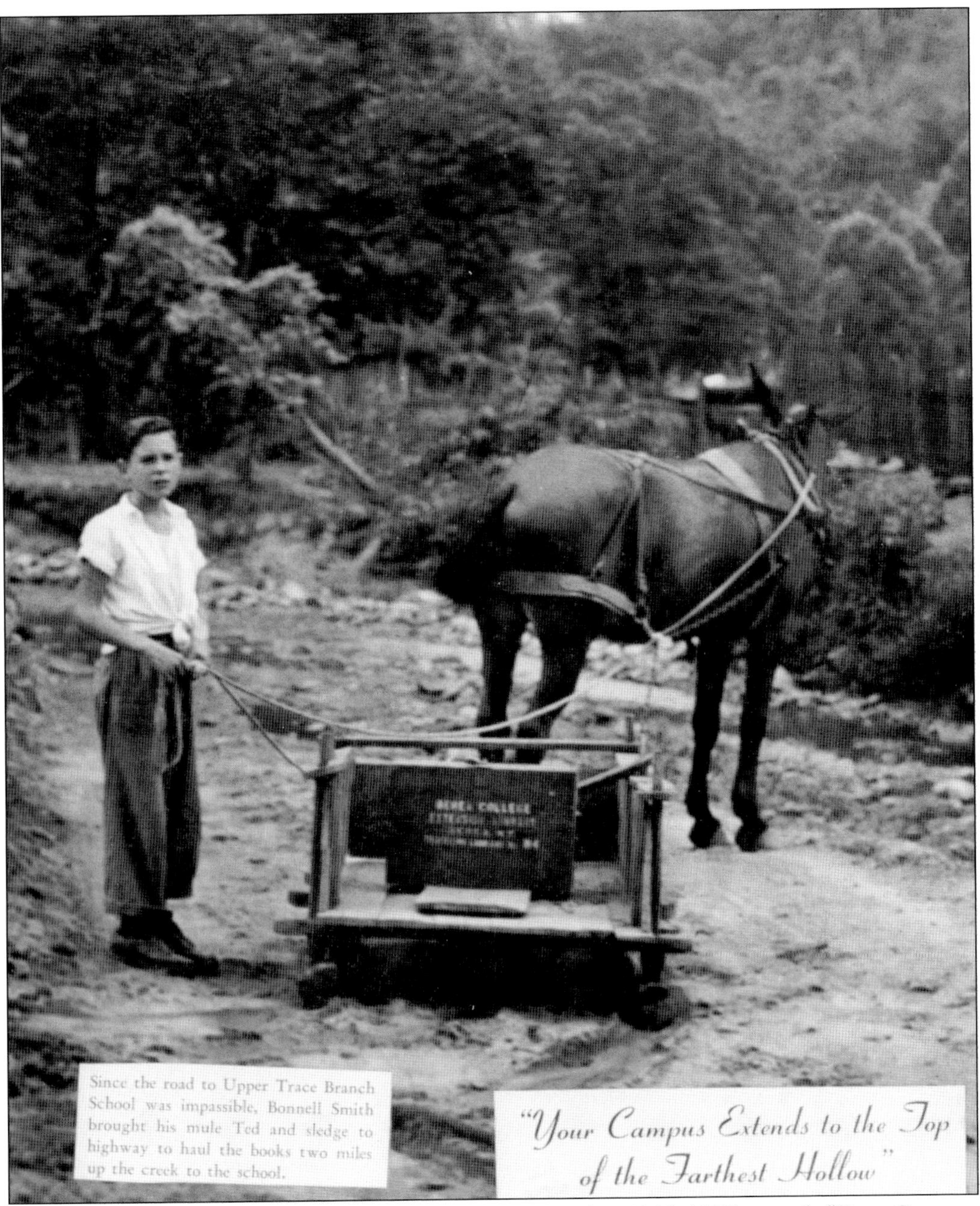

The Berea College Extension Library in Berea, Kentucky, 1915–1925, stated, "Your Campus Extends to the Top of the Farthest Hollow." Bonnell Smith brought his mule, Ted, and a sledge to the highway to haul books two miles up the creek to the Upper Trace Branch School since the road was impassable. In the fifth year of the extension library, delivering books home to home was discontinued so they could reach more schools. Trustworthy patrons were responsible for collections of books. This gave them opportunities to help others by delivering books instead of being recipients only. (Courtesy of Berea College Special Collections and Archives.)

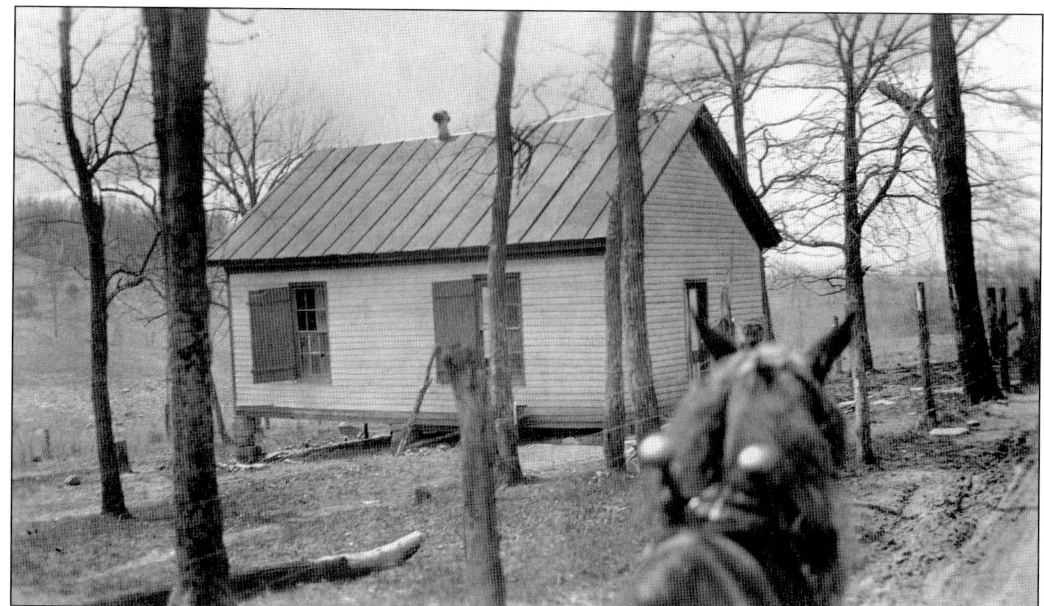

A schoolhouse came in view as the Berea College book wagon approached sometime between 1915 and 1925. For a period of three to four months in the winter, it was impossible to send children to school due to the weather and impassable roads. The college's book wagons attempted to visit homes during these months and to schools when they were in session. (Courtesy of Berea College Special Collections and Archives.)

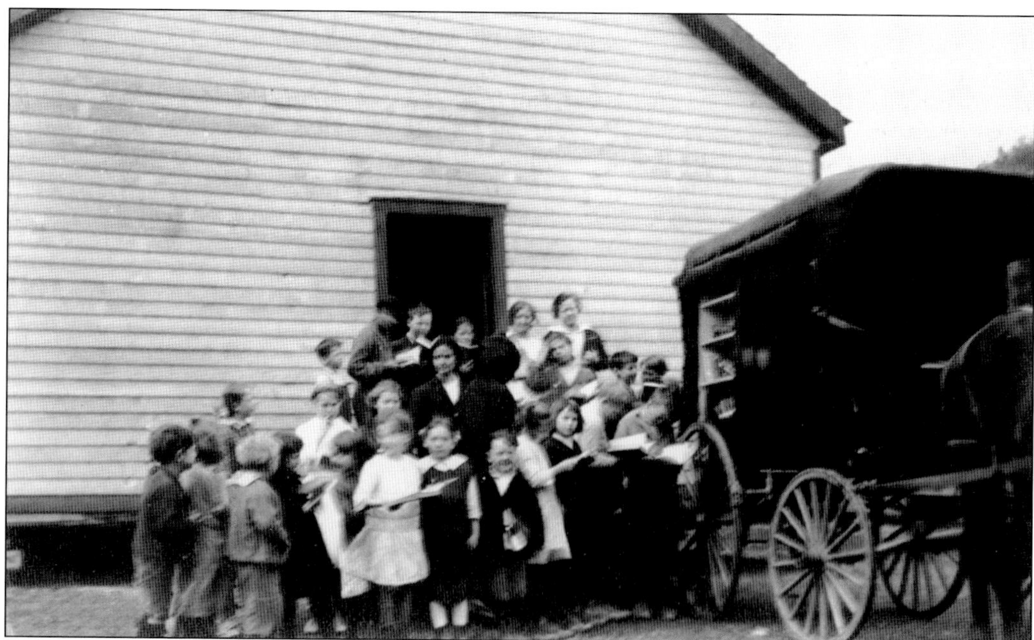

Librarian Mrs. Ridgway's head is wrapped to stay warm due to the high winds as she visited the schoolhouse. During 1919–1920, three routes totaling 19 trips were made serving 150 families and eight schools. An average trip cost $8–$9 to circulate approximately 126 volumes. Therefore, it cost 7¢ per month to loan out one book. (Courtesy of Berea College Special Collections and Archives.)

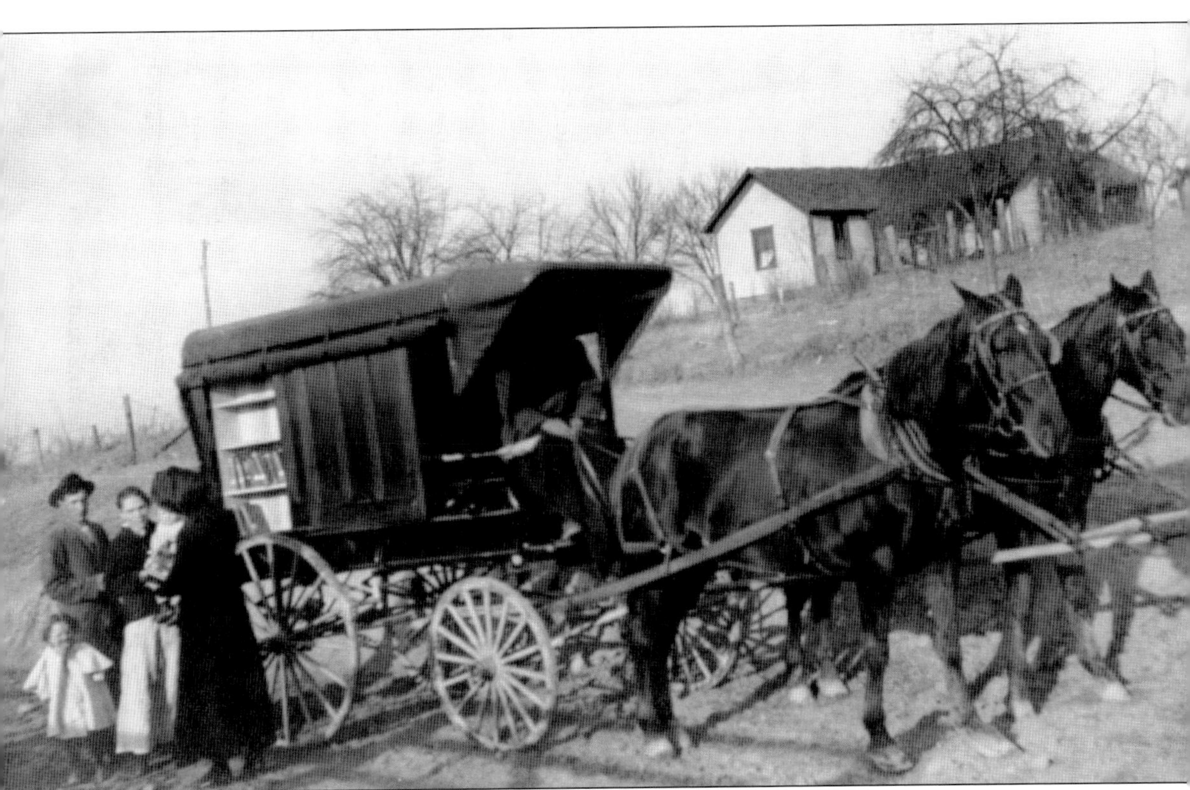

People shared their gratitude. "It's the nicest thing I know the way you folks haul around books for us to read," a patron declared with a sunshiny smile. Another stated, "I was proud to have them books to read when I couldn't get out anywhere when it was so cold." A mother of seven said, "You know what's good for 'em. Just fit 'em out, four to sixteen." One woman confessed, "My man never cared for readin' but all last winter I put a table by his chair before the fire and laid your books on it. He got in the way pickin' them up and now he likes to read." An elderly man commented, "Us folks ought to get mighty well eddicated along the road with the library wagon bringen us books." (Courtesy of Berea College Special Collections and Archives.)

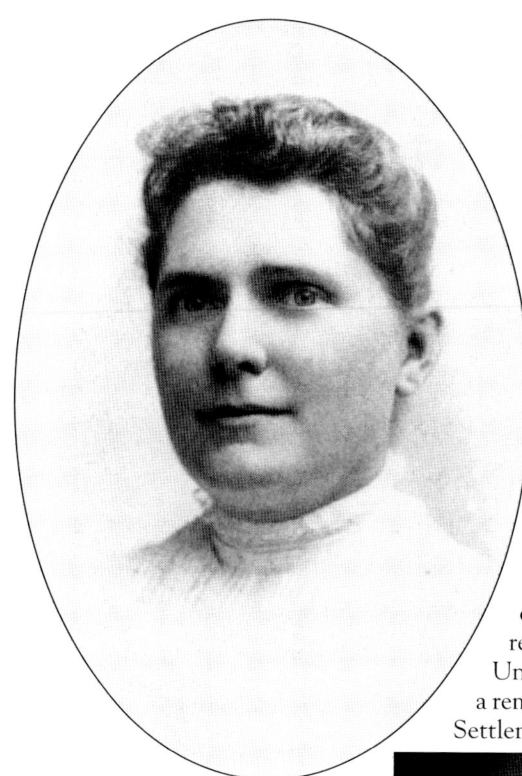

As the legend goes, Solomon Everidge was not able to read or write, and he desperately wanted literacy for his "greats" and "grands"—grandchildren and great-grandchildren—of Troublesome Creek in Hindman, Kentucky. Everidge walked 22 miles barefooted to the town of Hazard to get the educated women, Katherine Pettit (left) and May Stone (right), to come back with him to start the Hindman Settlement School and teach his descendants. Established in 1902, the Hindman Settlement School was the first rural social settlement school established in America. Pettit and Stone would refer to Everidge as Uncle Sol, the visionary founder. Uncle Sol's cabin still stands on the school's campus as a reminder of its roots. (Both, courtesy of the Hindman Settlement School.)

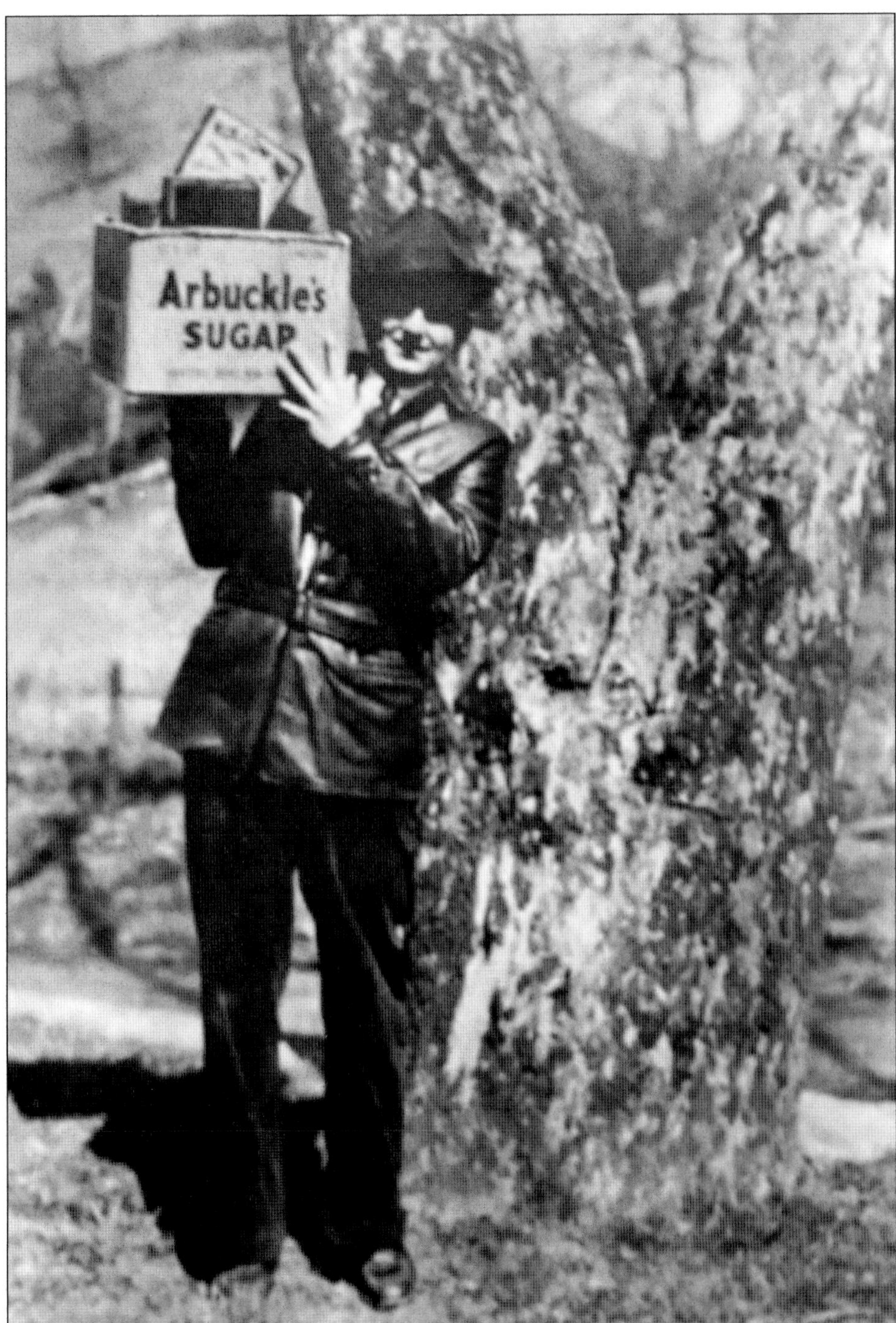

In 1931–1932, the first traveling library in Hindman, Kentucky, and the surrounding area was created. Librarian James Still carried books in an Arbuckle Sugar box in 1933. Still was a poet, novelist, short story writer, and folklorist who came to Hindman for a summer program in 1931 and returned in 1933 as the full-time librarian. He would wake early in the morning to take books to more isolated schools that did not have access to books like Hindman Settlement School. (Courtesy of the 1955 Bookmobile Project Collection of the Louisa St. Clair Archive, the Hindman Settlement School.)

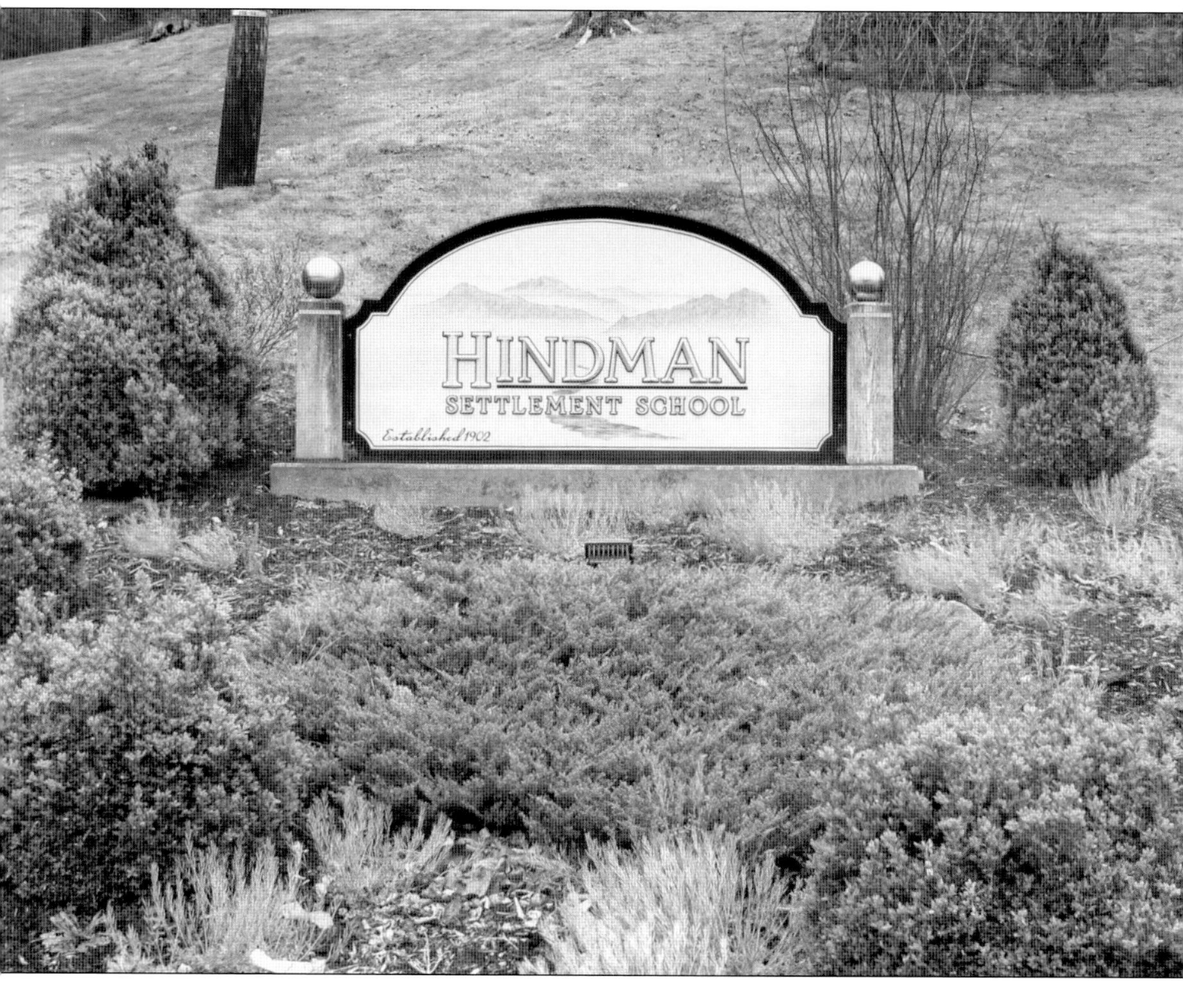

In 1933, the state's traveling library programs, like Berea College Extension Library and Hindman Settlement School, ended, and Kentucky counties had no access to library books until Pres. Franklin D. Roosevelt's administration and the Works Progress Administration under the New Deal. (Photograph by Nicki Jacobsmeyer; courtesy of Hindman Settlement School.)

Two

Cracking Hard Times

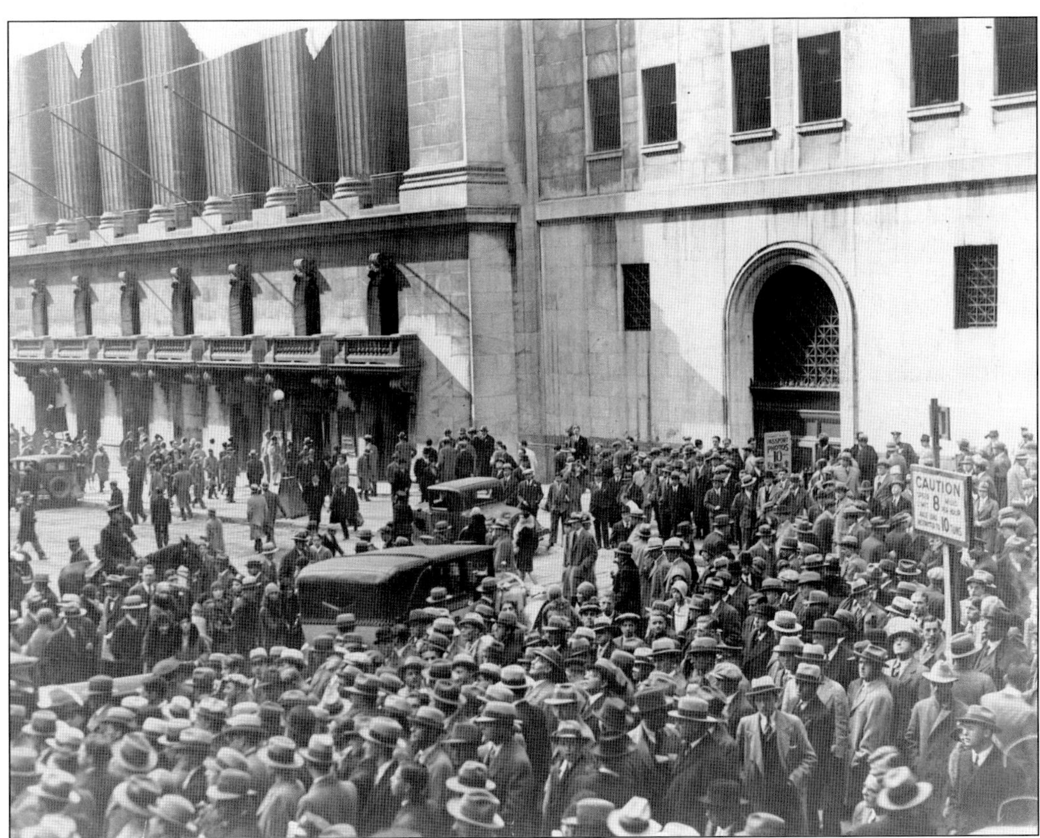

Eight months after Herbert Hoover was elected president, the world shifted. The stock market crash of 1929, also known as Black Tuesday, occurred on October 29, 1929, when Wall Street investors traded millions of shares on the New York Stock Exchange in a single day. The economy plummeted and contributed to the Great Depression of the 1930s. (Courtesy of the Library of Congress.)

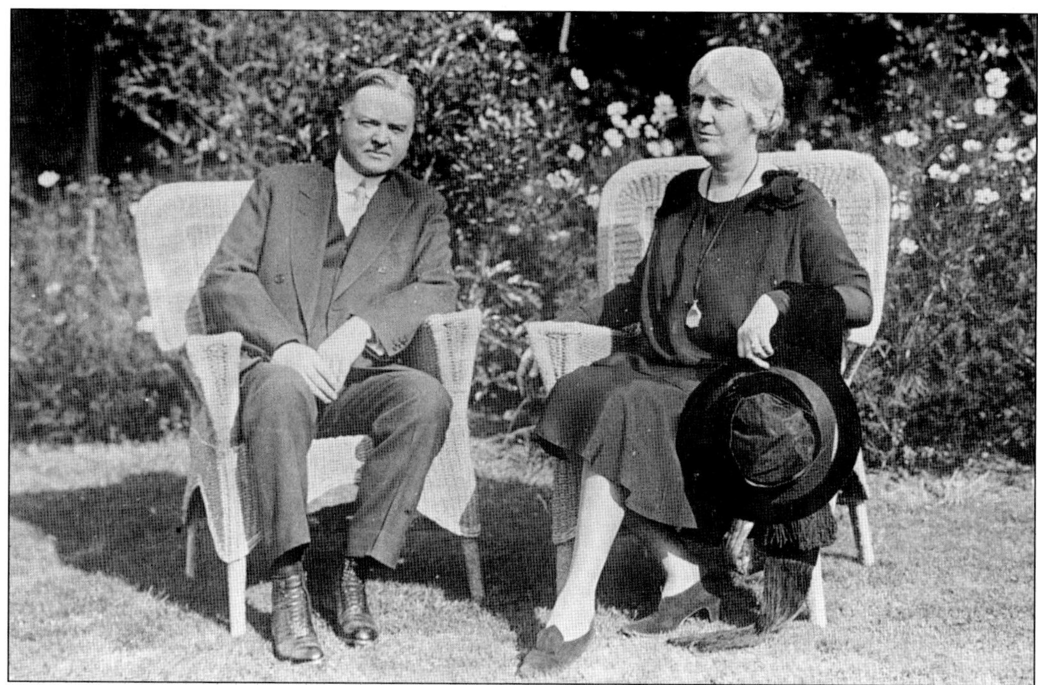

In President Hoover's campaign he said, "We in America today are nearer to the final triumph over poverty than ever before in the history of any land." Sadly, the stock market crashed soon after, and his plan to overcome the Great Depression did not prevail. Due to this outcome, he was not elected for another term. (Courtesy of the Library of Congress.)

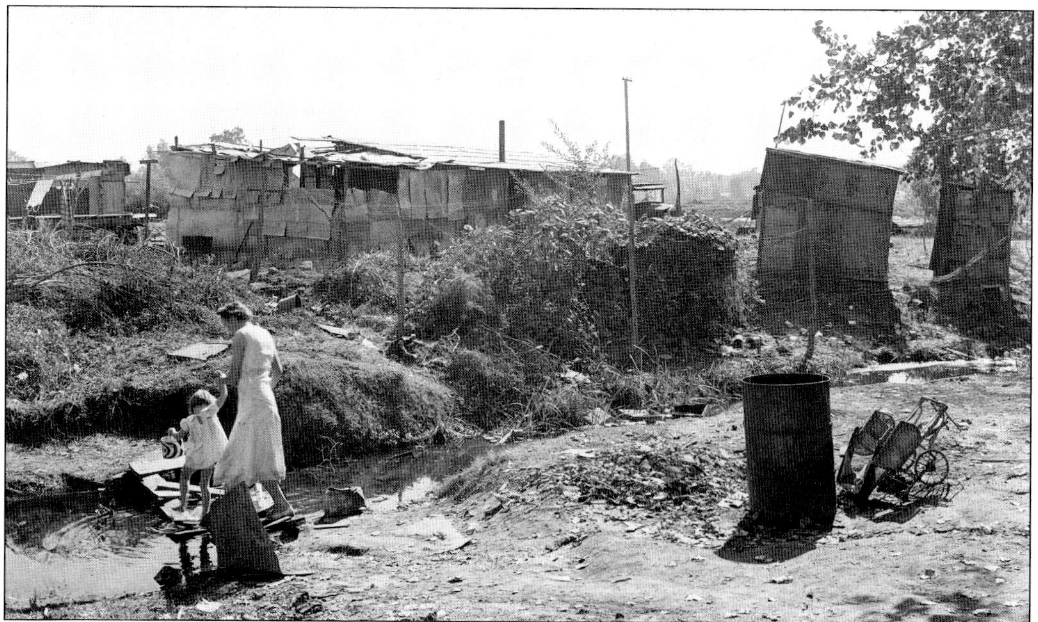

After the stock market crashed, unemployed people were evicted from their homes, and shantytowns showed up across the country. As the Depression worsened in the 1930s, people looked to the federal government for help. When no relief was provided, people blamed President Hoover and replaced the name of shantytowns with Hoovervilles. (Courtesy of the Library of Congress.)

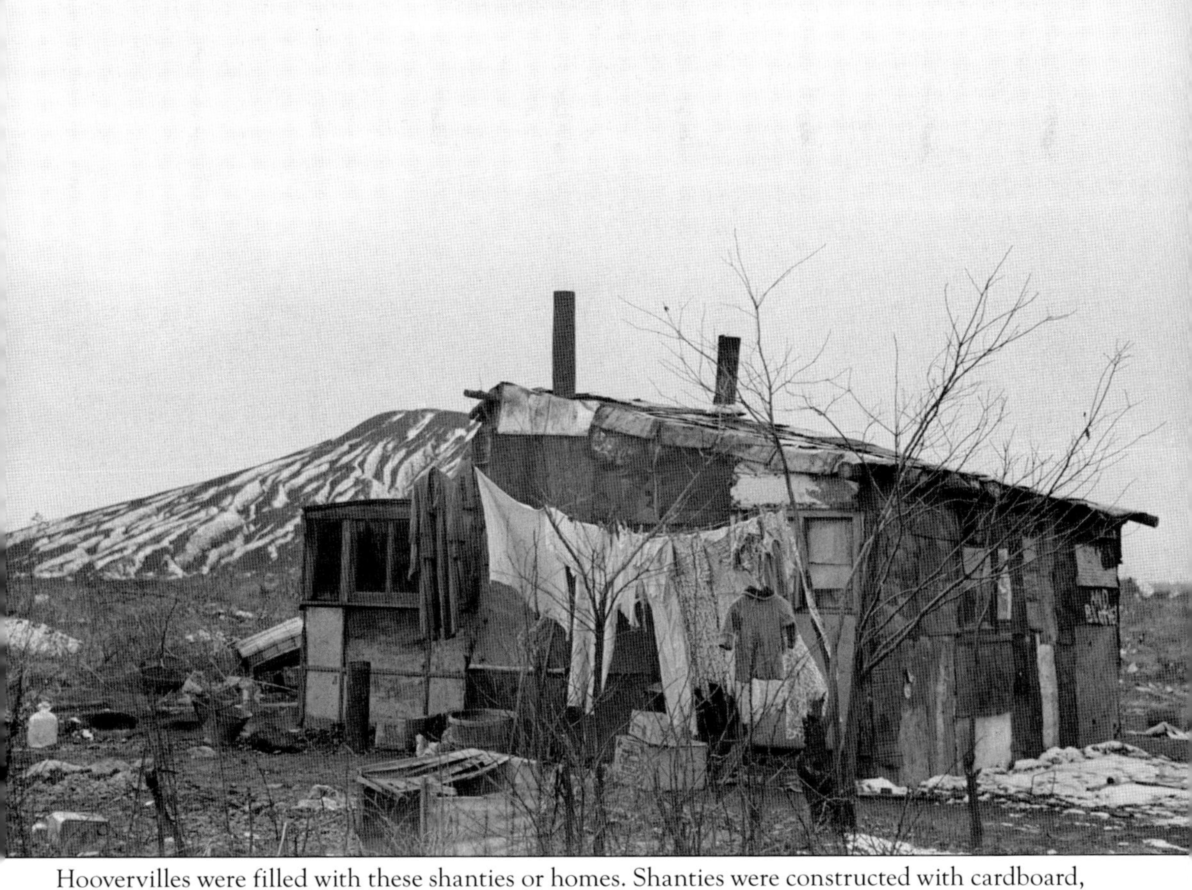

Hoovervilles were filled with these shanties or homes. Shanties were constructed with cardboard, tin, glass, tar paper, and any other available materials. They continuously needed to be repaired and rebuilt. Hooverville camps ranged in size and population throughout the United States. Setting up camp near a water source, if possible, was a huge advantage. Having water was one less necessity to worry about. Although thc camps were bleak and unclean, people had nowhere else to go. (Courtesy of the Library of Congress.)

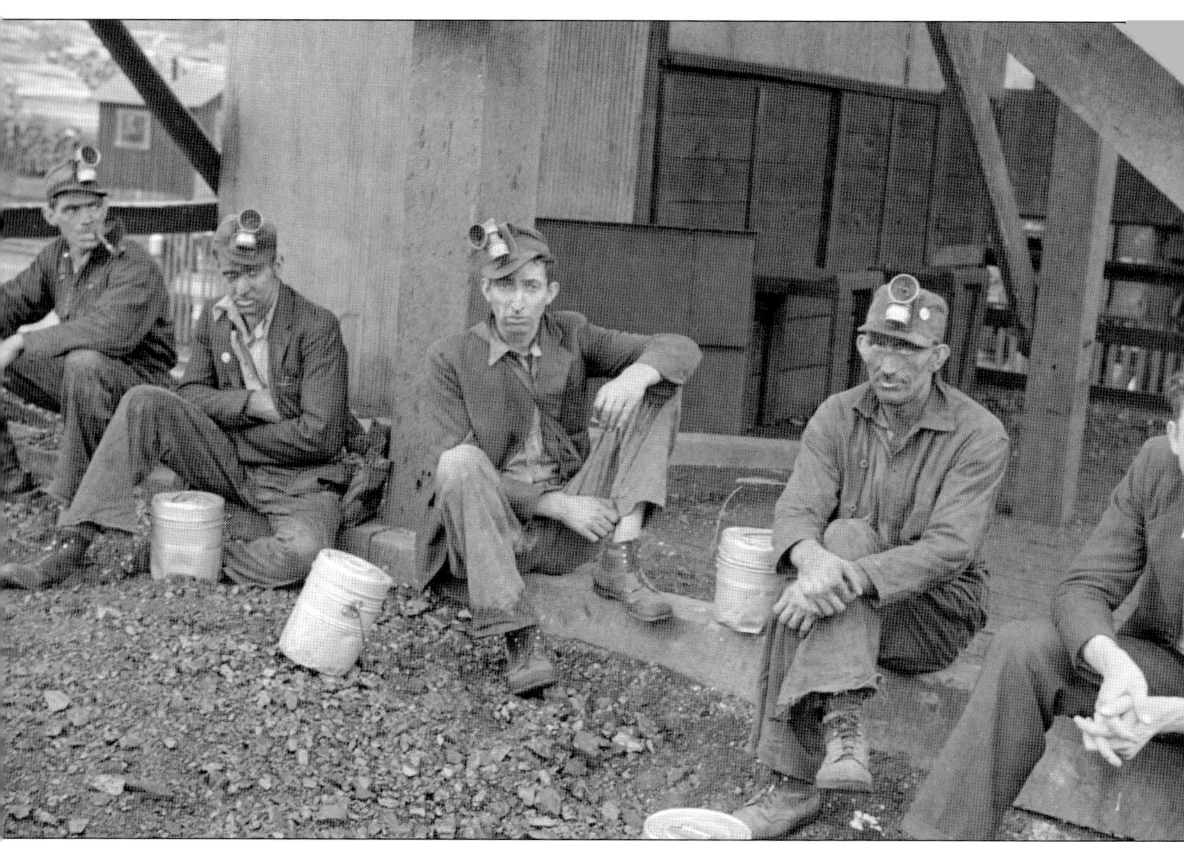

Miners took a break in the southeastern town of Jenkins, Kentucky, in Letcher County. Jenkins is located at the foot of Pine Mountain, a ridge in the Appalachian Mountains. Due to the increased use of natural gas for heating, coal orders had dropped since 1927. Rather than large-scale layoffs, companies worked miners fewer hours at first. However, by 1933, half the region's coal mines were closed, and unemployment had risen to 40 percent in Appalachia. Some men left their country homes and traveled to the city to find work, but few jobs were available. People referred to the Great Depression as "cracking hard times" and did whatever was needed to survive. (Courtesy of the Library of Congress.)

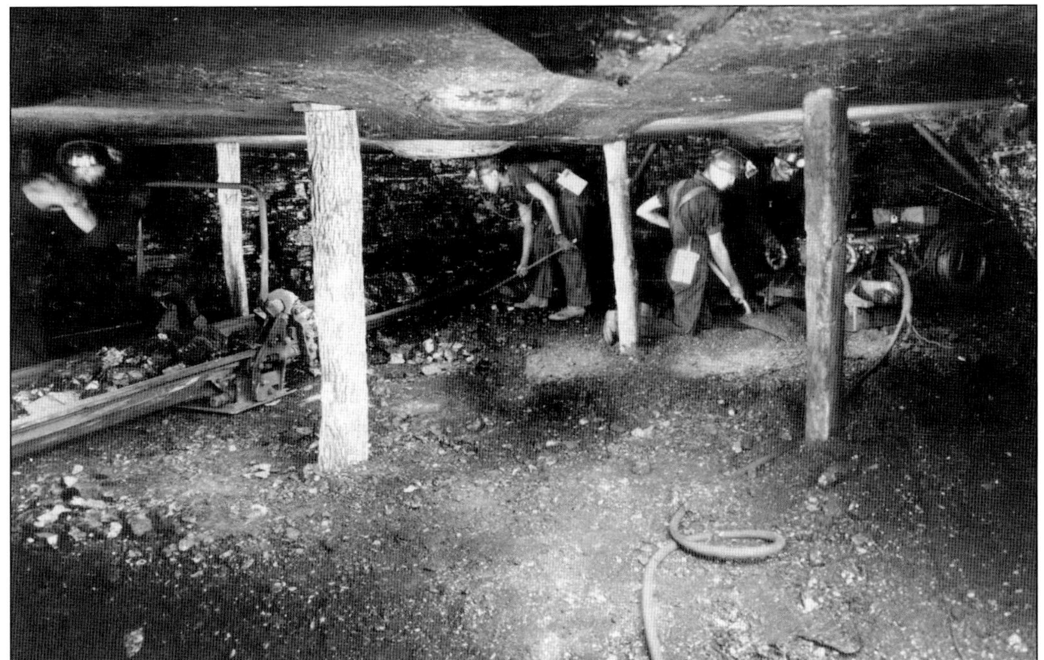

Working in coal mines was dark, dirty, and dangerous. Miners labored with the threat of toxic gases and being crushed or injured from fires and explosions. However, mining had been a family tradition over generations for many. The pay provided for many families, especially during those tough times. (Courtesy of WPA collection, Archives and Records Management Division, Kentucky Department for Libraries and Archives.)

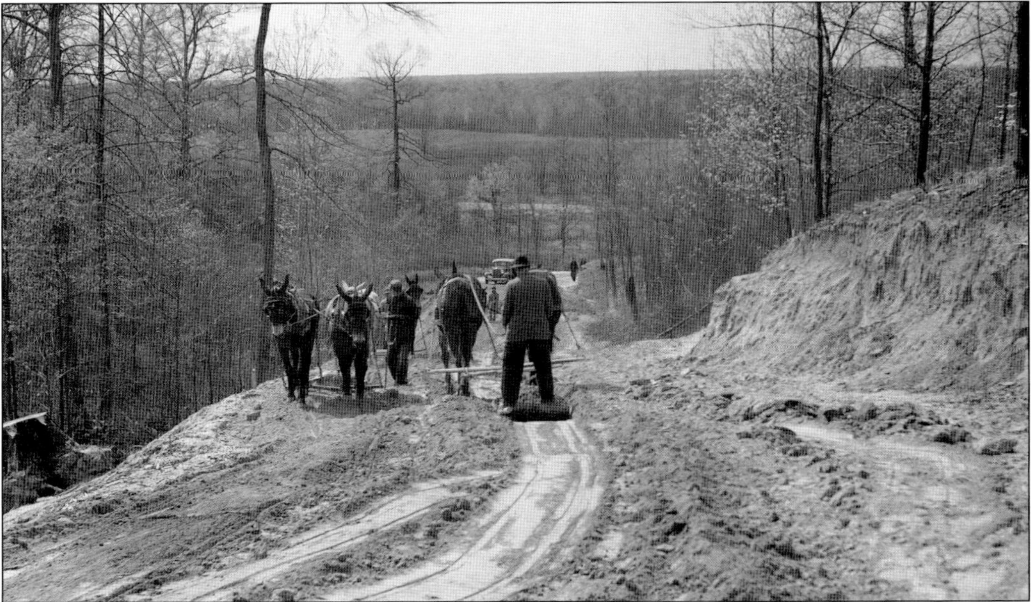

In the 1930s, men were considered the breadwinners, someone who earned the money for the household. Most of the work required physical labor such as mining or building roads, schools, and plants. Men built roads in rural communities with horses and plows through the dirt and dust. (Courtesy of the Library of Congress.)

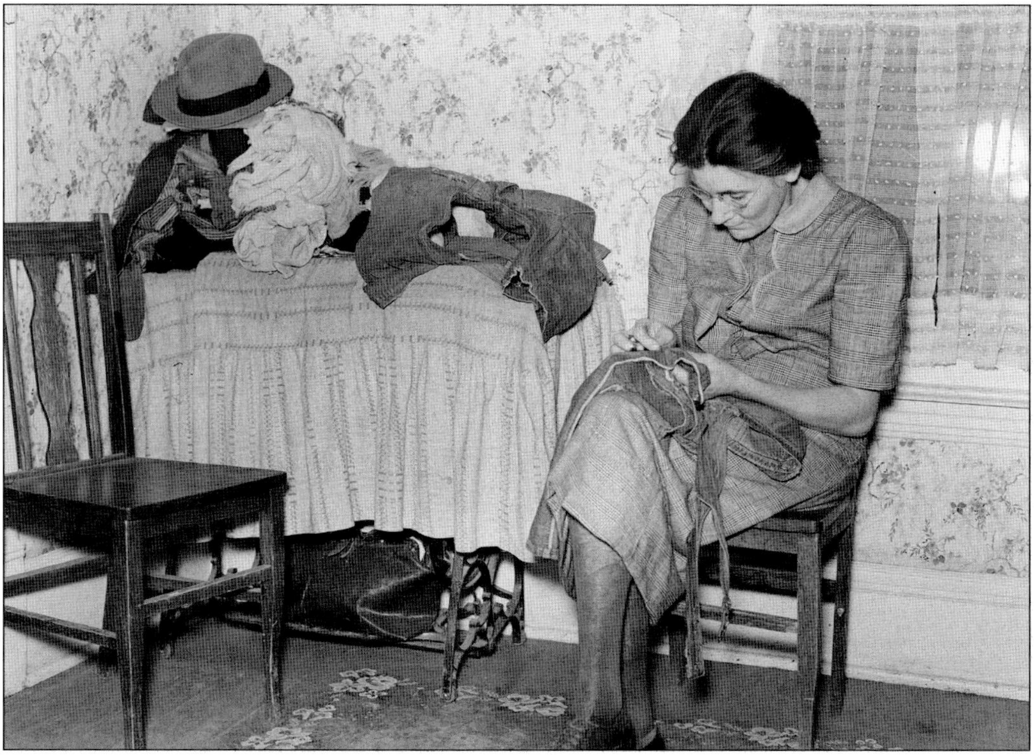

When the economy tanked and these jobs were eliminated, men lost their livelihood. The household had to find other ways to make money. In order to make ends meet, women and children worked. Women would clean houses, do laundry, sew, and make quilts for a wage. (Courtesy of the Library of Congress.)

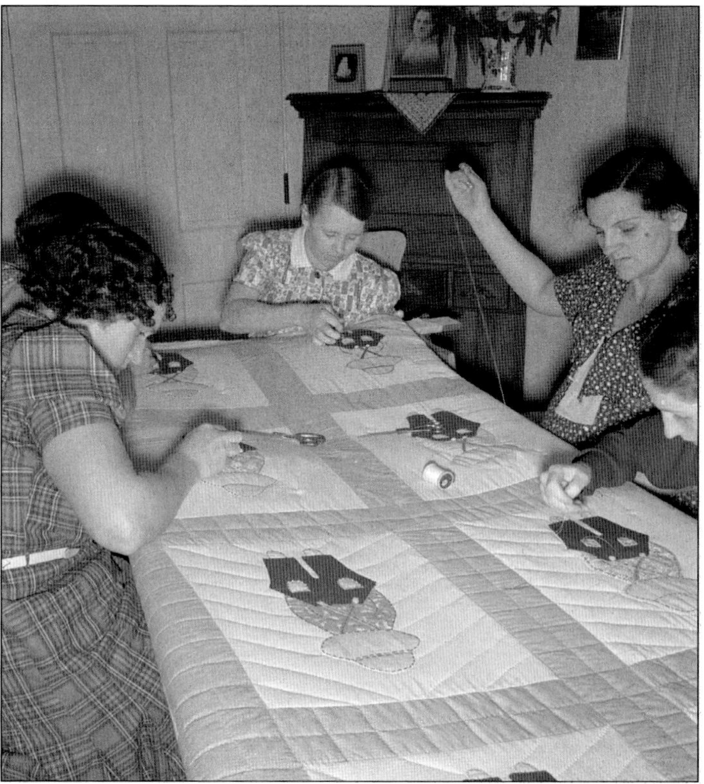

Women gathered around a table to put the finishing touches on a quilt. For practical purposes, quilt making provided work. Symbolically, the handmade comforter represented making something beautiful and useful out of nothing. Quilt making was a coveted job by women and helped them support their families. (Courtesy of the Library of Congress.)

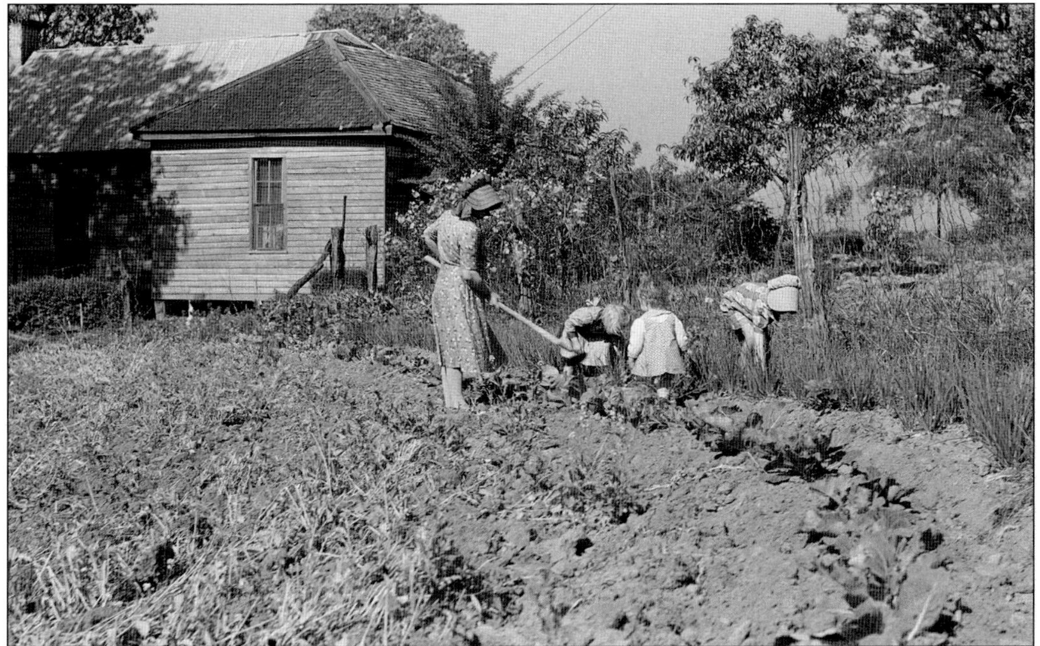

Children did their fair share of work to help their families make and save money. Ways to save money included eating from backyard gardens and canning to preserve their food and harvest. Making food last, especially through the winter, kept bellies full. Children sold their homegrown fruits and vegetables at stands or by going door-to-door. (Courtesy of the Library of Congress.)

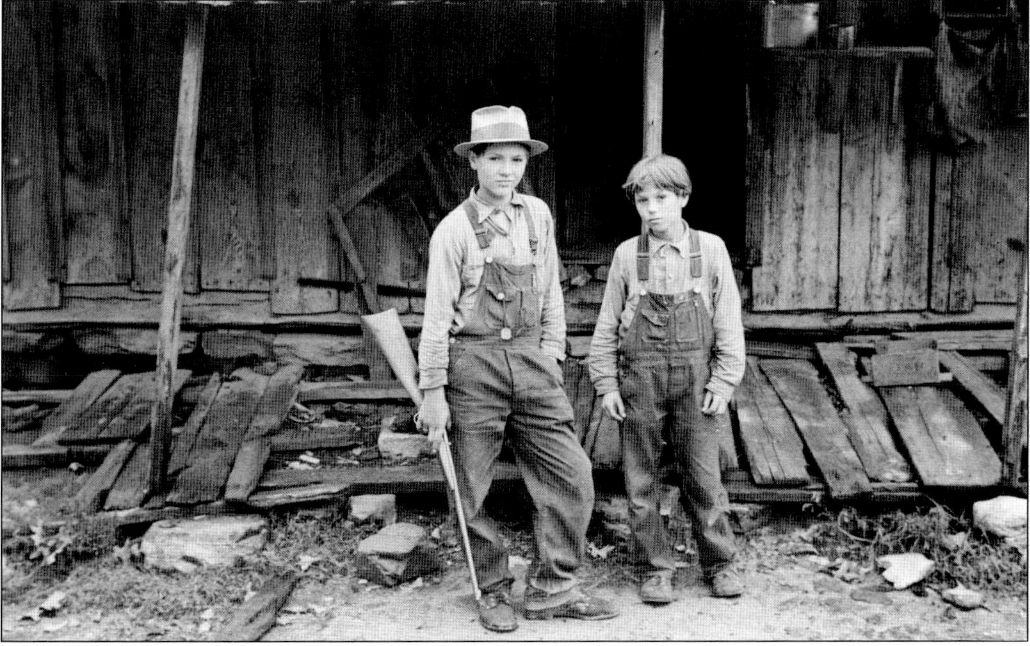

Boys hunted in the forest and trapped animals, which they then sold the furs. Kids scoured the fields and woods for food like nuts, berries, and roots for their family to eat. They fished in nearby streams hoping for a fresh catch. If they were old enough and able, every member of the family would work to contribute to their livelihood. (Courtesy of the Library of Congress.)

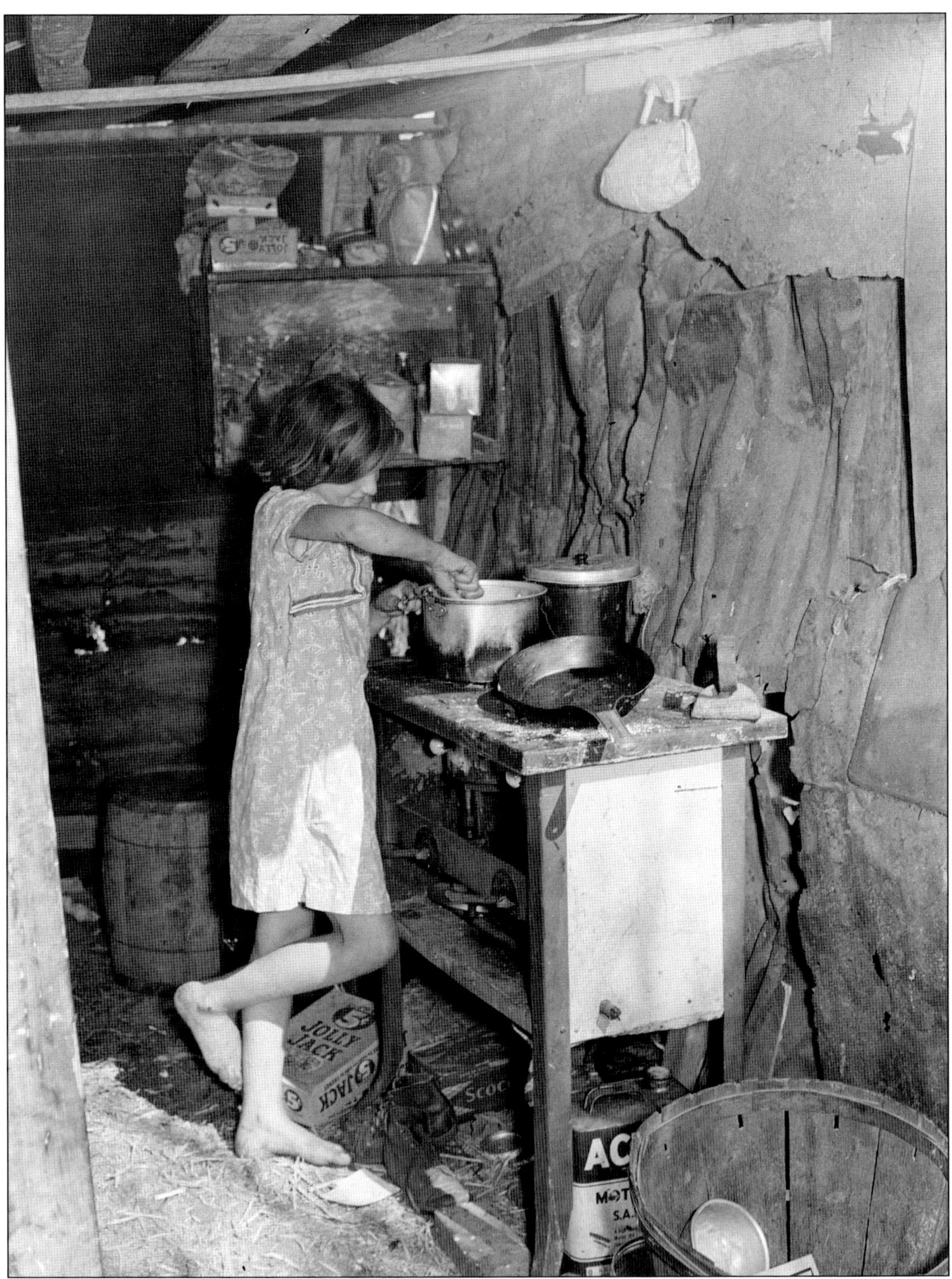

A girl prepared a meal, stirring the contents in a metal pot in the kitchen area of the house. A box of Jolly Jack sugar and Scoco shortening laid at her feet. Girls completed chores around the house, including watching their siblings, cleaning, and cooking meals to be ready when their parents came home from work. They earned money by babysitting or doing chores for other families. (Courtesy of the Library of Congress.)

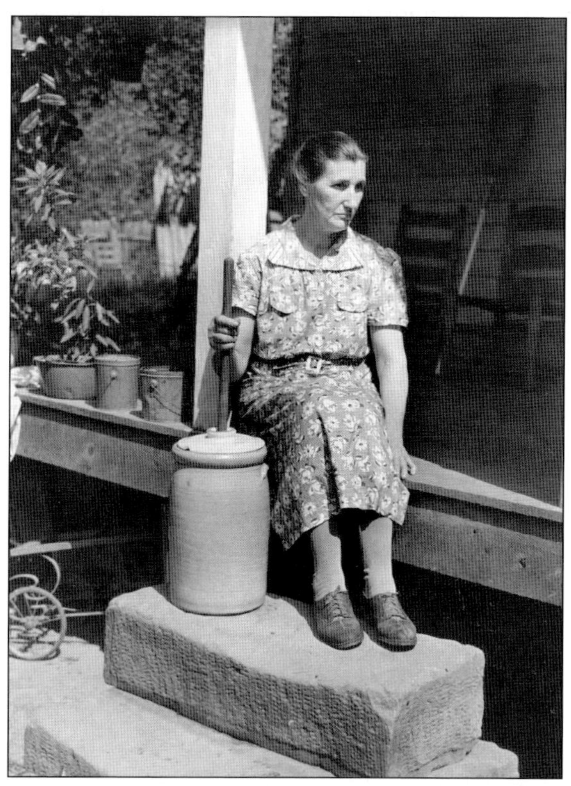

Instead of spending money, people traded goods and services. Farming families exchanged their churned butter, heavy cream, or fresh farm eggs with a store owner for coffee, sugar, or flour. Some would be paid in food for their hours of labor. (Courtesy of WPA collection, Archives and Records Management Division, Kentucky Department for Libraries and Archives.)

In the 1930s during the Great Depression, 25 percent of the nation's children starved. For children in the Appalachian Mountains, the numbers climbed to 90 percent. Little ones showed signs of malnutrition with curved legs and gaunt features. Adults also suffered from a lack of food. Men got lost in their overalls, and women swam in their dresses and skirts. (Courtesy of the Library of Congress.)

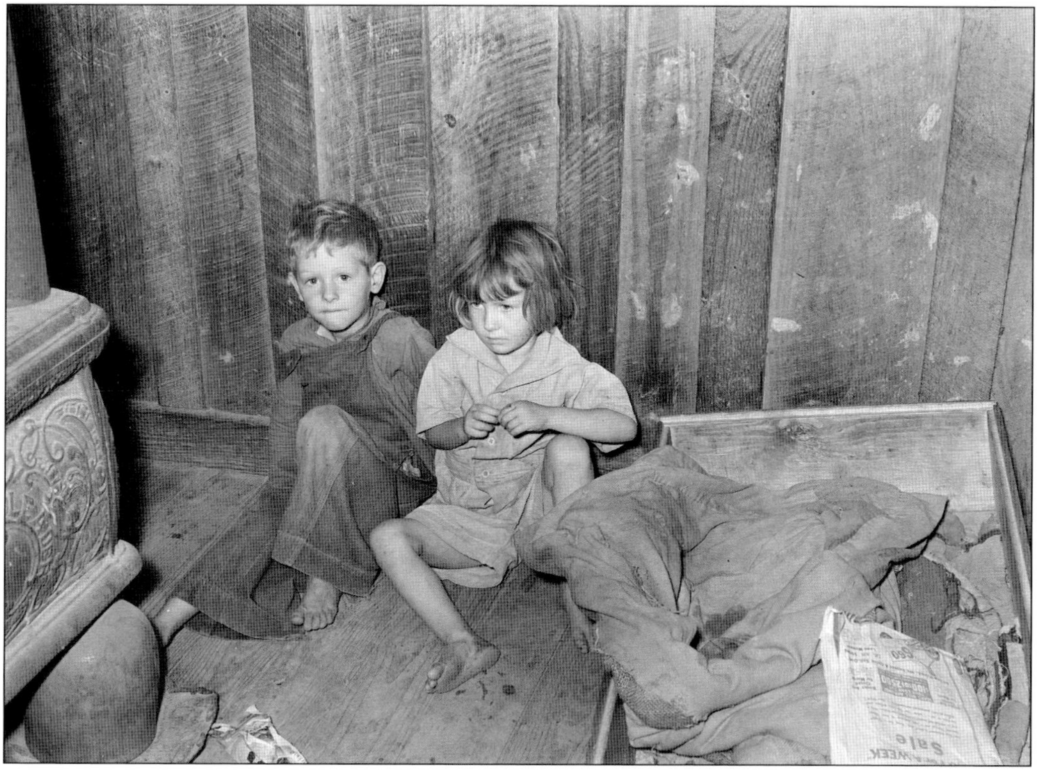

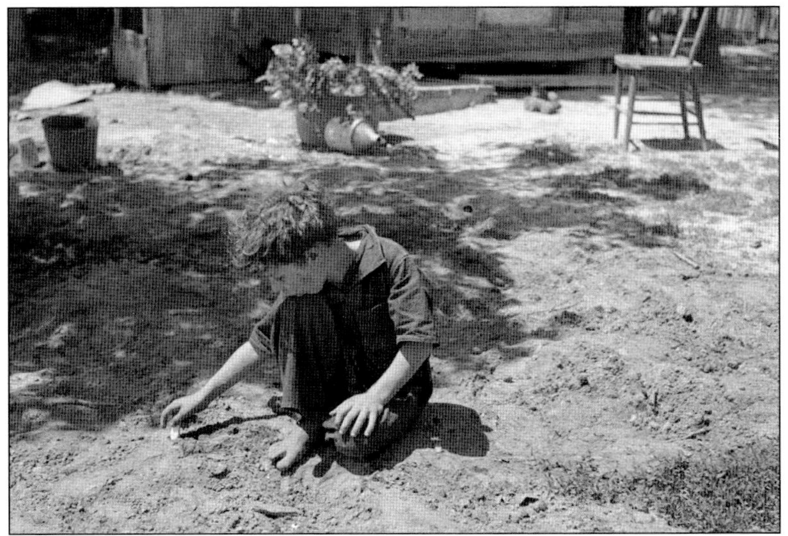

Sometimes people could not afford meals and looked to alternative solutions to fill their empty stomachs. One choice would be to eat red clay from the earth to keep their stomachs from rumbling. A "clay eater" was recognized by the reddish color and puddy texture of their skin. (Courtesy of the Library of Congress.)

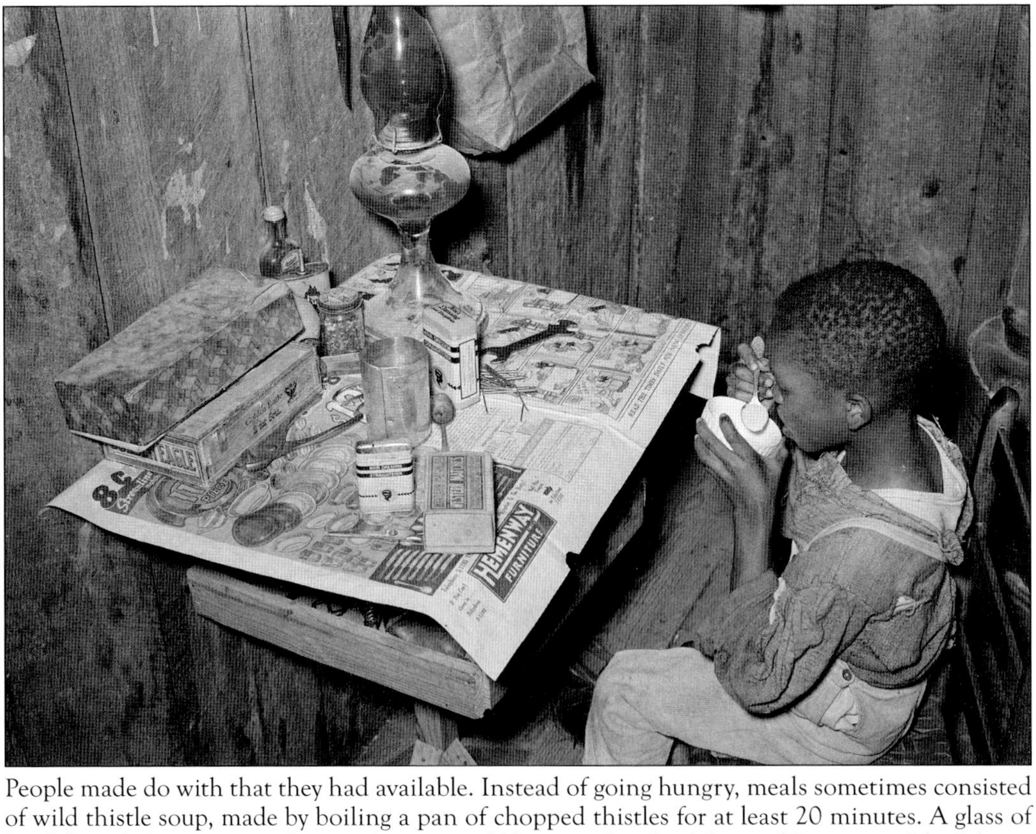

People made do with that they had available. Instead of going hungry, meals sometimes consisted of wild thistle soup, made by boiling a pan of chopped thistles for at least 20 minutes. A glass of "milk" made from mixing flour and water could be considered a delicacy. (Courtesy of the Library of Congress.)

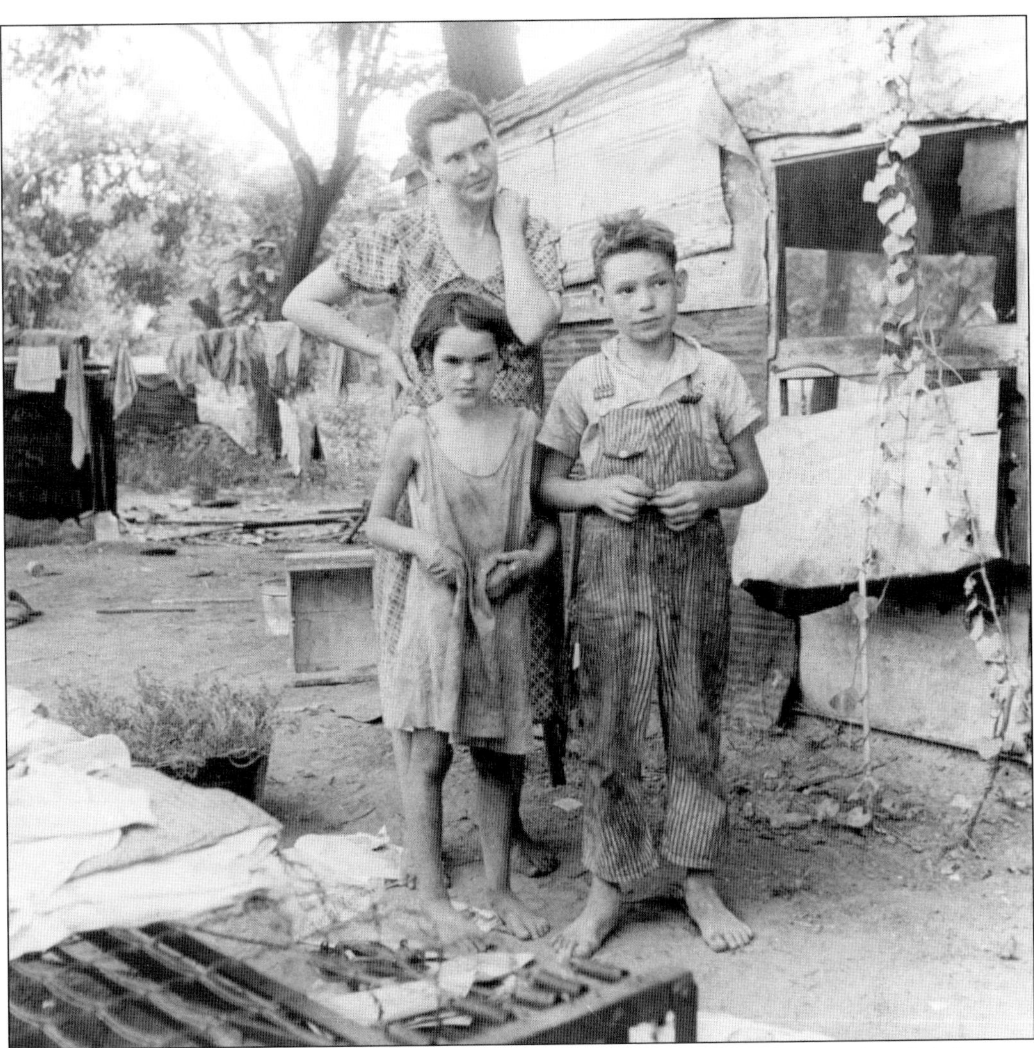

Clothes needed to last as long as possible. Holes were patched, and items were handed down to siblings or swapped with other families once they no longer fit. People were resourceful, and nothing went to waste. Empty flour sacks made for durable shirts, skirts, dish towels, and underwear. Strings for shoelaces and cardboard for shoe soles extended the life of footwear. If a sturdy boot was needed, heavy burlap over a shoe did the trick. (Courtesy of the Library of Congress.)

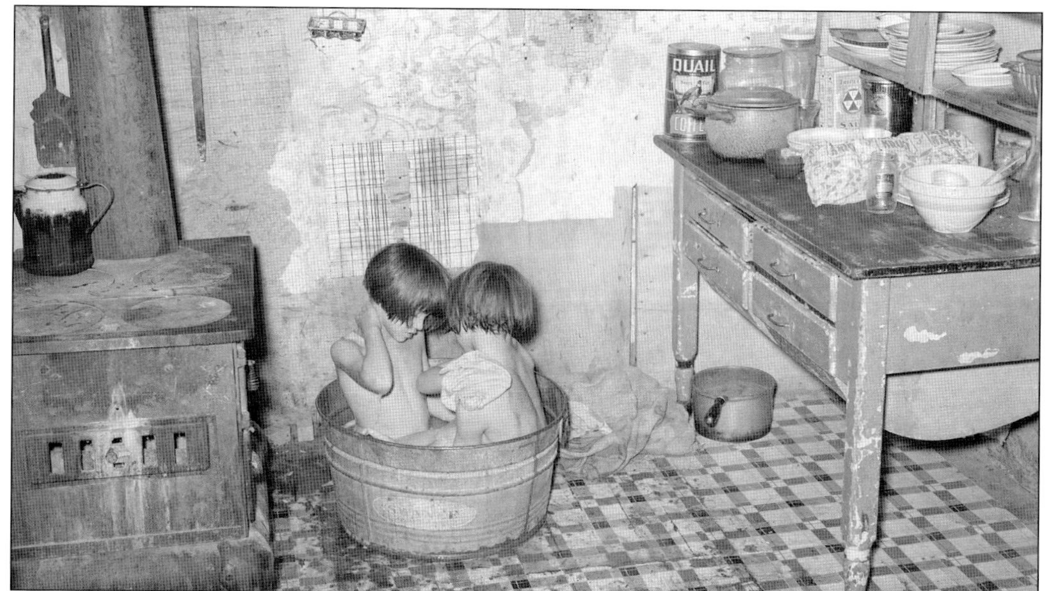

Two children enjoyed a bath in a tin tub in their kitchen. Most water had to be brought in from the well outside. For hot water, one would boil it in the kettle or put the tub in front of a coal fire and the back boiler would heat the water. Bathing did not happen daily, sometimes it was on a weekly basis or longer. (Courtesy of the Library of Congress.)

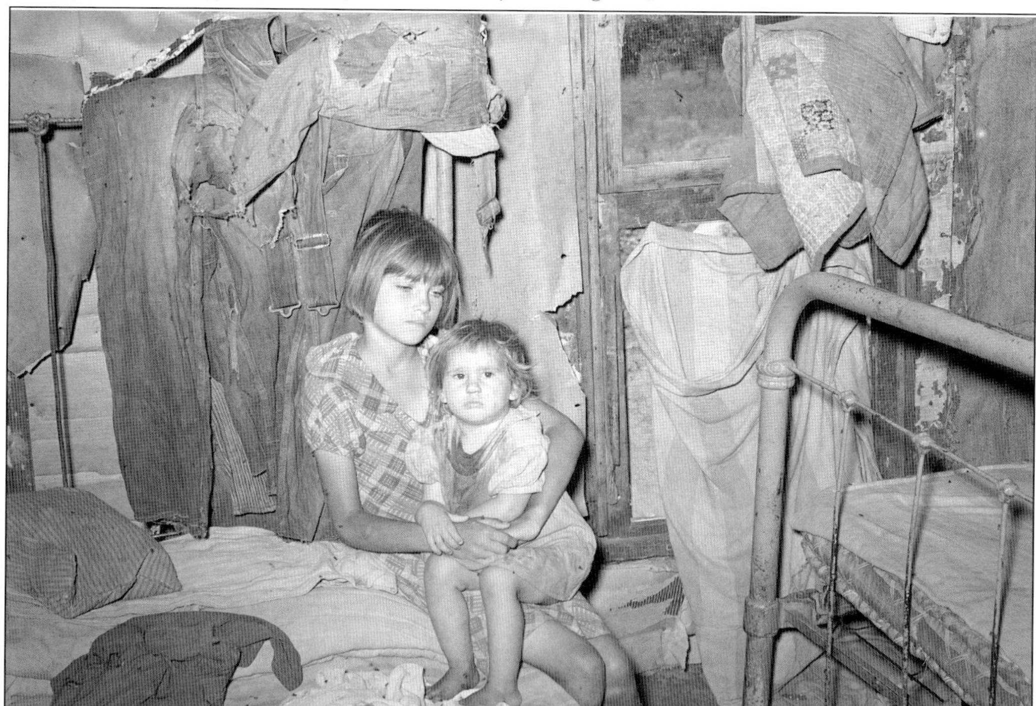
The beloved quilt had many uses in mountain homes. Mostly, they were used as bed coverings, but they also hung to cover the openings of doors and windows. The quilt repelled the wind, rain, snow, and chill that whipped through the cabin homes and was a cost-effective solution. (Courtesy of the Library of Congress.)

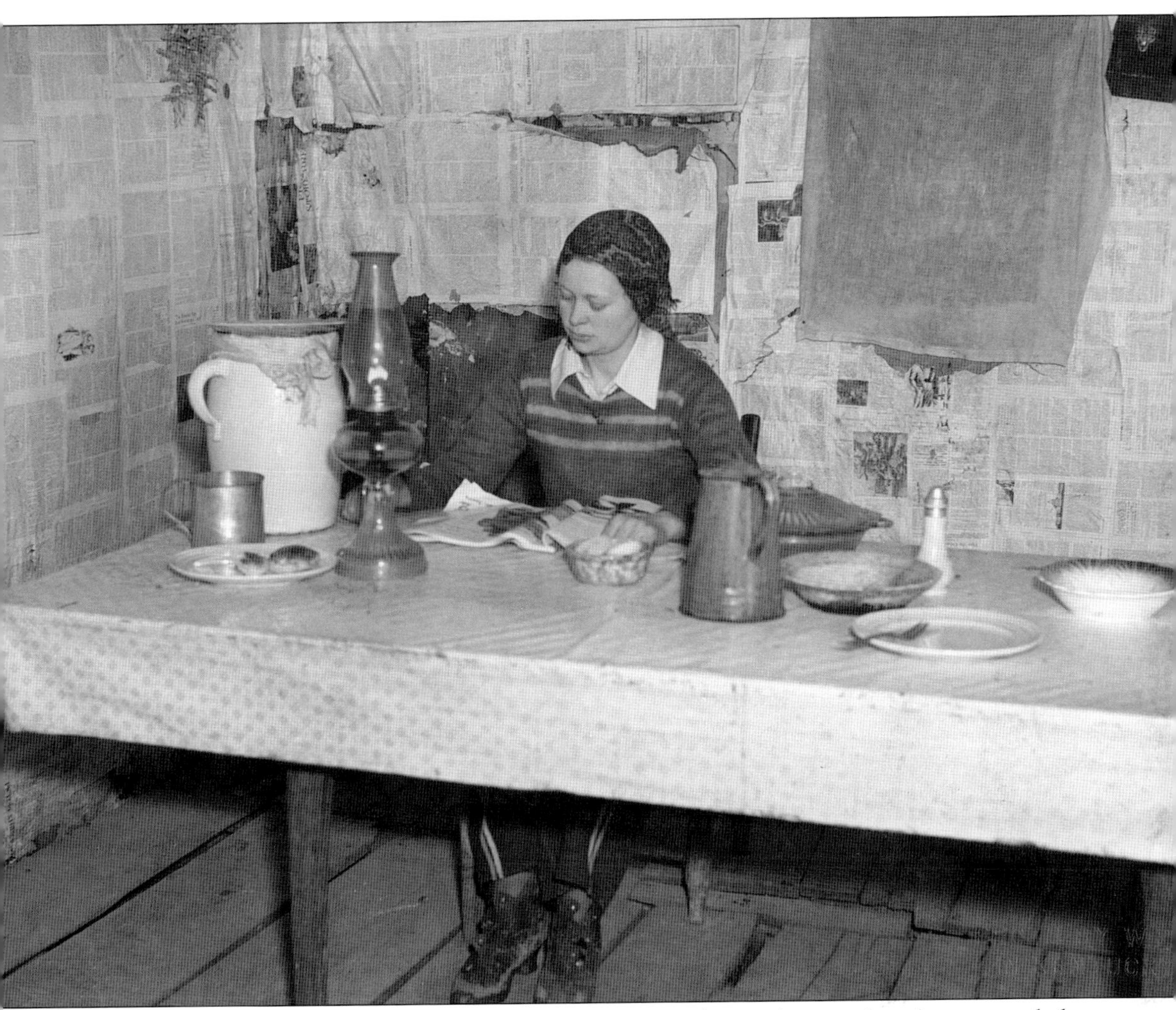

When old newspapers or magazines had been read by family members and no longer needed, people would not throw them out. They repurposed and reused all that they had. The newspapers were often used to wallpaper the rooms in their homes for insulation. If repairs were needed, one wadded up the paper and patched any holes or gaps in the walls. Newspapers could also be used to line shelves and drawers, clean windows without leaving streaks, start a fire, or store fruit. (Courtesy of WPA collection, Archives and Records Management Division, Kentucky Department for Libraries and Archives.)

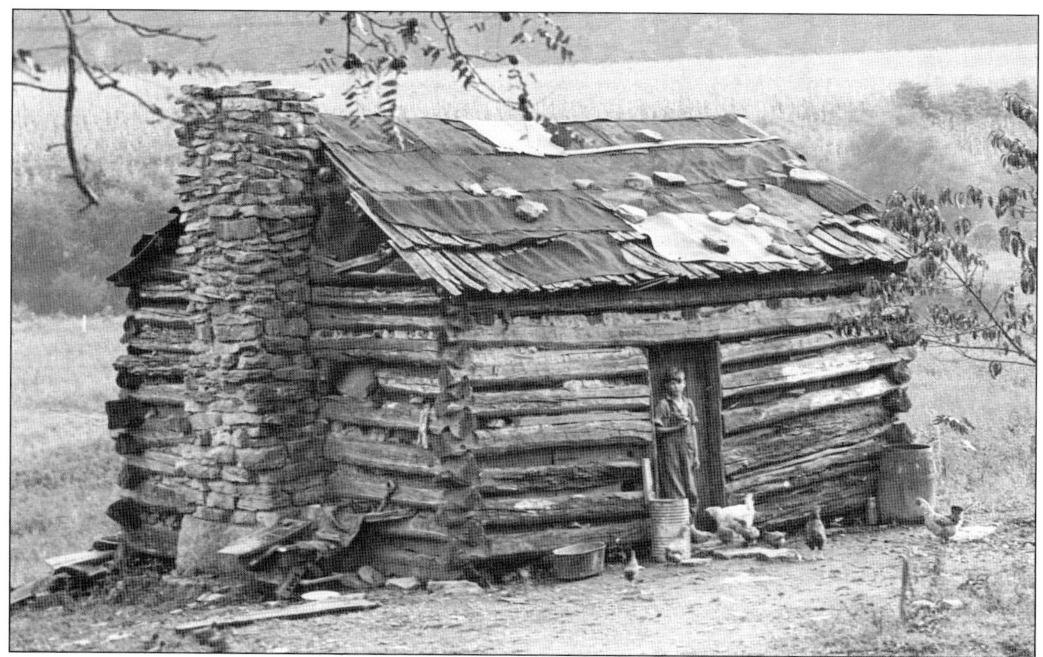

Newspapers were useful for external needs as well. Sheets of paper and rocks would be used to cover up openings in the roof instead of replacing the planks. The extra insulation helped keep the home dry and warm, especially during the winter months. (Courtesy of WPA collection, Archives and Records Management Division, Kentucky Department for Libraries and Archives.)

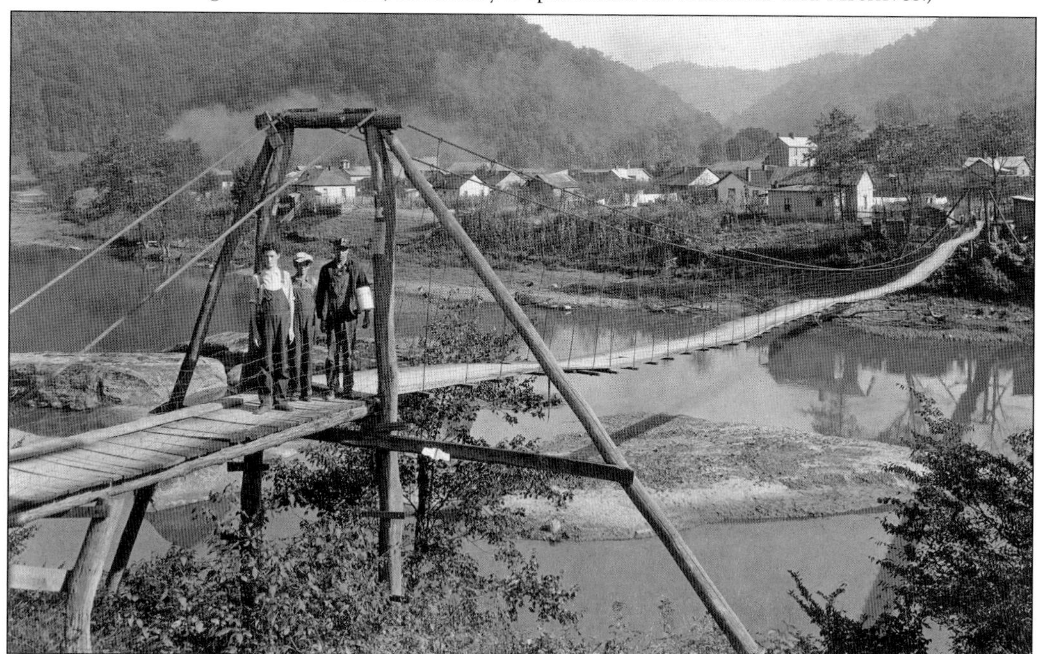

Half of American youth dropped out of school during the Great Depression. Many reasons contributed, including children needing to work for money during the day, and school had to be put on hold to make ends meet. (Courtesy of WPA collection, Archives and Records Management Division, Kentucky Department for Libraries and Archives.)

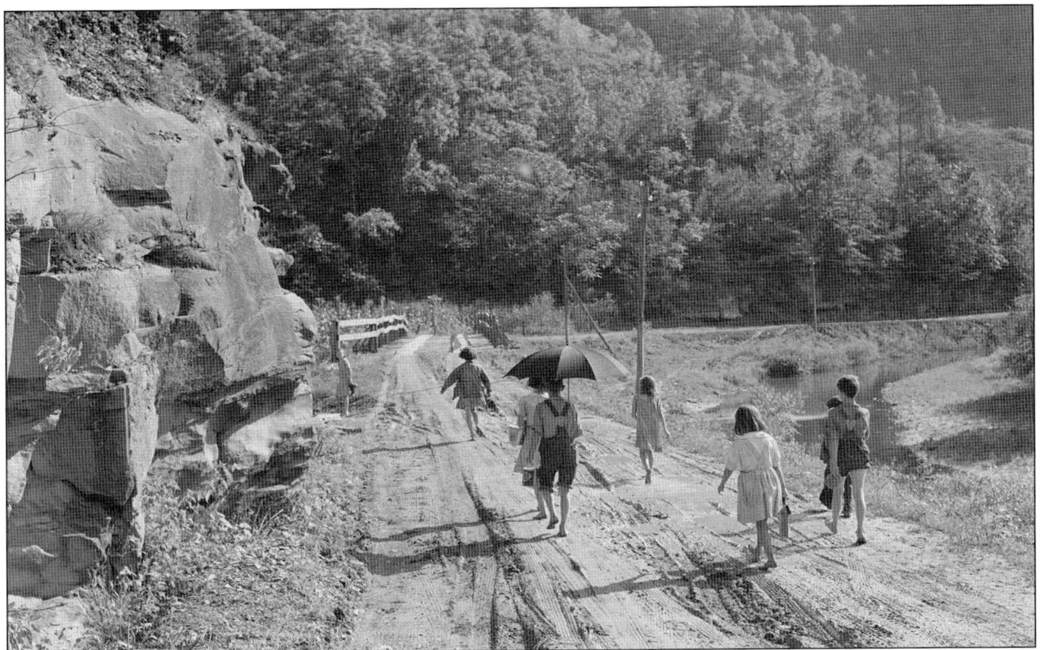

Some students lived too far away from school to walk, and their family did not have a horse, wagon, or car to get them there because they sold it for much-needed cash. Other reasons included schools being closed due to funding or the county could not pay the teachers. (Courtesy of the Library of Congress.)

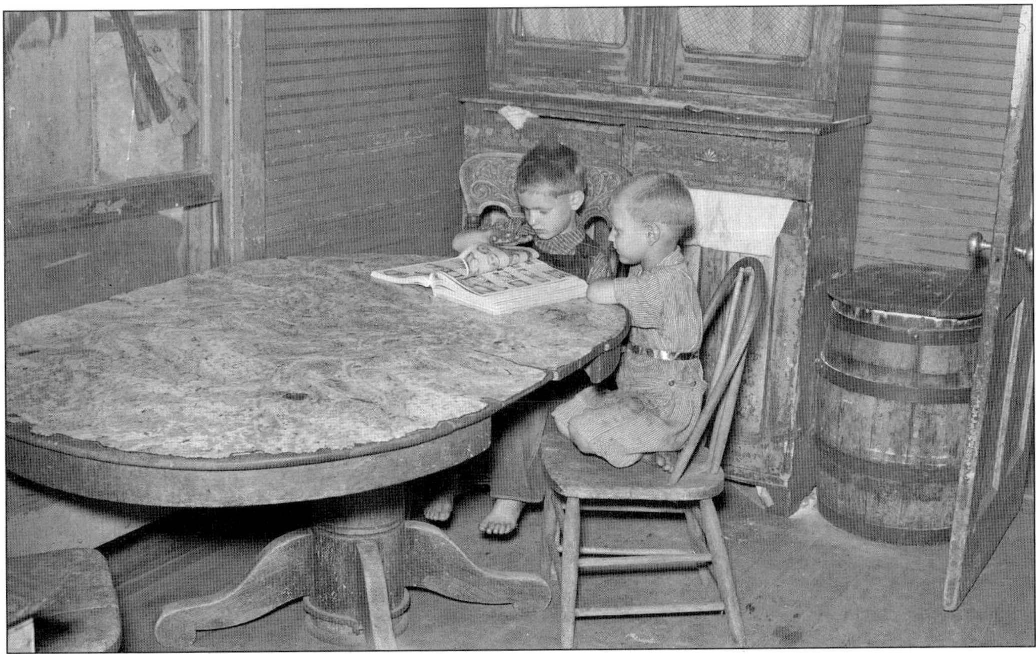

When thousands of people did not have telephones, radios, or television, they had to get creative about entertainment. Children made paper figures or dolls from magazines or catalogs. They pasted the cutout pictures on cardboard and dressed them up with magazine accessories. Wood scraps and rags would be used to make toys and clothes too. (Courtesy of the Library of Congress.)

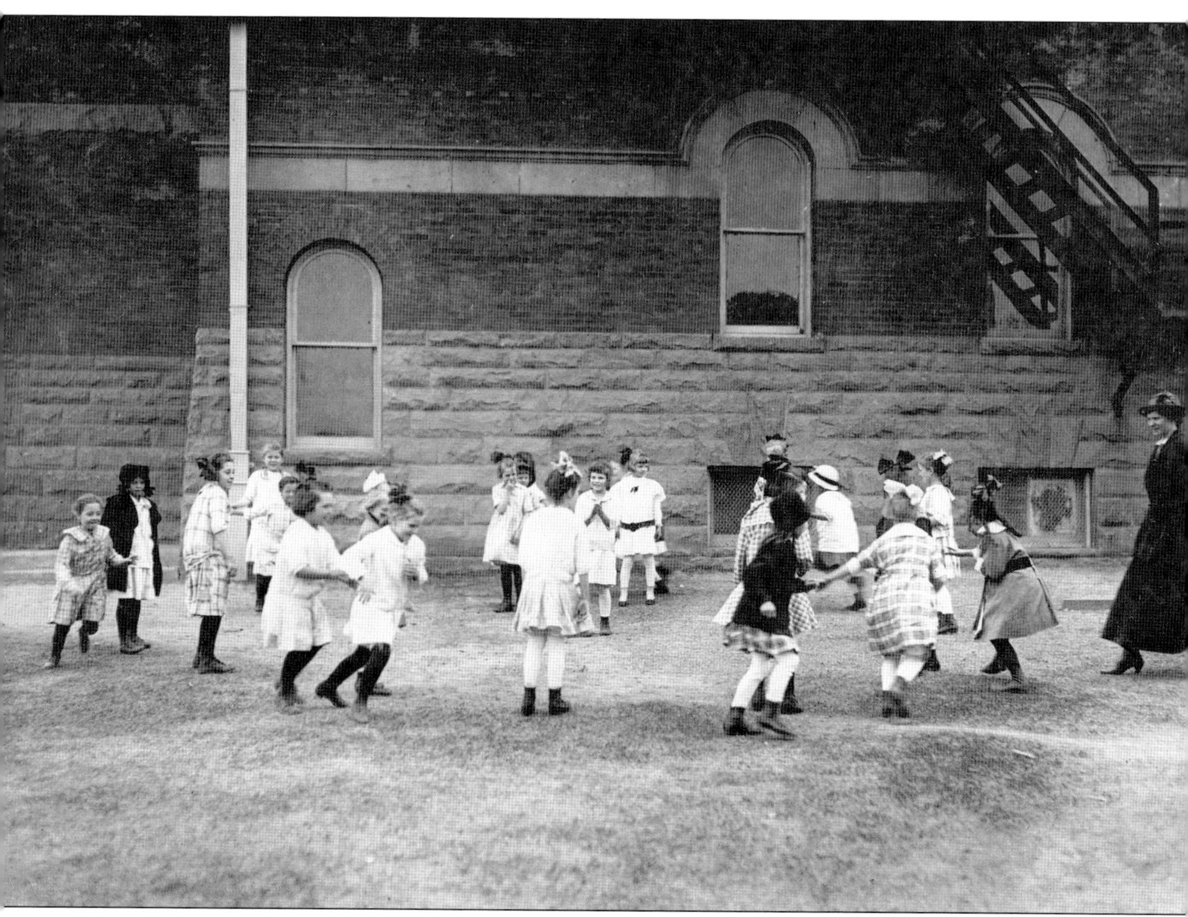

The children in this circle played pom pom pull away outside school with their teacher looking on. Much like the red rover game, five or more children lined up in an open space. One child stayed in the center, called any player by name, and added a line. For instance, "John Smith, Pom Pom pull away! Come away, or I'll fetch you away!" Then the child who was called, ran to the other side and tried not to get tagged. If they did, they had to stand in the middle with the caller and help tag others. If they were not called, they cheered on their classmates to join them on their side. The caller repeated with another name until all the players were caught. The first player caught was the caller for the next game. Other schoolyard games included hopscotch; "Mother May I;" seven-up; tetherball; and red light, green light. (Courtesy of the Library of Congress.)

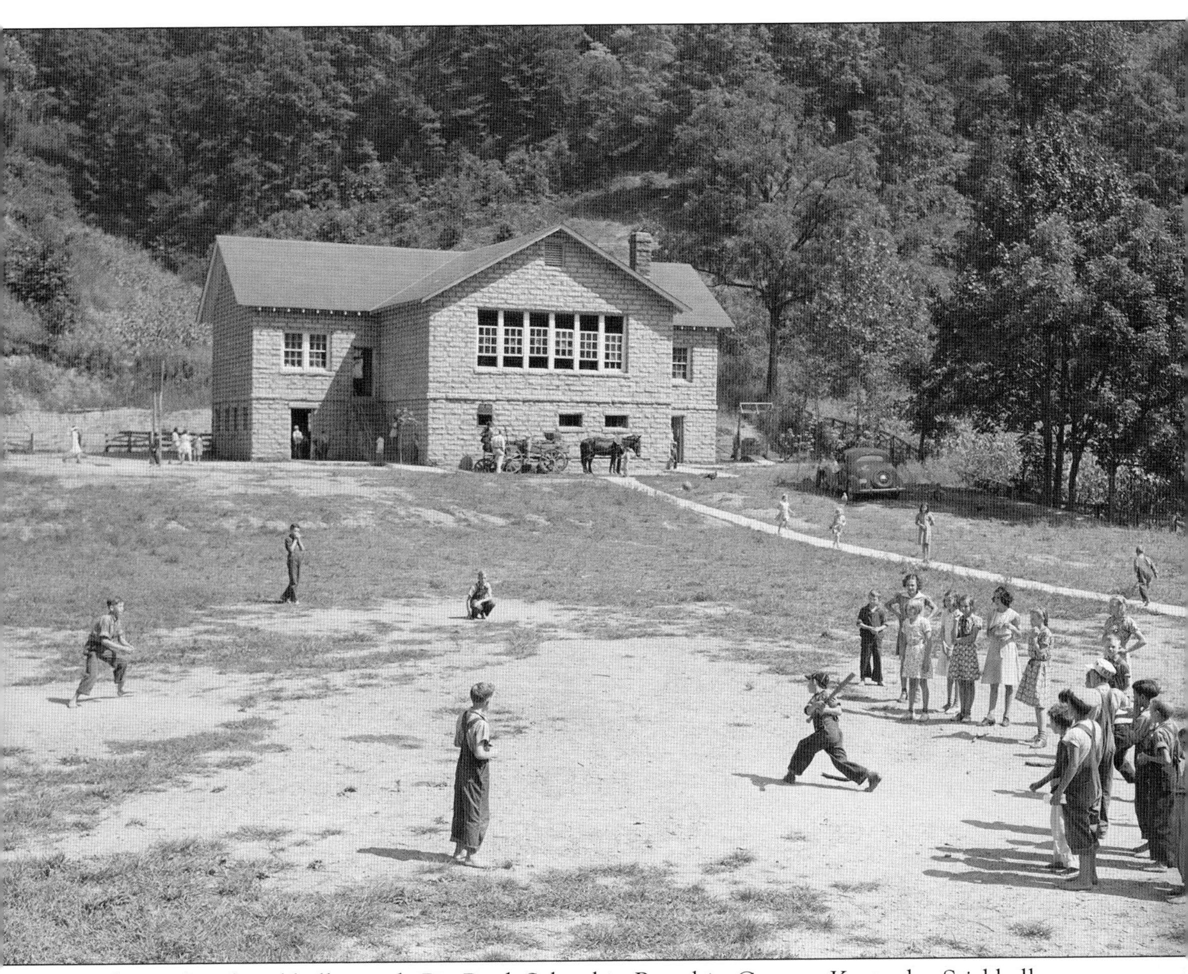

Students played stickball outside Big Rock School in Breathitt County, Kentucky. Stickball was a street game similar to baseball but without the same equipment. Rural kids could also play in the schoolyards, fields, and backyards. Instead of a bat, they used a stick or a broom handle; instead of a ball, a rock or rubber ball. The rules were adjusted to fit the location of the game. Tree stumps or sewer hole covers were used as bases, buildings for foul lines, etc. With stickball, the batter is out if the opposing team catches the ball on the fly or after a single bounce. If the ball hits a roof, porch, or breaks a window, it is often ruled a home run. Since many kids did not have radios or televisions, stickball was a popular form of entertainment. (Courtesy of the Library of Congress.)

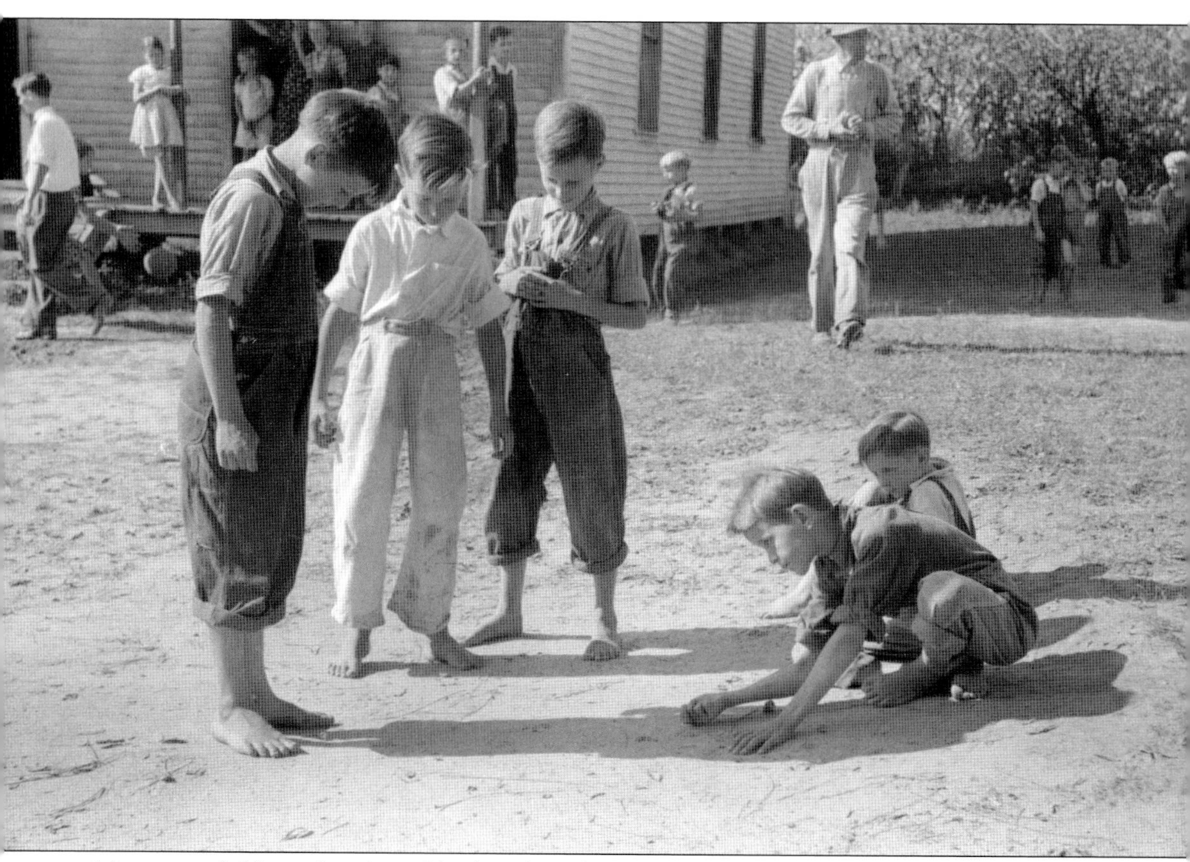

Mountain children played marbles barefooted after school in the dusty schoolyard in Breathitt County, Kentucky. There are dozens of informal games that can be played with marbles, which is one of the reasons for their popularity. Due to the ability to mass produce marbles by a machine, they were relatively easy to make and therefore inexpensive. They could be played almost anywhere but damp sand, dusty, or hard surfaces were favored. The game involved two opposing teams, which could be played with singles or up to six players per team. The objective for each team was to knock the most marbles outside the ring, which is about six feet in diameter. The person or team who collected the most marbles won. Of course, there are variations of this game with different playing area sizes and number of marbles used. (Courtesy of the Library of Congress.)

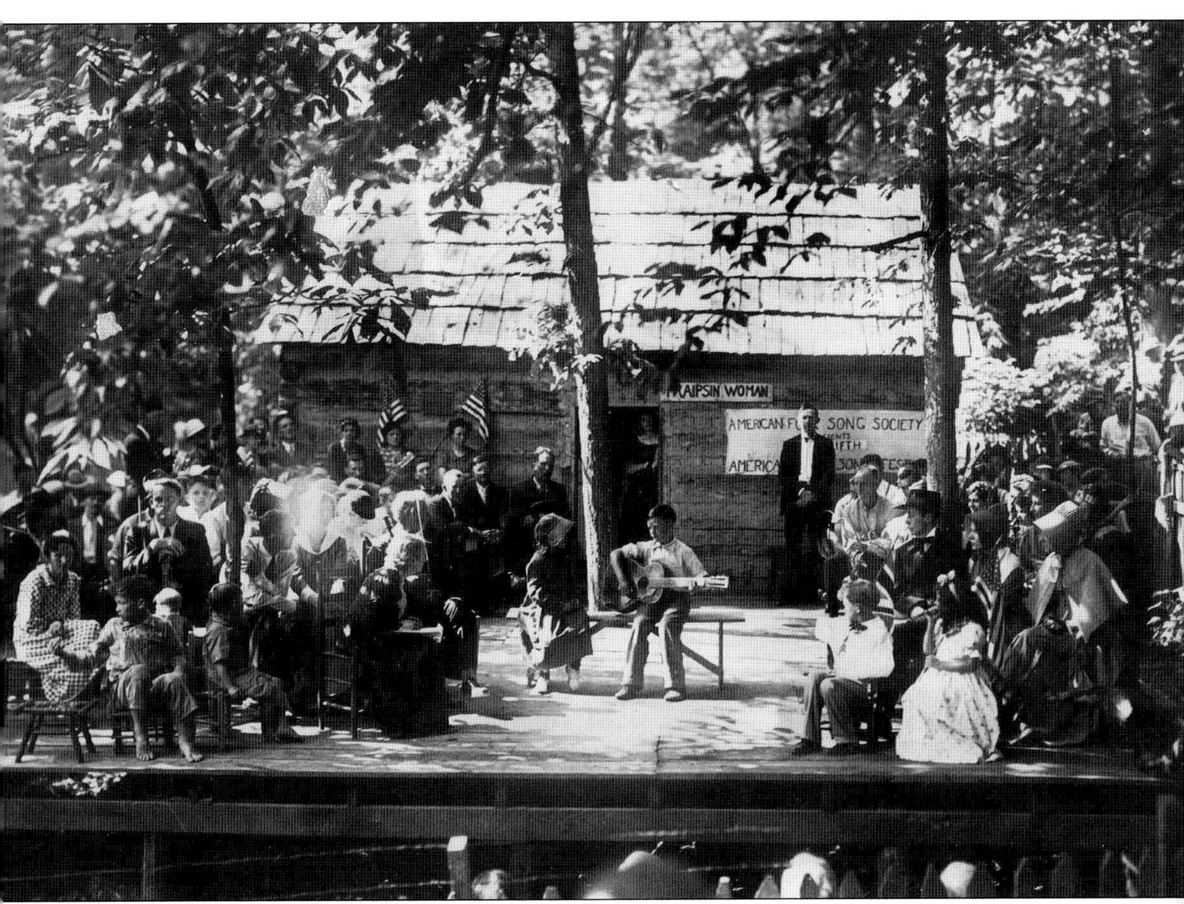

A boy strummed his guitar while the girl sang at the American Folk Song Festival at the Traipsin' Woman Cabin on the Mayo Trail near Ashland, Kentucky, in Boyd County. Musicians performed ballads and hymns that soothed the soul and brought amusement and entertainment to attendees. The first American Folk Song Festival was held in 1932 in the home of Jean Thomas and featured 18 acts. The festival was held annually, with the exception of the years 1943–1948, until Thomas retired in 1972. (Courtesy of WPA collection, Archives and Records Management Division, Kentucky Department for Libraries and Archives.)

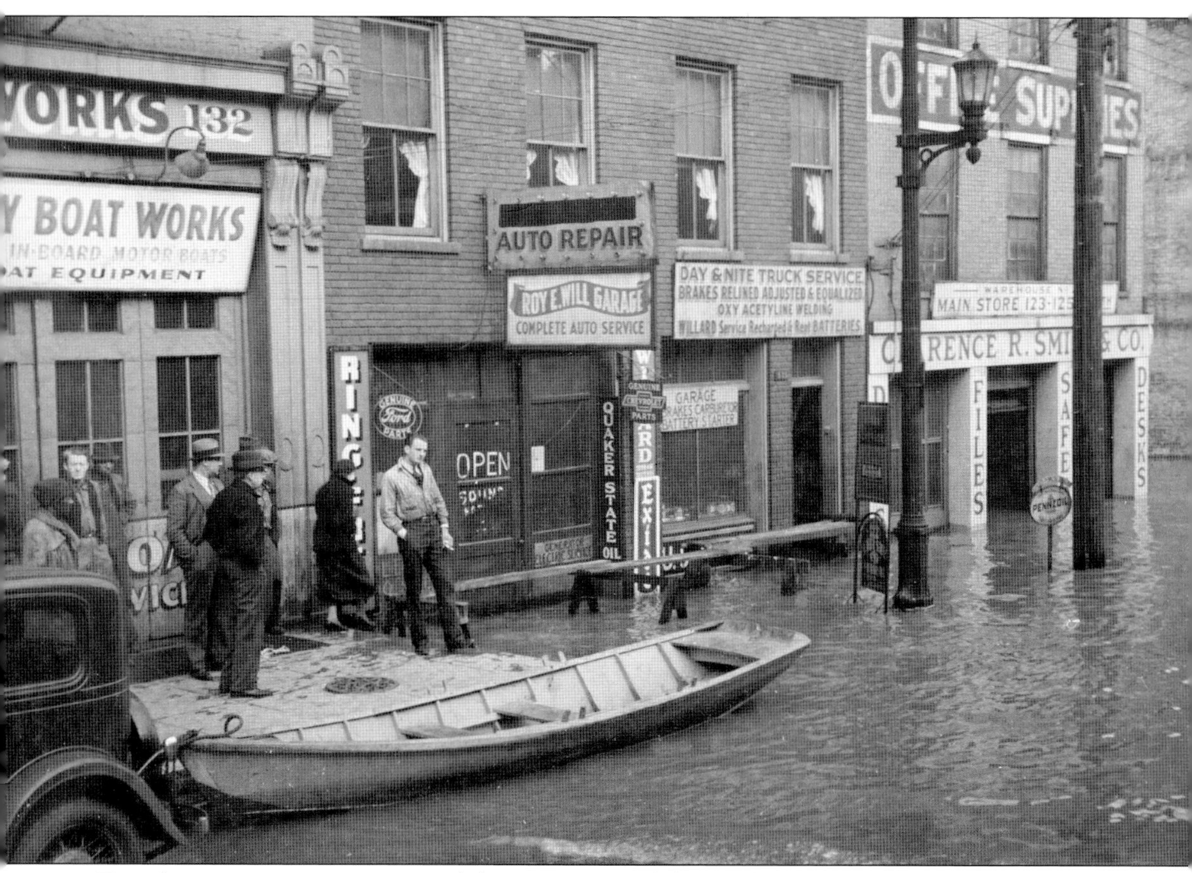

To make matters worse, two natural disasters occurred during the Depression also. The Ohio River floods of 1930 and 1937. Residents in downtown Louisville, Kentucky, traveled by boat to evacuate during the Ohio River flood of 1937. Water began to rise on January 5, 1937, and record rainfalls were recorded for the next several weeks. In January and February, 27 square miles of Louisville was put under water. It was the most destructive flood in the history of the United States at that time. (Courtesy of the Library of Congress.)

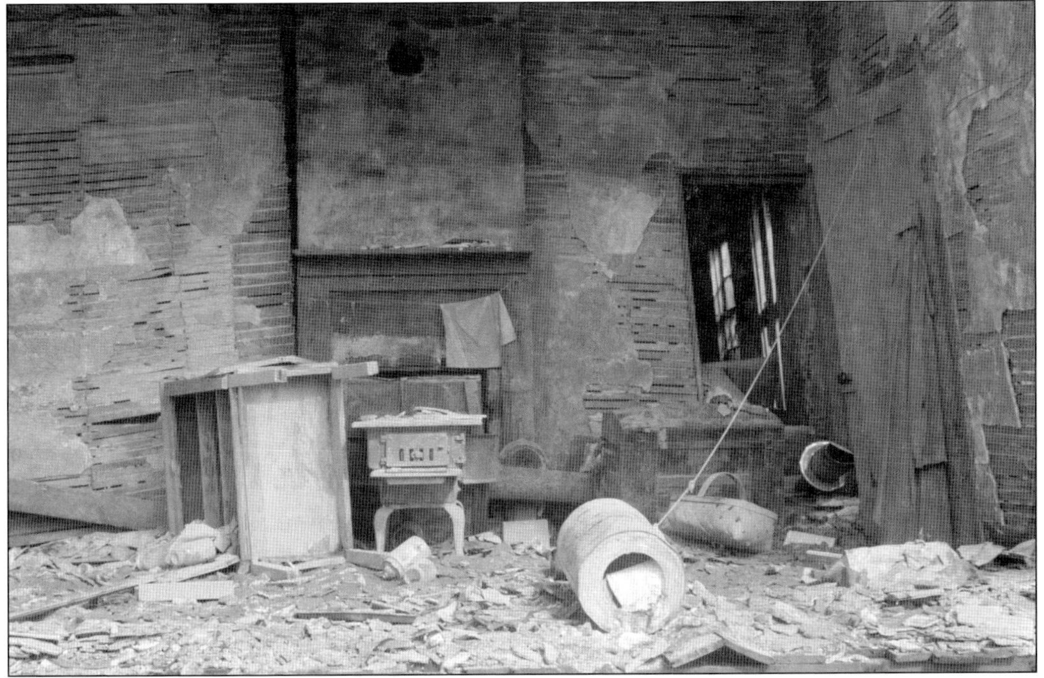

The interior of a house demolished by the Ohio River flood of 1937 in Smithland, Kentucky, in Livingston County left residents homeless. More than 150 cities along the Ohio River were flooded, driving hundreds of thousands from their homes and resulting in hundreds of lives lost and over $8 billion in damages. (Courtesy of the Library of Congress.)

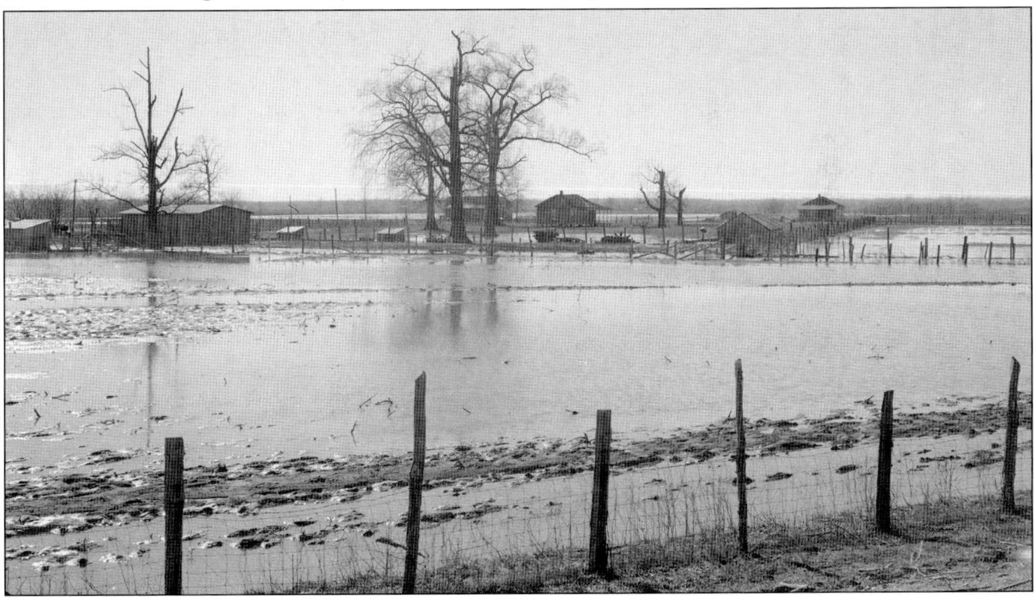

Farmland was submerged by the Ohio River flood of 1937 at Bessie Levee's farm near Tiptonville, Tennessee, near the Kentucky state line. By the end of January, the Ohio River overflowed fast and backed up connected rivers, causing farmers serious problems. They could not get livestock to high ground in time, and the water washed topsoil away for planting crops. (Courtesy of the Library of Congress.)

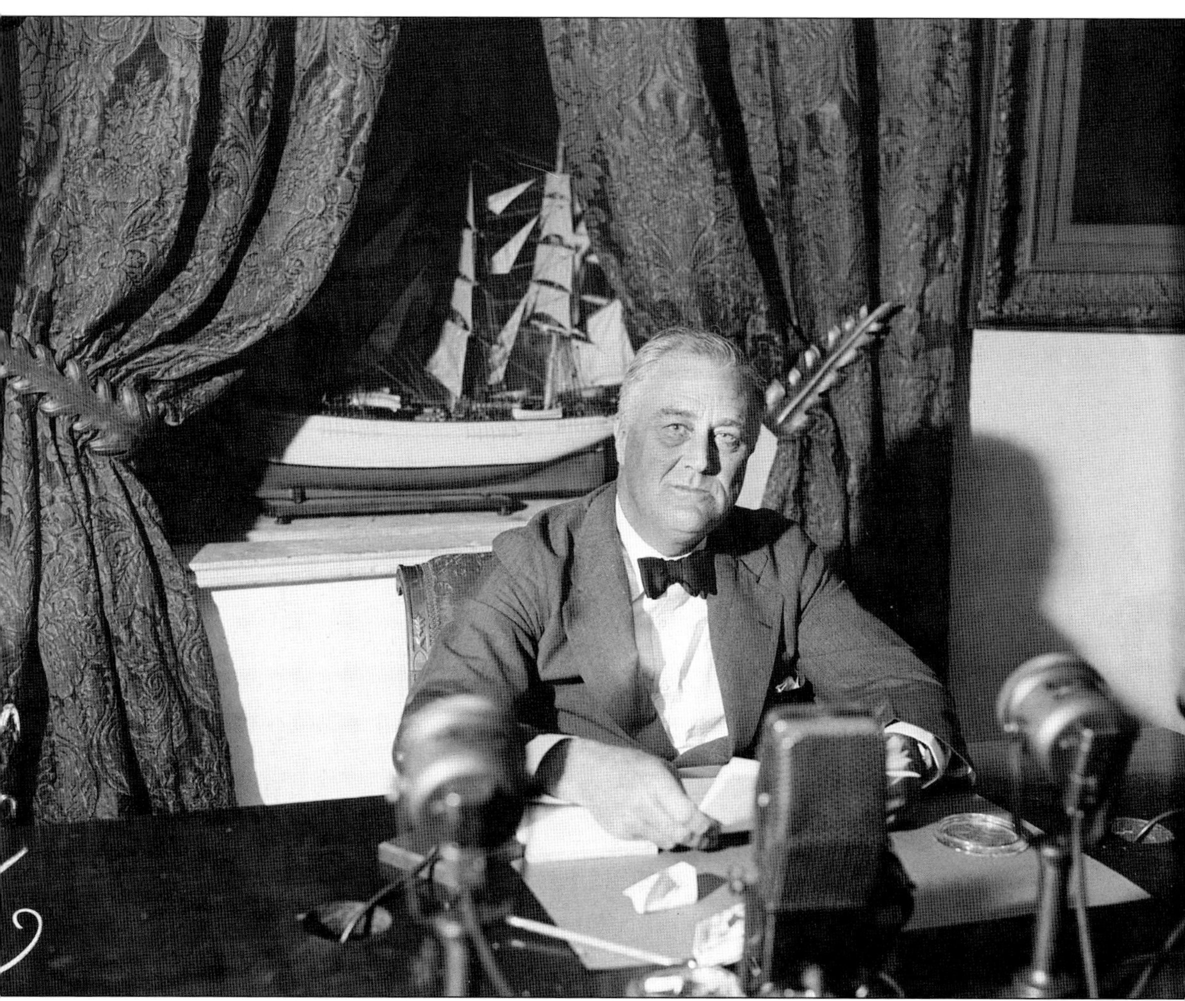

In 1932, Franklin D. Roosevelt became the 32nd president, defeating Herbert Hoover in a landslide victory. During his first 100 days, he implemented the policies that got people back to work. Roosevelt delivered radio speeches or "fireside chats" to the American people, giving them hope: "There is nothing to fear but fear itself." In 1933, President Roosevelt passed the New Deal, a series of programs to help tackle the Great Depression. Part of the New Deal were the Works Progress Administration (WPA) programs, which were initiated in 1935. The programs gave jobs with small salaries to people who needed work and promoted social and cultural awareness of art, theater, and literature. Due to his efforts, Roosevelt was reelected for president in 1936, 1940, and 1944. He was the only American president in history to be elected four times. (Courtesy of the Library of Congress.)

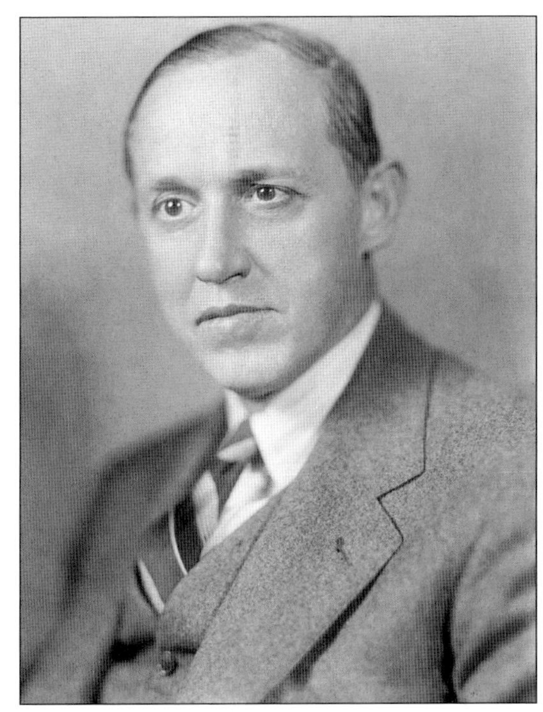

Harold "Harry" Hopkins was an American statesman, public administrator, and a presidential advisor to Roosevelt. As the head of the WPA and other federal programs, Hopkins believed government jobs were the solution to the economic crisis. During the seven years of the WPA, the programs employed 8.5 million people and worked on 1.4 million projects, including the repairs of roads, schools, hospitals, and more. (Courtesy of the Library of Congress.)

Ellen Woodward, a Mississippi state legislator, served on the state's Board of Public Welfare. The New Deal tapped Woodward to assist Hopkins with the WPA program concentrating on work for women, especially from the South, including her native state of Mississippi. She worked diligently for 30-plus years as a public servant until retiring in the 1950s. (Courtesy of the Library of Congress.)

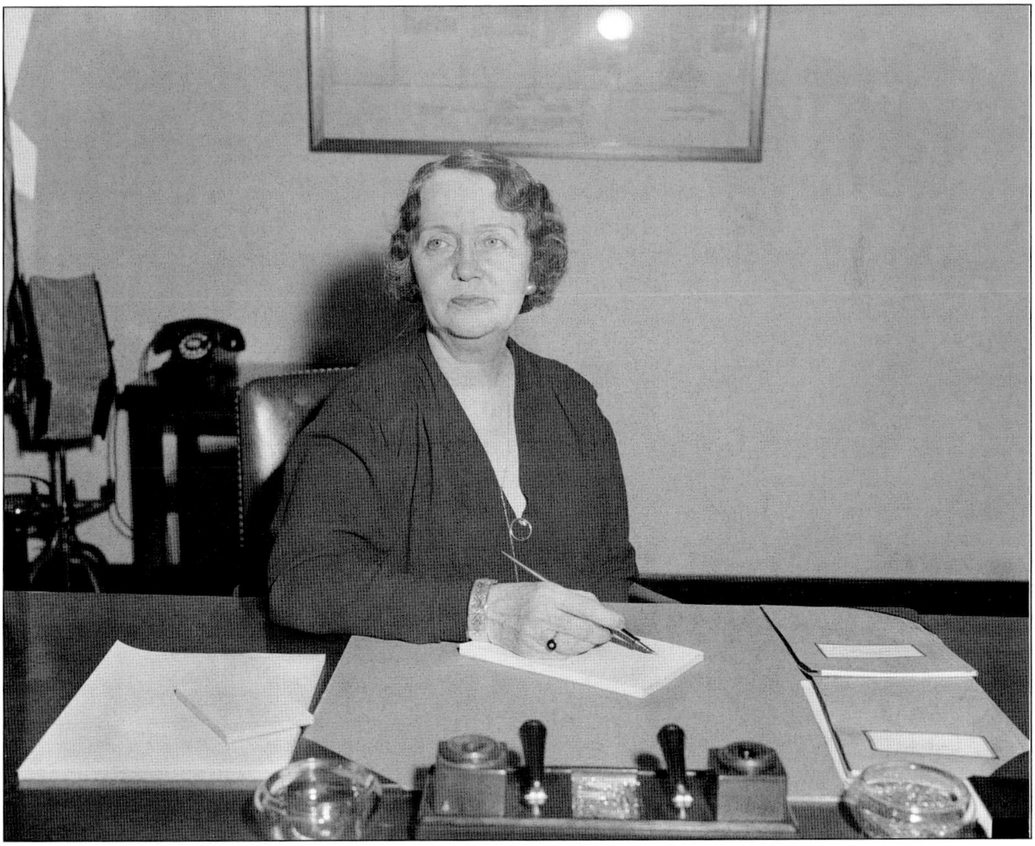

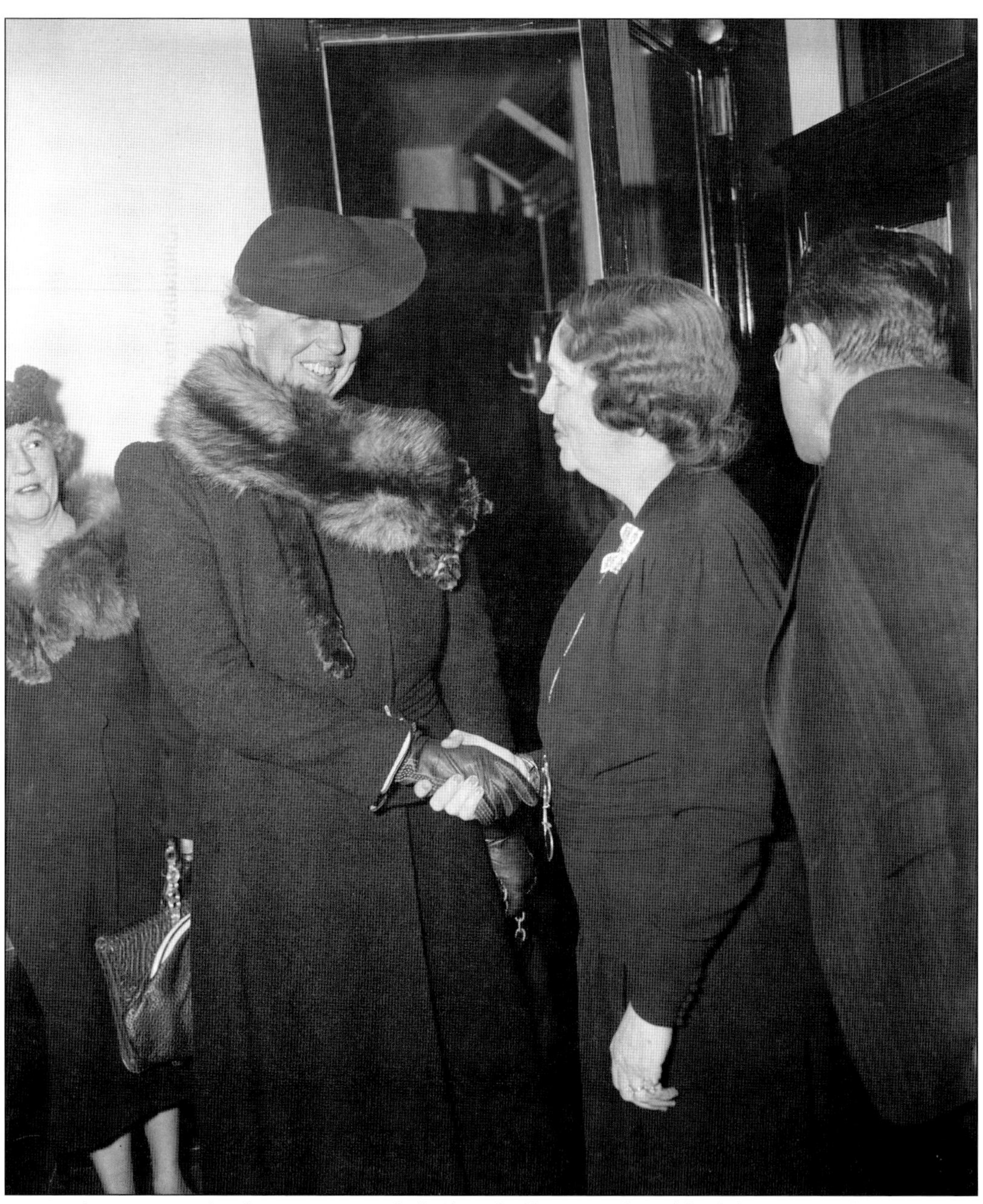

Pictured are First Lady Eleanor Roosevelt (left) and Ellen Woodward (right) in 1938. The First Lady sought out opportunities for women whenever possible. As the director of work relief programs for women, Woodward sought out an agreement with Appalachia women to deliver books through the Packhorse Library Project. The Kentucky region reminded her of Mississippi. Although her home state's library project built new libraries, the solution was different in Kentucky. The folks that needed loaned books the most lived miles from a town and deep in the mountains. The First Lady and Woodward were some of the most influential women in the WPA programs. (Courtesy of the Library of Congress.)

Increasing literacy was focused across the country through the WPA programs. The Illinois WPA Federal Art Project poster in 1940 read, "For greater knowledge on more subjects use your library often!," a quote by V. Donaghue. The man shown in the poster promoting library use is based on Auguste Rodin's *The Thinker* sculpture. (Courtesy of the Library of Congress.)

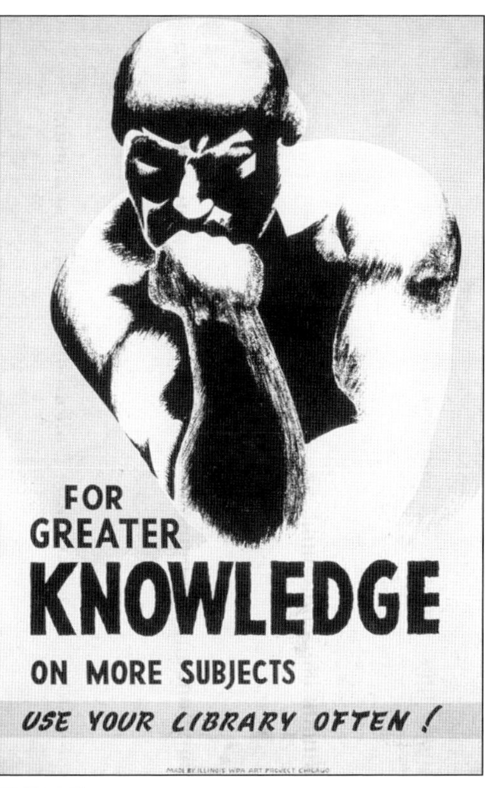

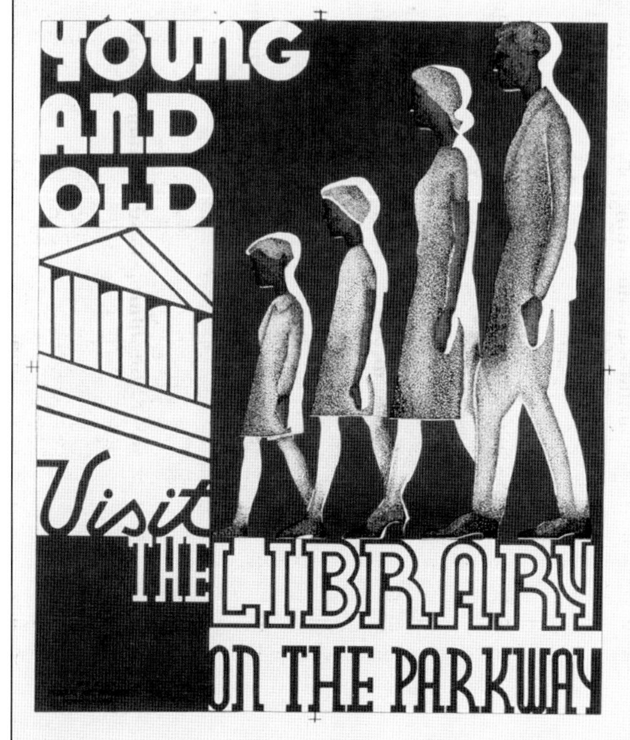

The Pennsylvania WPA Federal Art Project poster of 1936–1937 read, "Young and old visit the library on the Parkway." The artist Nathan Sherman showed a family going to the library together. The group of poster artists also designed posters for art programs, public parks, and health and education organizations. (Courtesy of the Library of Congress.)

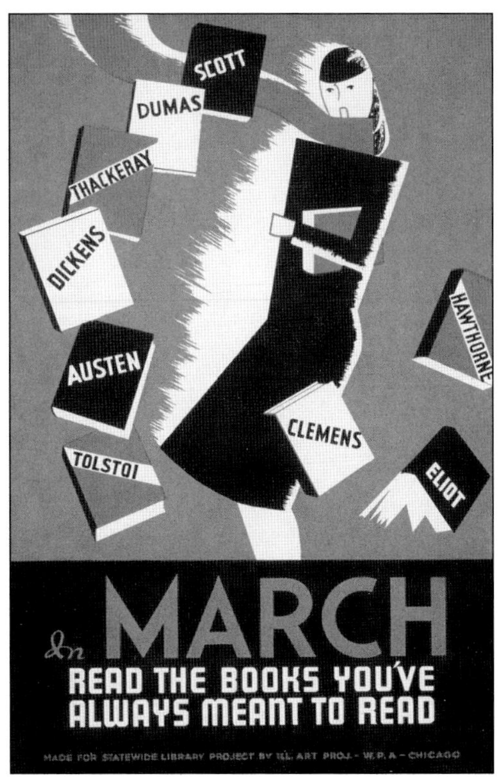

This poster enticed readers to grab a book during the month of March 1941: "In March read the books you've always meant to read." These posters were first made by hand but eventually moved to the silk screen process, which allowed for more to be printed. From 1936 to 1943, over two million posters were printed. (Courtesy of the Library of Congress.)

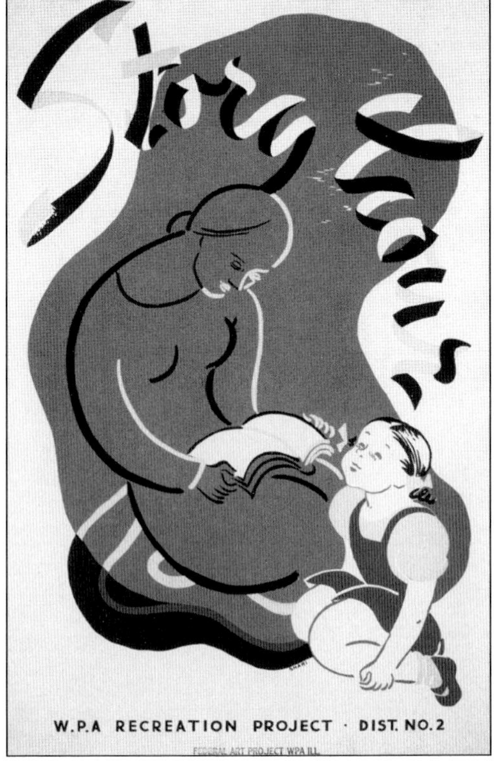

"Story hour W.P.A recreation project–Dist. No. 2" was a poster designed by Shari Weisberg in 1939 of a girl sitting at the knees of a woman holding an open book. The WPA posters were created for programs in 17 states and the District of Columbia. (Courtesy of the Library of Congress.)

The Iowa WPA Federal Art Project poster read, "The vacation reading club—join now at your public library." The 1939 poster enticed readers to take a "vacation" by reading a book with others. The states with the strongest poster representation were California, Illinois, New York, Ohio, and Pennsylvania. (Courtesy of the Library of Congress.)

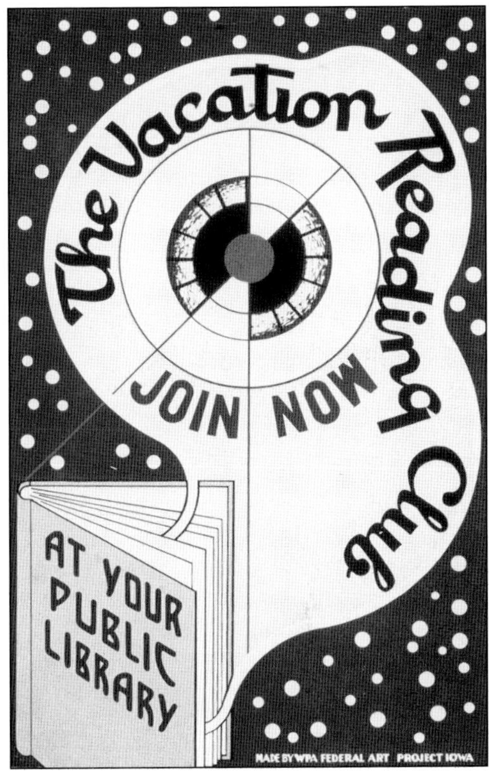

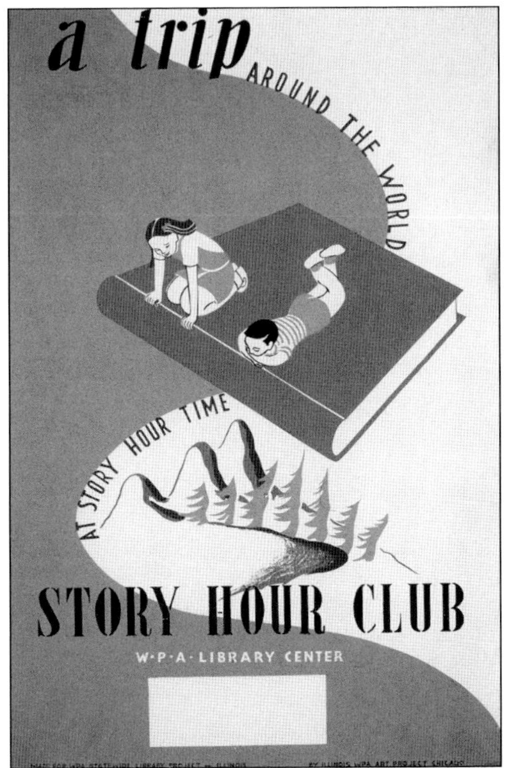

Another WPA poster designed by Shari Weisberg read, "A trip around the world at story hour time Story Hour Club—W.P.A Library Center." The poster was created and displayed between 1936 and 1940 and promoted the statewide library project, showing two children on a large book peering down at mountains and trees. (Courtesy of the Library of Congress.)

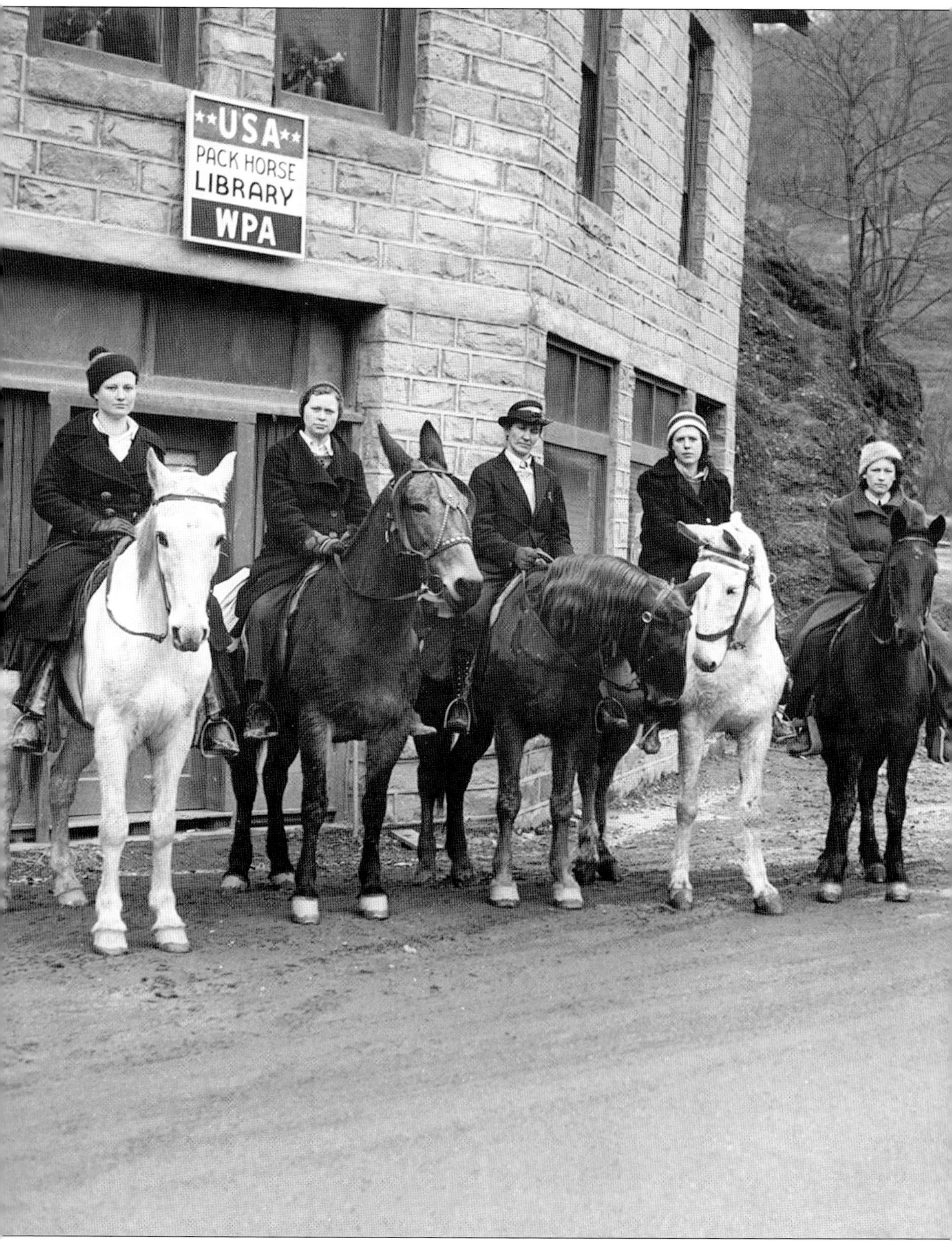
USA
PACK HORSE
LIBRARY
WPA

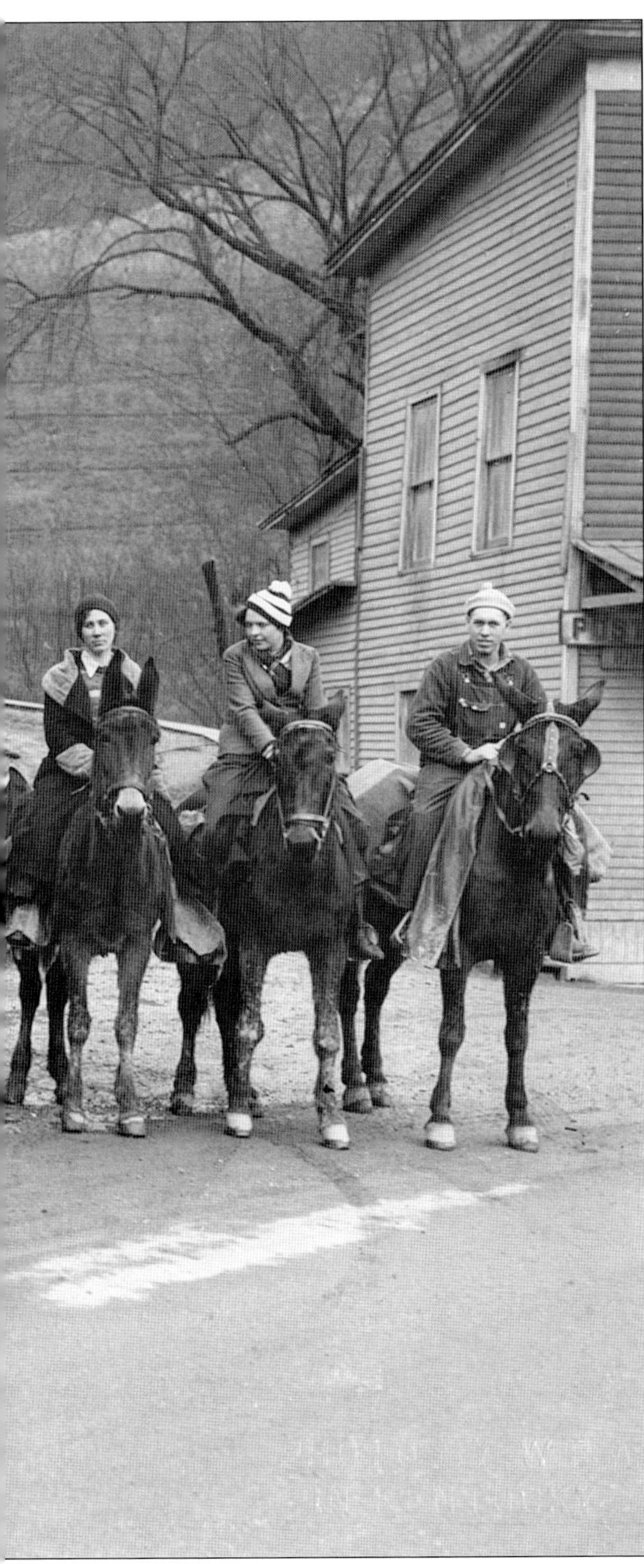

One of the WPA programs focusing on literacy was the Packhorse Library Project, which began in 1935. The WPA packhorse librarians of Hindman, Kentucky, in Knott County posed for a photograph in front of their central library in downtown Hindman. Next door to the post office, the library was housed in an office building. The space donated by a businessman allowed the librarians to serve homes and schools in Hindman and also the surrounding areas. The Packhorse Library Project brought literacy to people during grim times. (Courtesy of WPA collection, Archives and Records Management Division, Kentucky Department for Libraries and Archives.)

W. P. A.

STATE EXHIBIT

June 10 and 11

at

Pack Horse Library

Opposite Sandy Valley Grocery Co.

Main St. PAINTSVILLE, KY.

Handicrafts, Weaving, Basketry

and Other Salable Articles

Puppet Show - Drum and Bugle Corps

Everything FREE! Everybody INVITED!

The WPA State Exhibit poster advertised various programs, including homecrafts, weaving, basketry, puppet shows, and the drum and bugle corps in Paintsville, Kentucky. The event took place at the Packhorse Library on Main Street opposite Sandy Valley Grocery Company. Everything was free and everyone was invited. With the New Deal, posters in different states across the nation promoted jobs for women, offering "good pay, good meals, good surroundings, and good working conditions." They found employment in domestics, heath services, sewing projects, school lunch programs, and libraries. (Left, courtesy of Mallie Cody Turner Collection [MS049-1993], Morehead State University Special Collections and Archives; below, courtesy of the Library of Congress.)

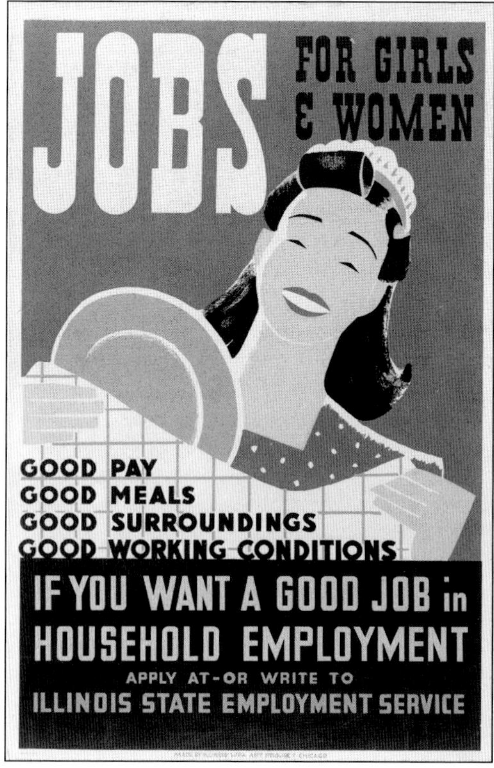

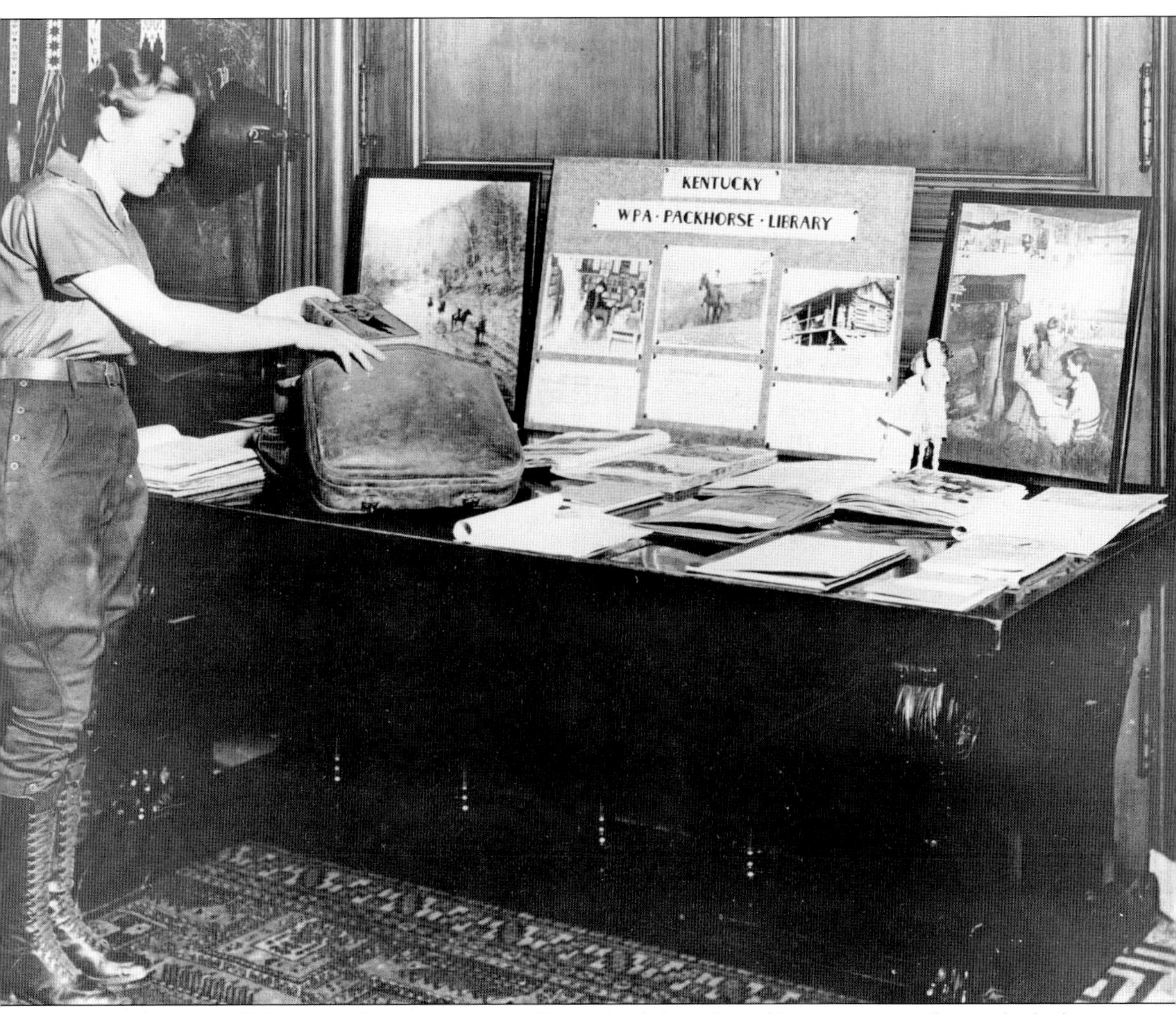

During the early 1930s, sixty-three counties in Kentucky did not have library services due to the lack of gravel or paved roads. The Packhorse Library Project was a way to get books into people's hands across the state. A packhorse librarian proudly set up a table to display photographs and literature about the Packhorse Library Project. (Courtesy of Mallie Cody Turner Collection [MS049-1993], Morehead State University Special Collections and Archives.)

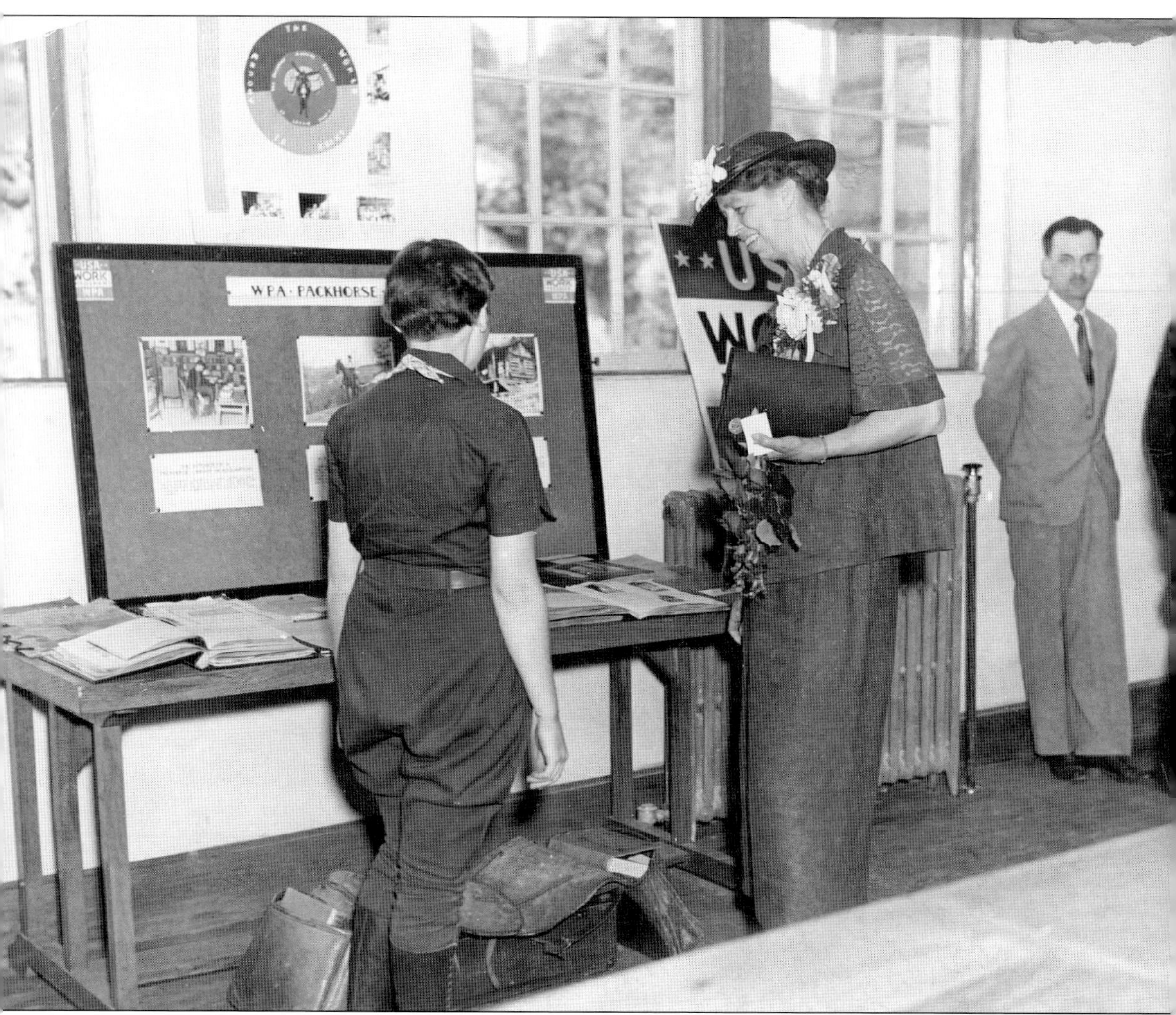

Since education was looked on as a way to escape poverty, First Lady Eleanor Roosevelt posed the question of how money could be found to "feed their minds?" The Packhorse Library Project was shared with a smiling First Lady and how literacy could fulfill this hunger. (Courtesy of Mallie Cody Turner Collection [MS049-1993], Morehead State University Special Collections and Archives.)

Three

HOPE ON HORSEBACK

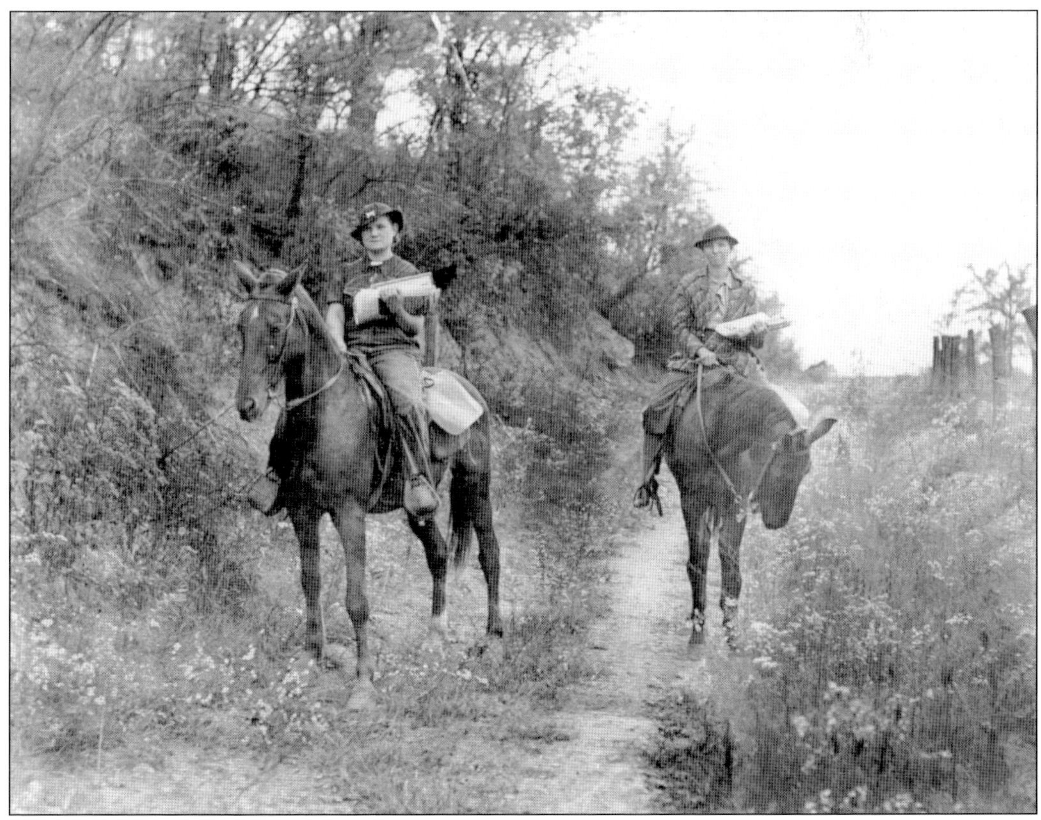

Two packhorse librarians crossed paths with their hands full of reading materials. The librarians had many names, including bookwomen, book ladies, packsaddle librarians, traveling librarians, and carriers. No matter which nickname patrons used, the librarians cherished hearing their name and eagerly wanted to help their communities. (Courtesy of Mallie Cody Turner Collection [MS049-1993], Morehead State University Special Collections and Archives.)

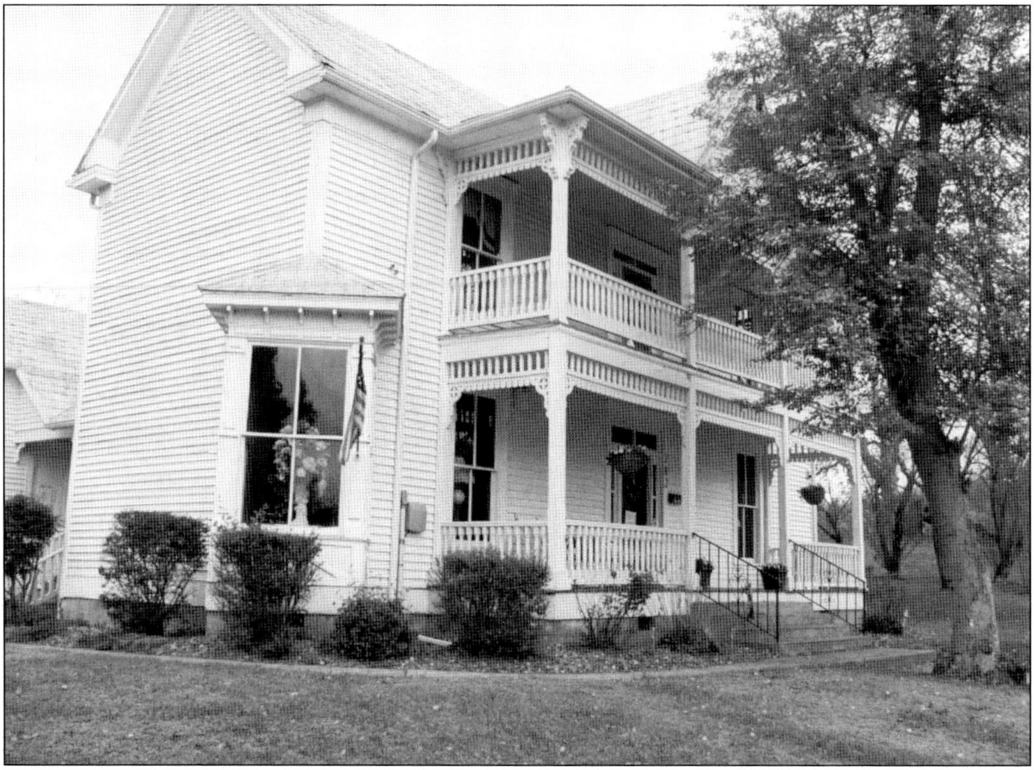

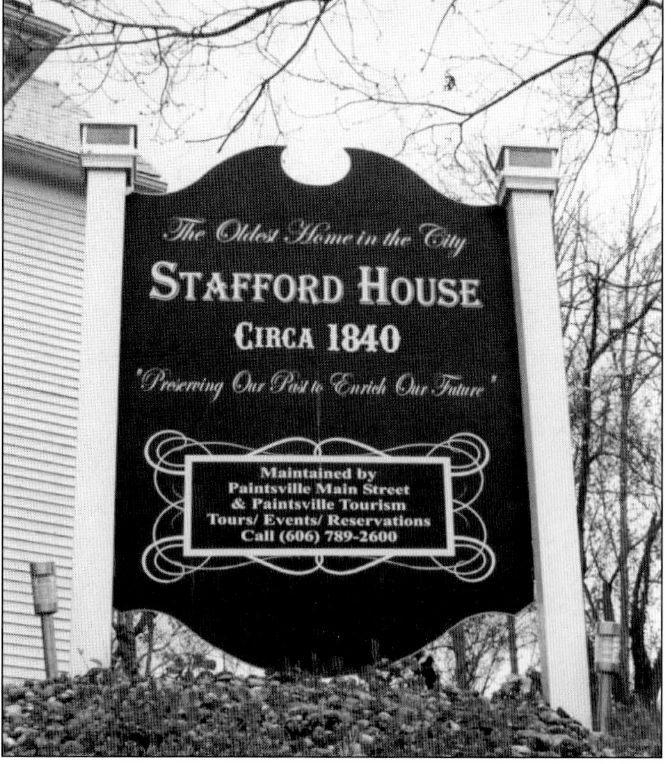

The Francis M. Stafford House is located at 102 Broadway Street in Paintsville, Kentucky, and is the oldest standing home in the city. The rear part of the home was built for John Stafford in 1843, when he helped establish Paintsville. In 1888, the front part was built by Stafford's son Francis, who he named the home after. At one time, the Stafford farm included a smokehouse, barn, corncrib, gristmill, storehouse, and a coal house, which was located below the home on Paint Creek. A holly tree planted in front of the house in 1861 still stands today. The home was added to the National Register of Historic Places in 1975. (Photographs by Nicki Jacobsmeyer; courtesy of Patty Reeves and Johnson County Public Library, Paintsville, Kentucky.)

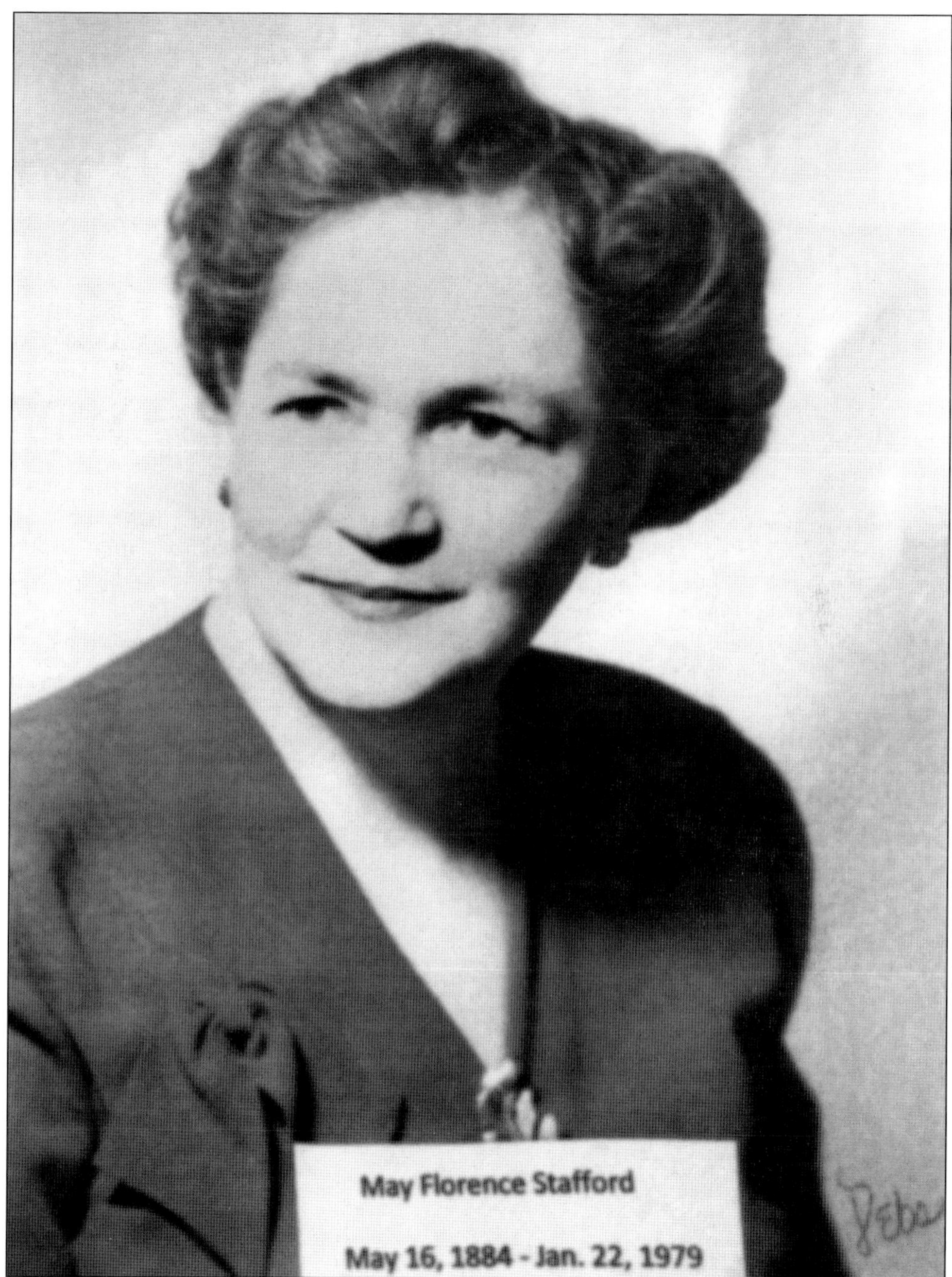

The packhorse librarians originated in Paintsville, Kentucky, and were started by May Florence Stafford. Francis Marion Stafford and his wife, Marietta Lavender, had 14 children. May was their 13th child and 11th daughter. She was the supervisor for the Paintsville and Johnson County Packhorse Libraries. She referred to them as one of her special projects. After attending college and teaching, May returned to Paintsville and restored the family's home in 1954–1955. She remained there for the rest of her life until she passed away in January 1978, four months before her 95th birthday. The community dearly misses May Stafford. (Courtesy of Patty Reeves and Johnson County Public Library, Paintsville, Kentucky.)

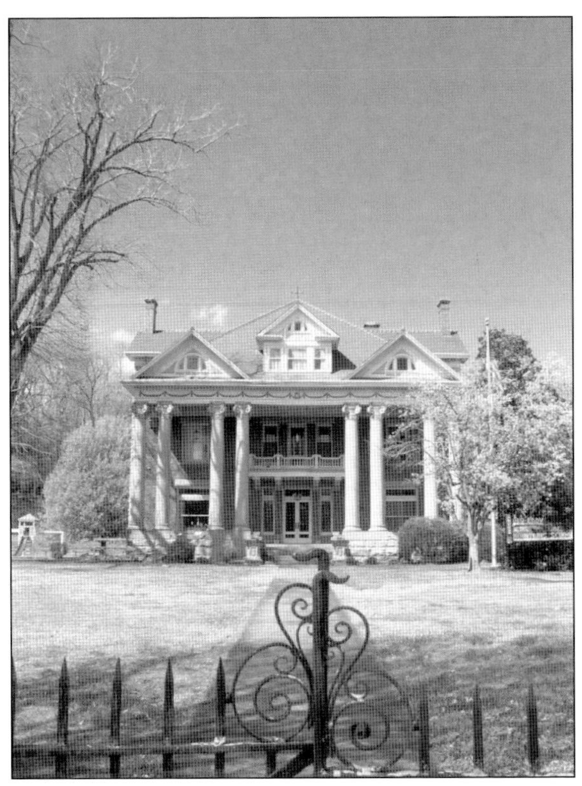

The Mayo Mansion is located at 405 Third Street in Paintsville, Kentucky. American entrepreneur John C.C. Mayo had it built from 1905 to 1912. An article titled "Pack-Horse Library Here" in the *Paintsville Herald* on January 6, 1938, informed the public that a new WPA project was to be directed by May Stafford and opened on December 20. The library was located in the Evans Mansion (formerly Mayo Mansion), donated by Mr. and Mrs. E.J. Evans. The collection began with around 200 donated books from the Ashland library and around 500 magazines. People of the town borrowed books and enjoyed the reading room. The mansion was added to the National Register of Historic Places in 1974 and is currently the home of Our Lady of the Mountains School. (Photographs by Nicki Jacobsmeyer; courtesy of Patty Reeves and Johnson County Public Library, Paintsville, Kentucky.)

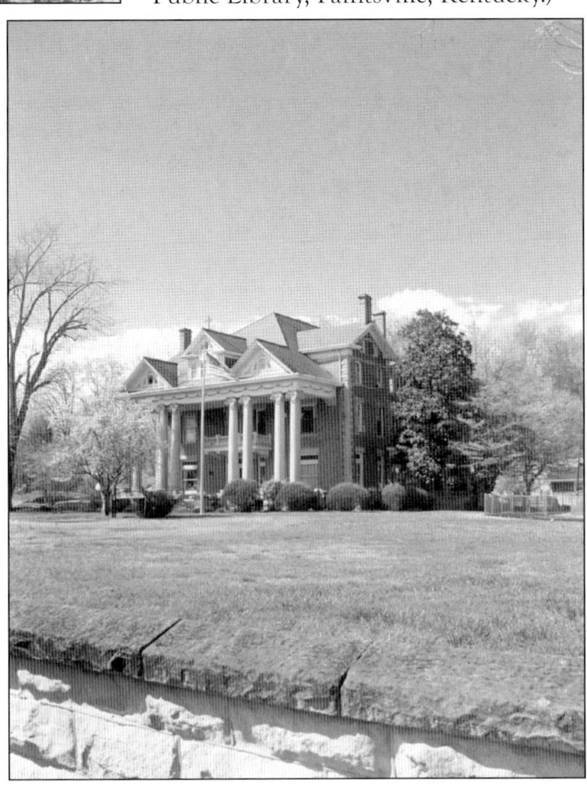

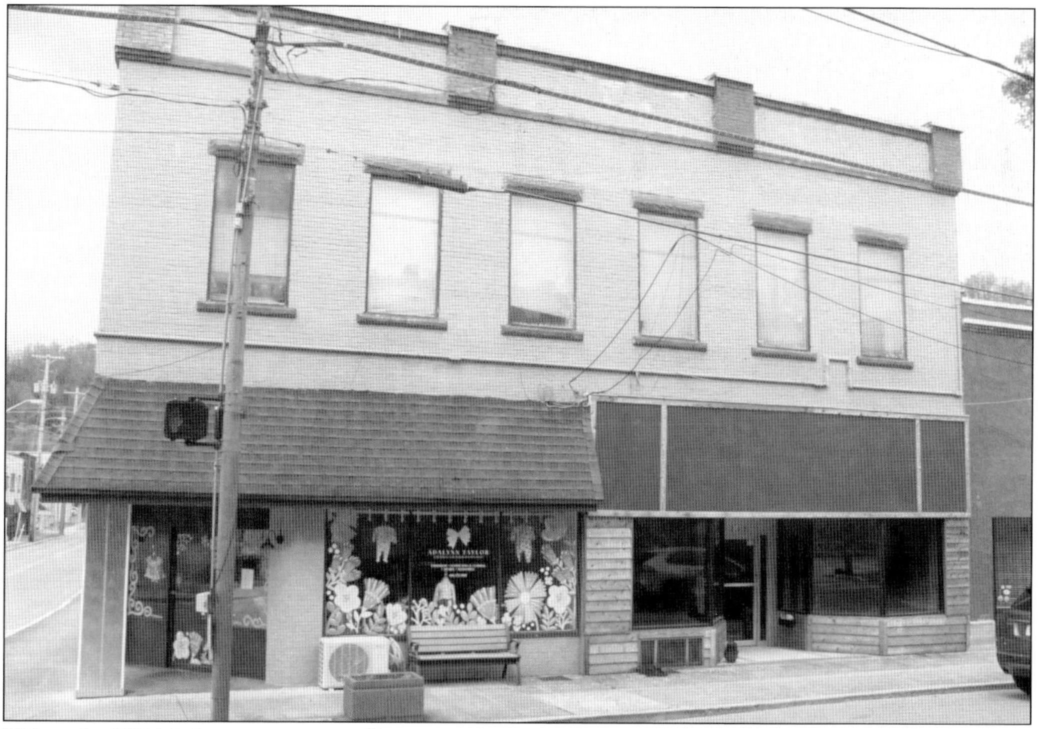

When the WPA Library in Paintsville, Kentucky, celebrated its first anniversary, it was located in this large building on Main Street. The owner of the building, H.M. Stafford, was librarian May Stafford's uncle and donated half of the value of the rent to the library. The collection had grown to 8,697 books and 13,551 magazines donated by 24 states. Types of books included classics, dictionaries, references, children, fiction, textbooks, travel, history, and religion, including Bibles in English, Hebrew, Greek, and German. The figures for one month reported 14 carriers, 1,702 homes visited, 352 schools visited, 1,858 miles traveled, and 29,656 books circulated. (Photographs by Nicki Jacobsmeyer; courtesy of Patty Reeves and Johnson County Public Library, Paintsville, Kentucky.)

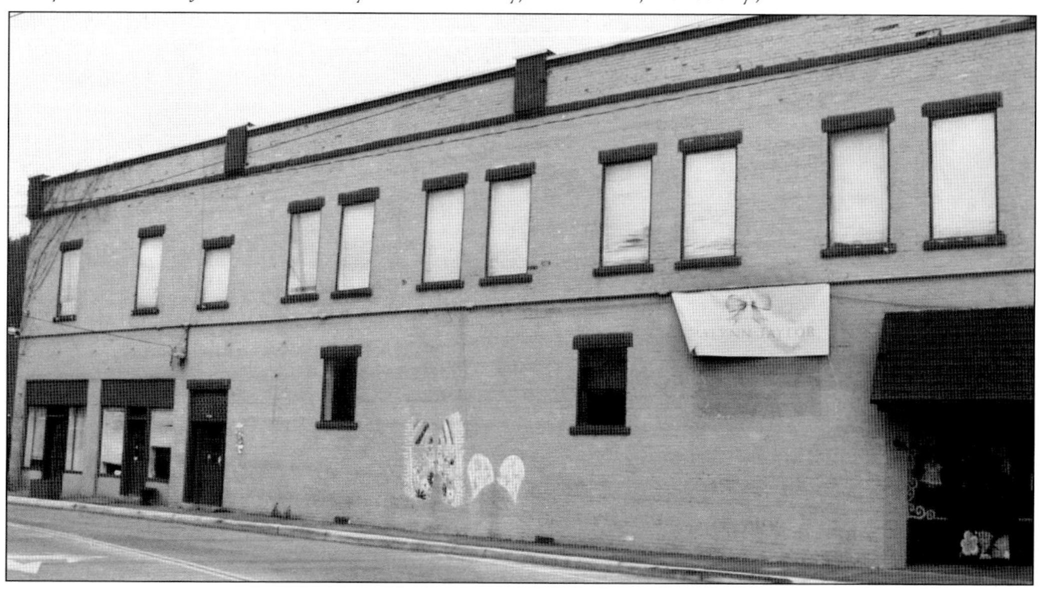

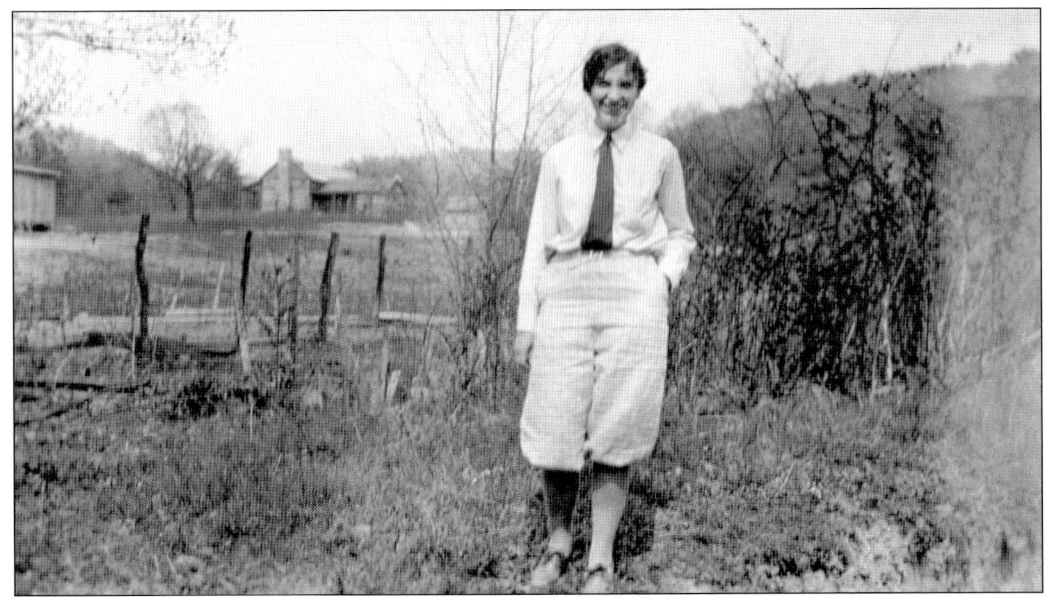

Librarian Marjorie Patch smiled for the camera in spring during the 1930s. Packhorse librarians wore rough, practical breeches and boots. With the miles and terrain traveled on horseback, they needed durable and comfortable attire. Their day started before the sun rose and often did not end until it set. (Courtesy of Berea College Special Collections and Archives.)

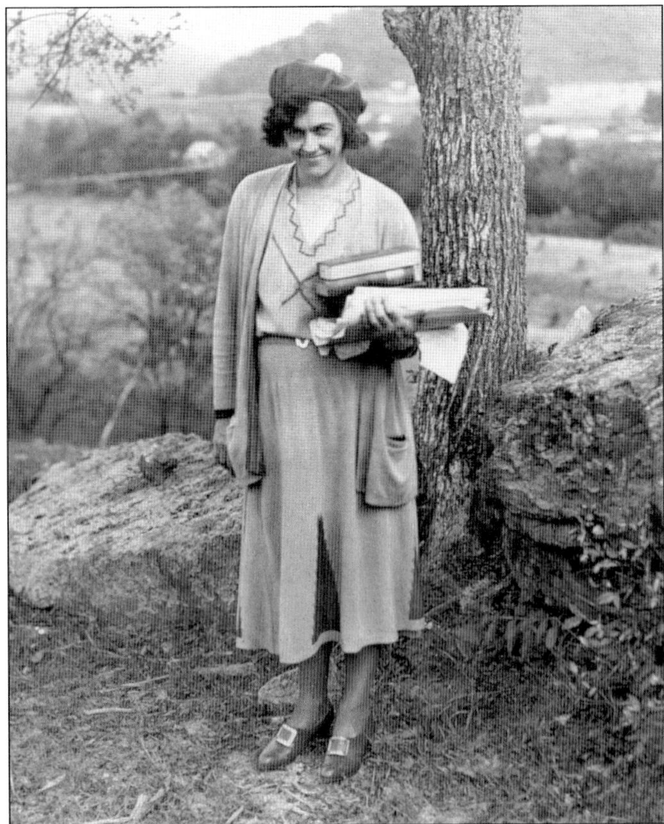

Most packhorse librarians were 25–35 years old, married, and the sole provider of the family. This librarian wore a skirt since she traveled on foot. Since she was without a horse and saddlebag, she carried her books and materials by hand. (Courtesy of Mallie Cody Turner Collection [MS049-1993], Morehead State University Special Collections and Archives.)

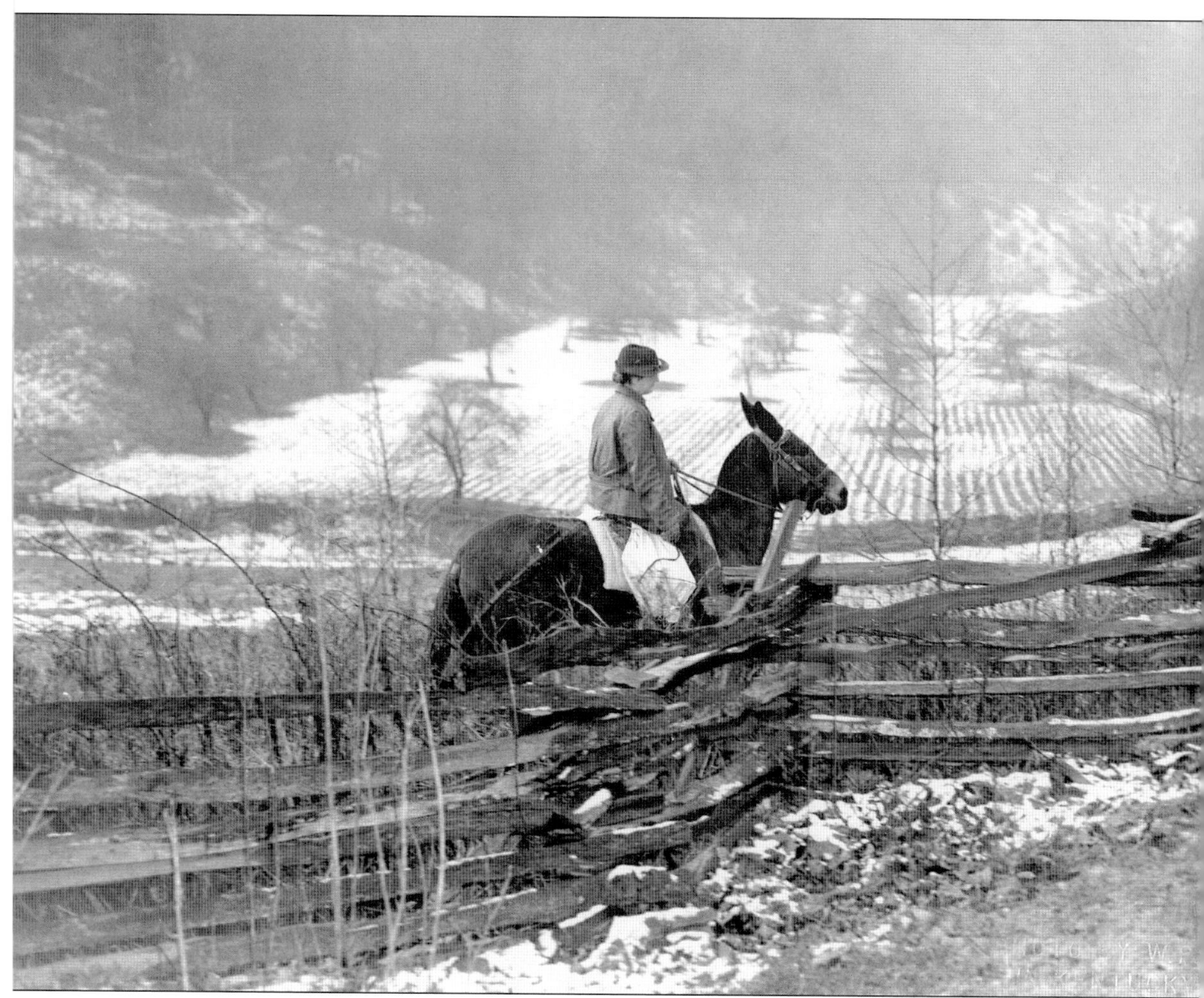

A packhorse librarian and her mule traversed the snowy hillside in winter with a sack full of books to deliver to her next patrons. Packhorse librarians received $28 per month for delivering books by horseback. In modern dollars, their salary was around $495 per month. This sum did not include if they needed to lease a horse or mule from a farmer. Nor did it include the animal's needs like food and water. Farmers were thrilled to lease out their animals. They simply had to hand over the reins and open the gate for the much-needed additional income. (Courtesy of Mallie Cody Turner Collection [MS049-1993], Morehead State University Special Collections and Archives.)

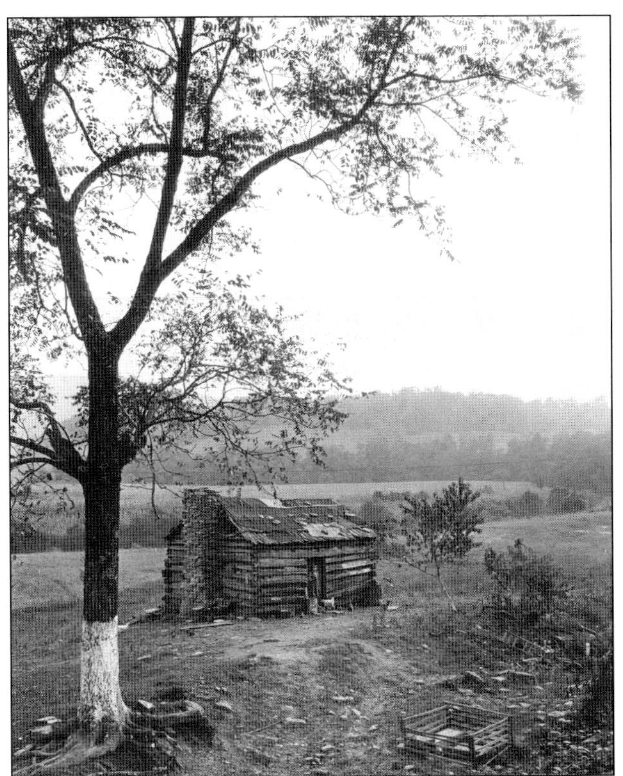

Each librarian was given a section of the county to cover. Their book routes averaged 100–120 miles per trip, which were repeated twice a month. They rode and walked an average of 4,905 miles per month. Packhorse librarians delivered to homes and schoolhouses. (Courtesy of WPA collection, Archives and Records Management Division, Kentucky Department for Libraries and Archives.)

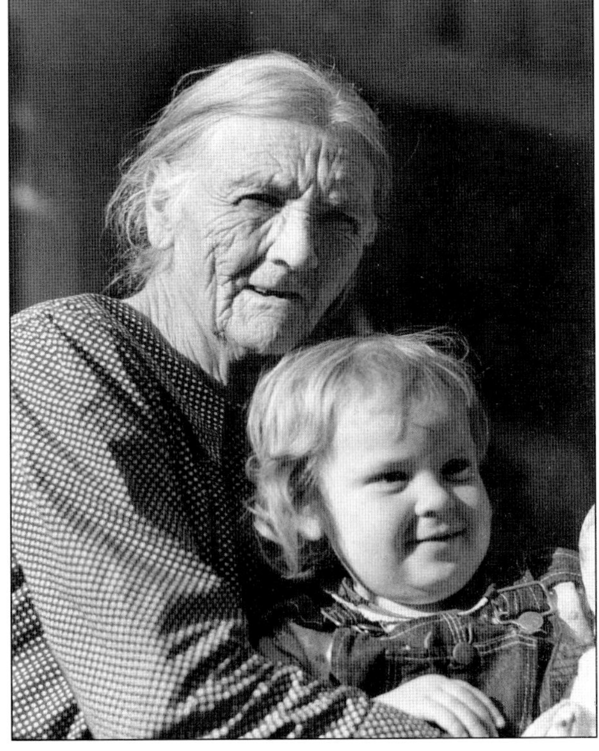

The Packhorse Library Project was successful because of the increased value of literacy among mountain folks. Folks wanted the best for their kin and craved education to be passed on to future generations. The librarians were accepted by people and became a part of daily life in the secluded and rugged Appalachian Mountains. (Courtesy of WPA collection, Archives and Records Management Division, Kentucky Department for Libraries and Archives.)

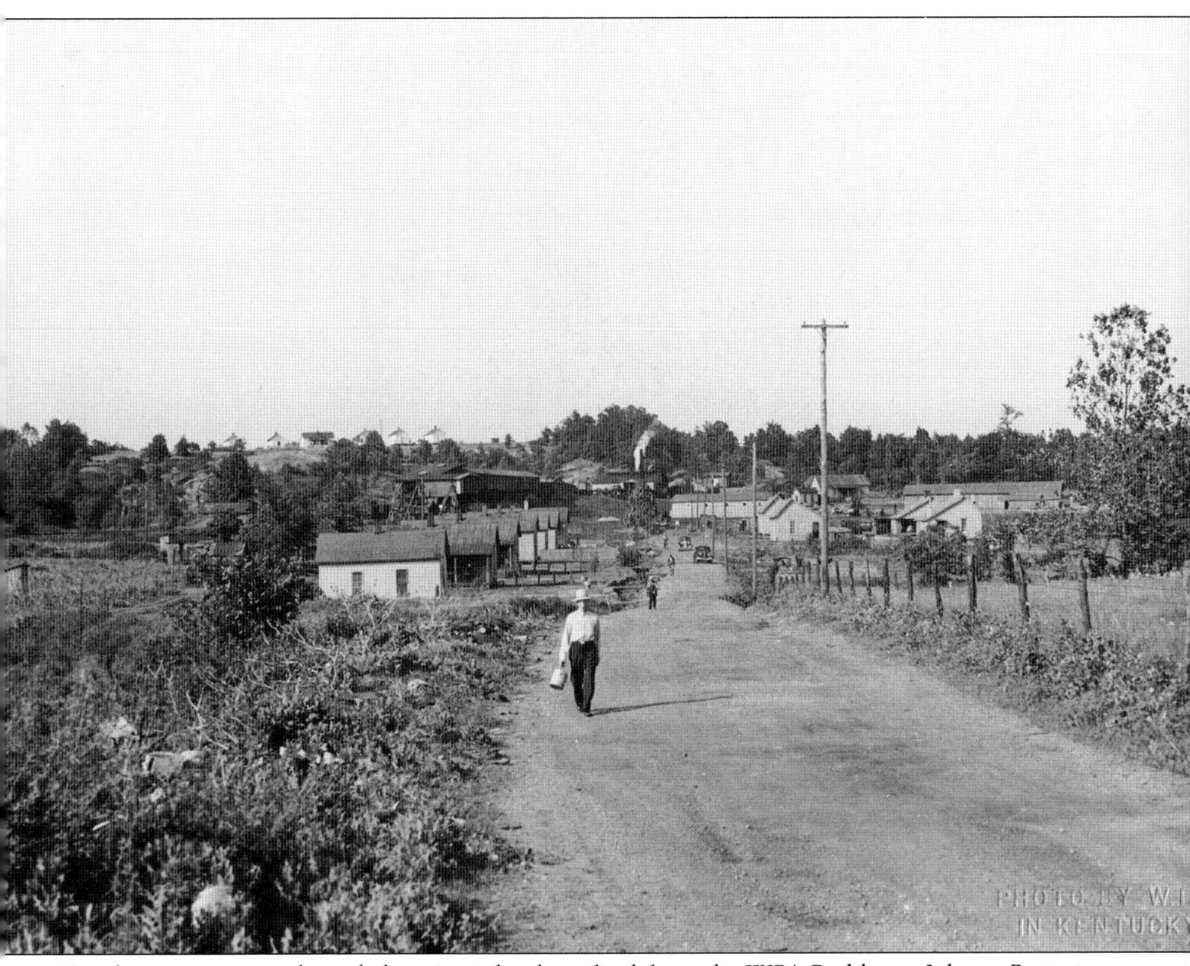

Rural areas were not the only locations that benefited from the WPA Packhorse Library Project; some small towns did as well. Branches of the main county library met those needs. Some counties had as many as 8 or 10 of these rural centers. The common goal to increase literacy across the country was reflected in these small town and rural library centers. (Courtesy of WPA collection, Archives and Records Management Division, Kentucky Department for Libraries and Archives.)

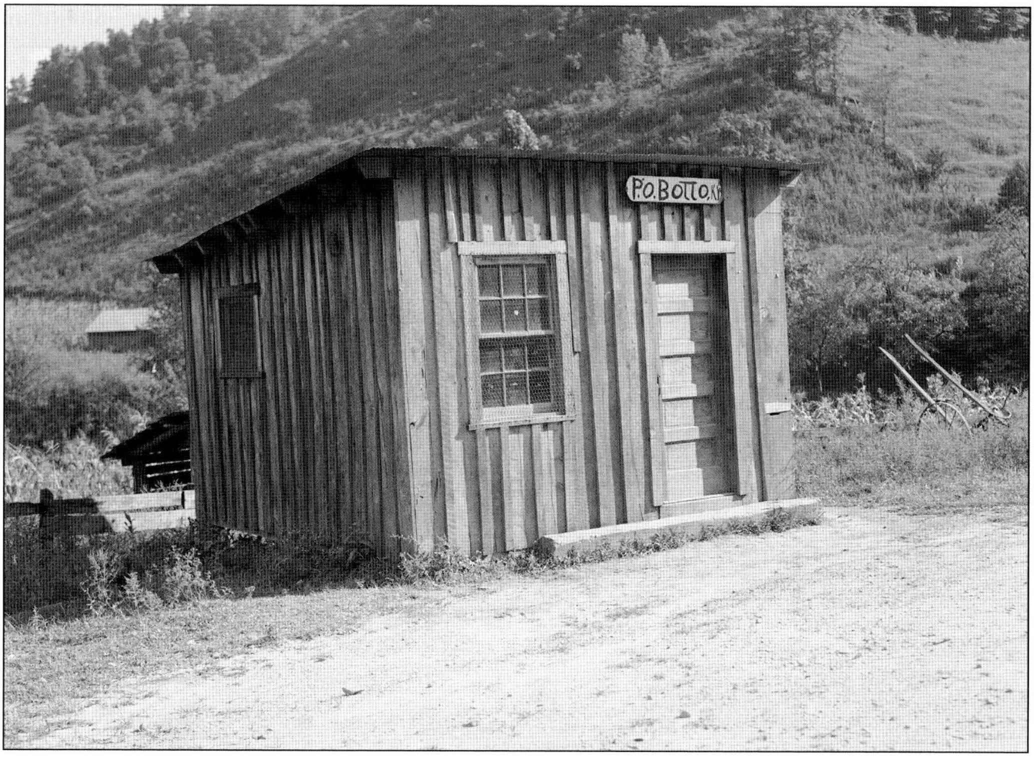

Central library branches were housed in facilities available by the community like this post office in Botto, Kentucky, of Letcher County. Other facilities included churches, schools, and businesses. The central library is where most of the reading materials were housed and the main meeting place for the packhorse librarians of that area and county. (Courtesy of the Library of Congress.)

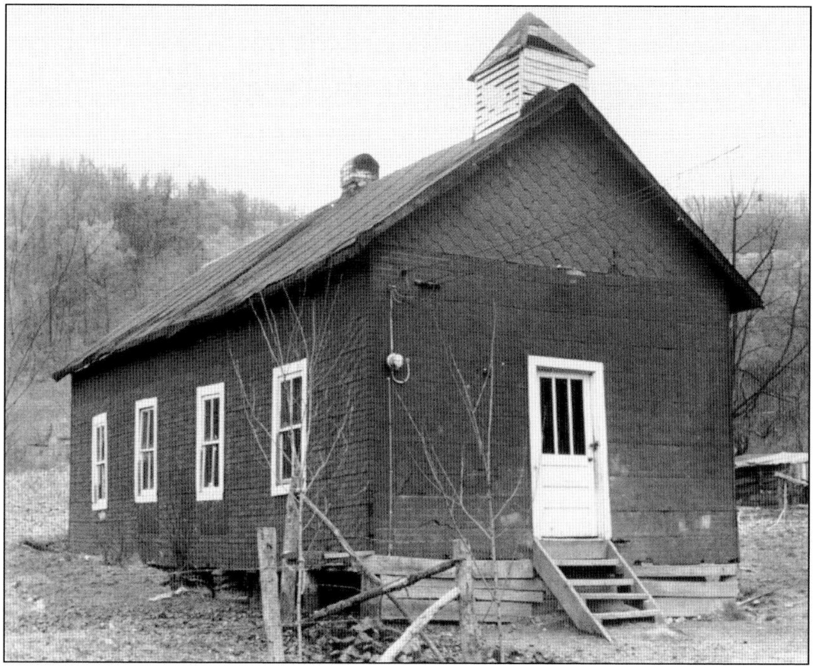

To run a central library facility, it cost around $40 per month in rent and utilities. However, local school districts provided rent, heating, and lighting for the library as long as the packhorse librarians would serve their rural schools by delivering reading materials. (Courtesy of Berea College Special Collections and Archives.)

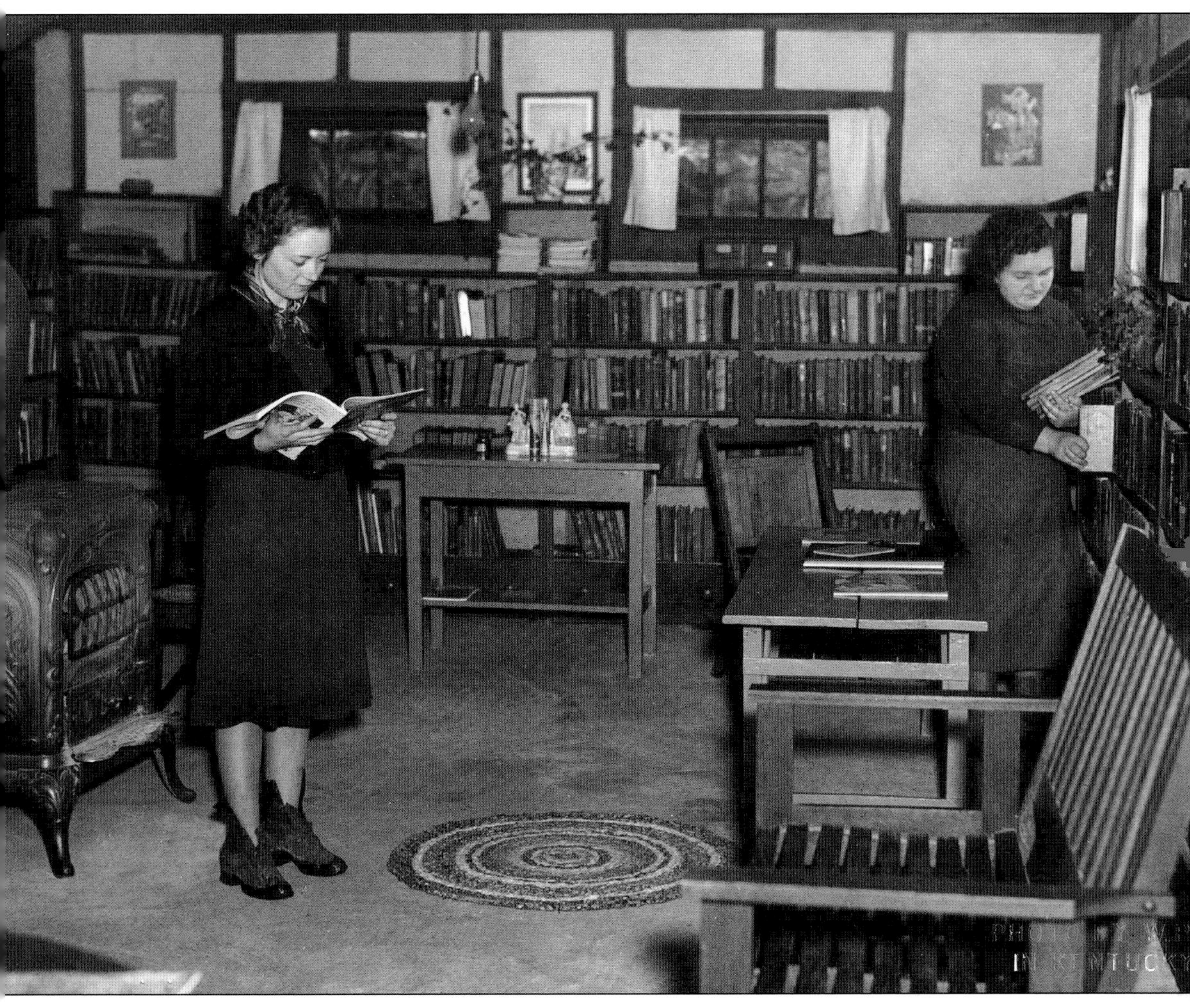

Librarians worked at the library center by shelving books recently returned or new to the collection and leafing through a magazine to determine which of her patrons would most enjoy checking it out. The WPA Packhorse Library Project opened 30 different libraries across rural Kentucky. These central libraries served around 155 schools and around 100,000 patrons. However, the companionship, encouragement, and hope the packhorse librarians provided was immeasurable. (Courtesy of WPA collection, Archives and Records Management Division, Kentucky Department for Libraries and Archives.)

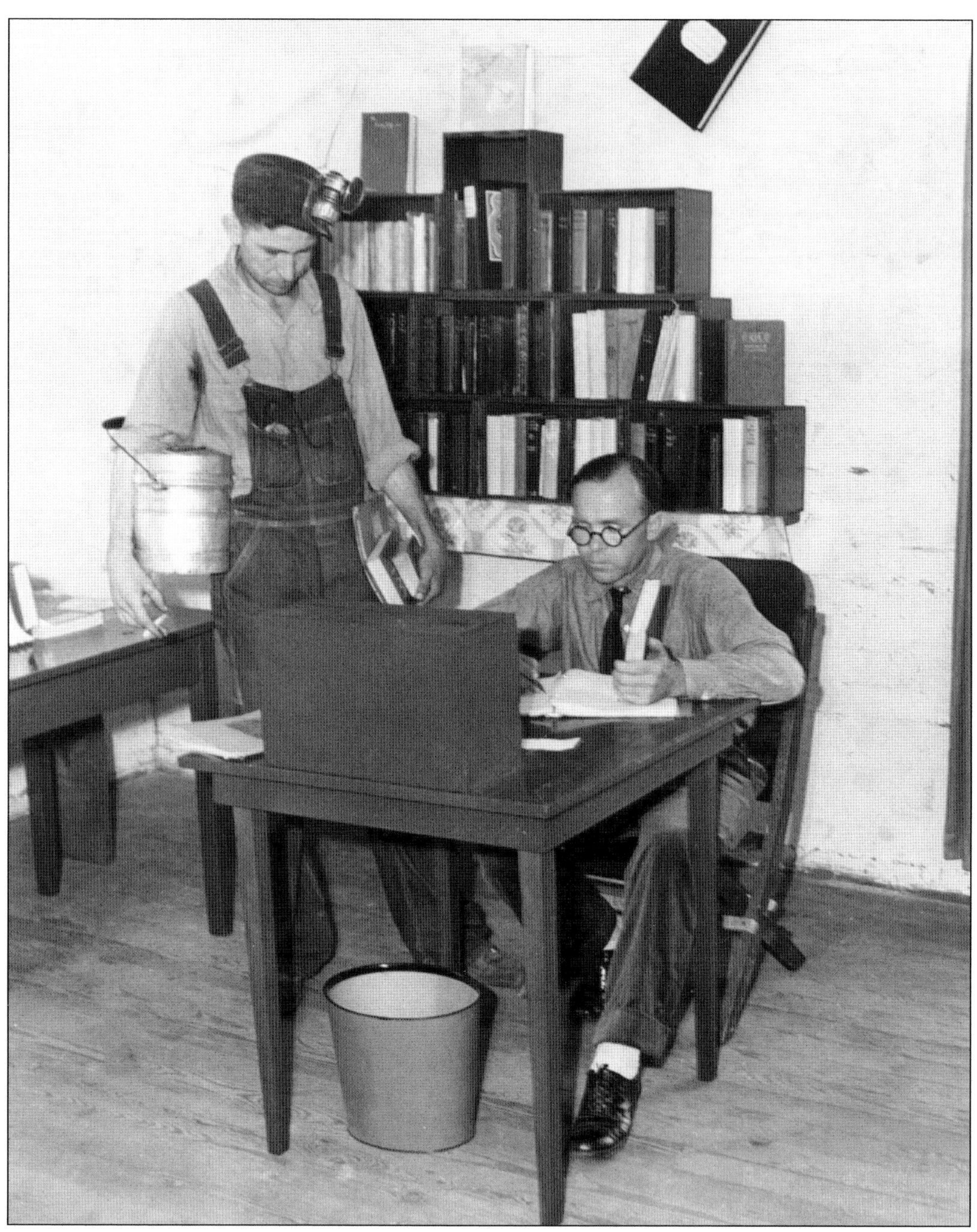

A coal miner checked out books at the local central library in his mining town. Coal miners spent their entire day down in the dark mines, craving the "light" books provided at night. Therefore, mining towns proved to be an ideal location for a library. (Courtesy of WPA collection, Archives and Records Management Division, Kentucky Department for Libraries and Archives.)

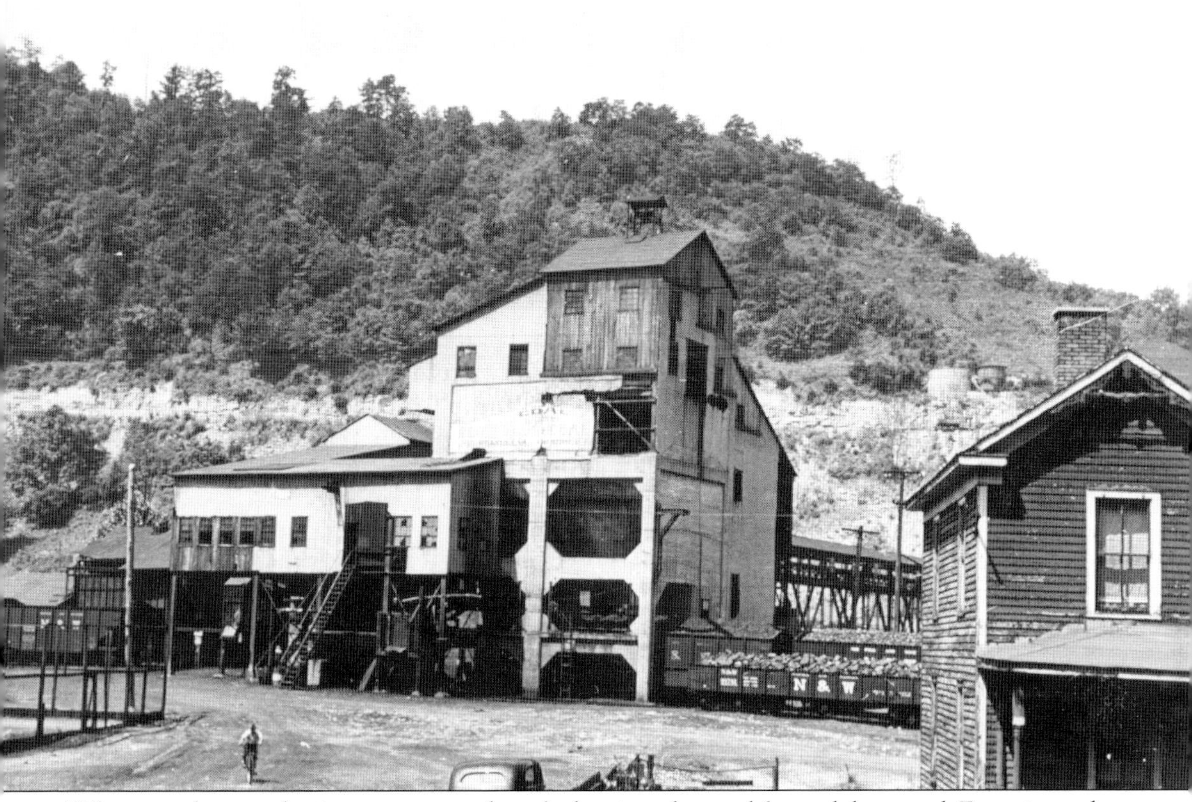

When people started using more natural gas for heating, the need for coal decreased. Factories and coal mines started closing, and the workers were laid off. The need for books and reading materials still remained, though, as these men needed to learn new skills in order to find work and provide for themselves and their family. (Courtesy of WPA collection, Archives and Records Management Division, Kentucky Department for Libraries and Archives.)

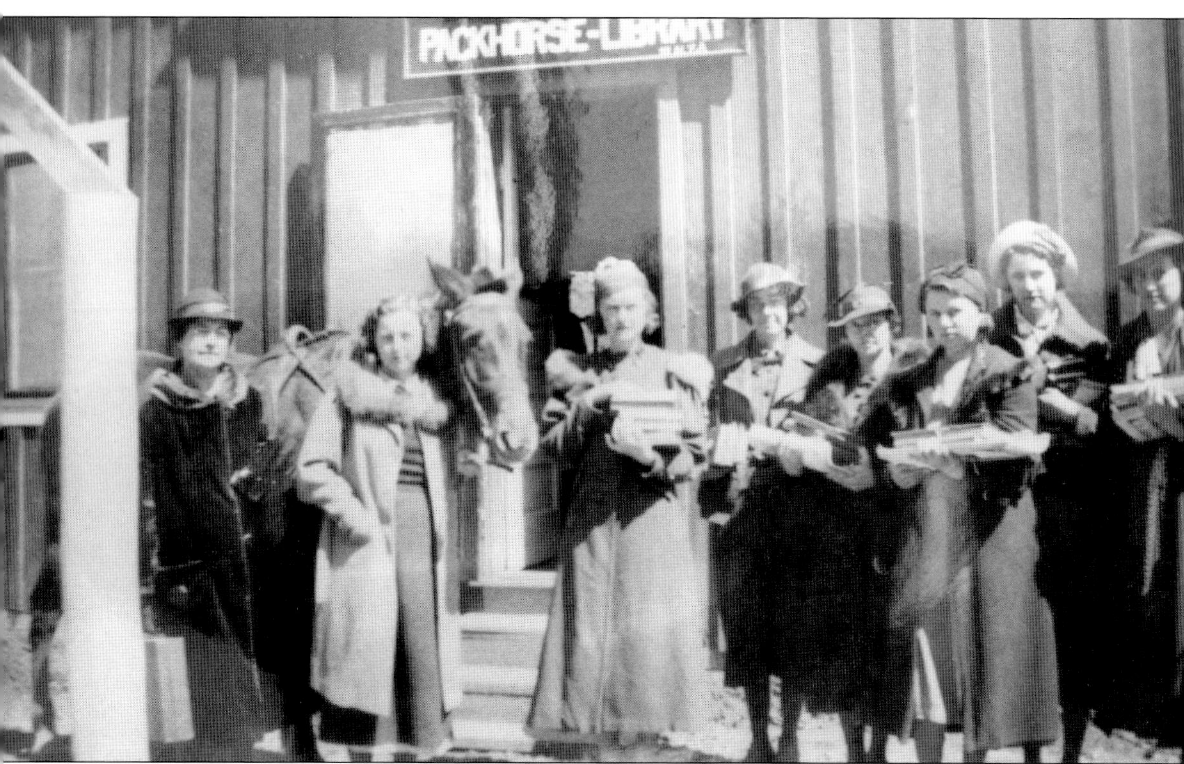

Packhorse librarians of Jackson County, Kentucky, posed in front of their central library headquarters. The carriers learned a photographer was visiting, so they got dressed up for the occasion. The Packhorse Library sign was made by the WPA National Youth Administration, which provided education and work for Americans ages 16–25. (Photograph by Prof. Jason Vance of Middle Tennessee State University; courtesy of the Franklin D. Roosevelt Presidential Library.)

Four

Grace and Grit

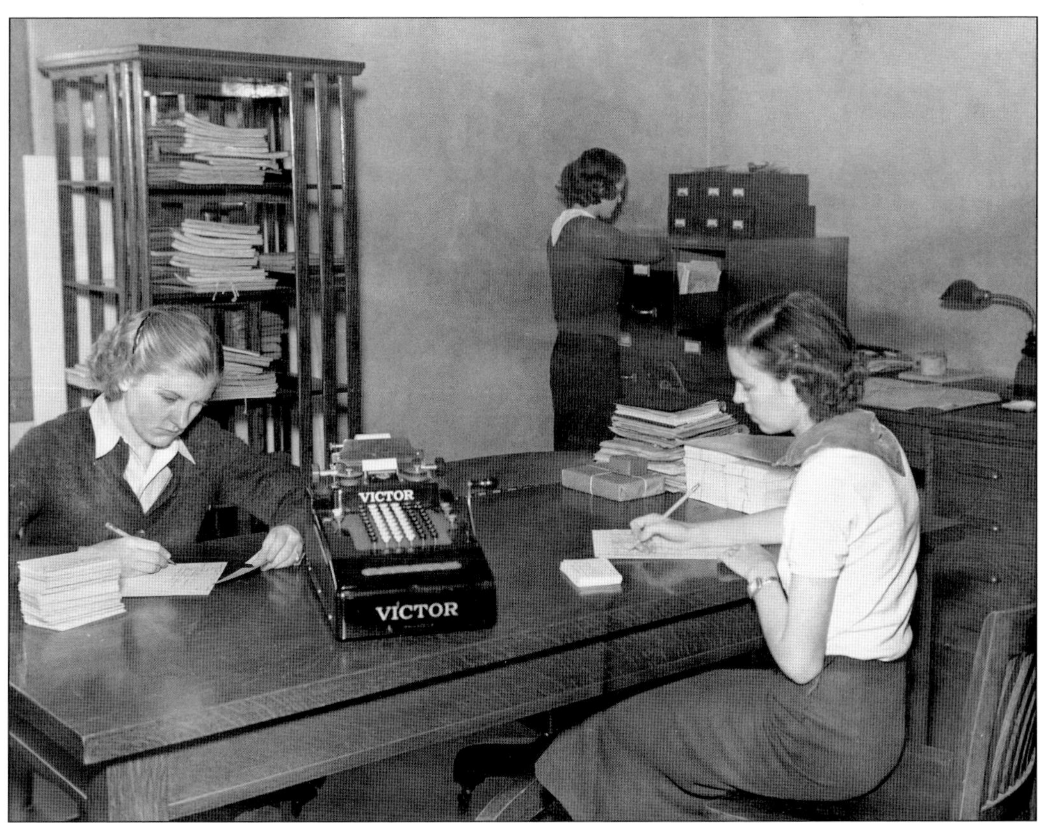

Central libraries staffed five to six packhorse librarians who delivered books. At least one librarian stayed at the library to organize and maintain the collection, recondition books and materials that needed mending, and formulate the carriers routes. (Courtesy of Mallie Cody Turner Collection [MS049-1993], Morehead State University Special Collections and Archives.)

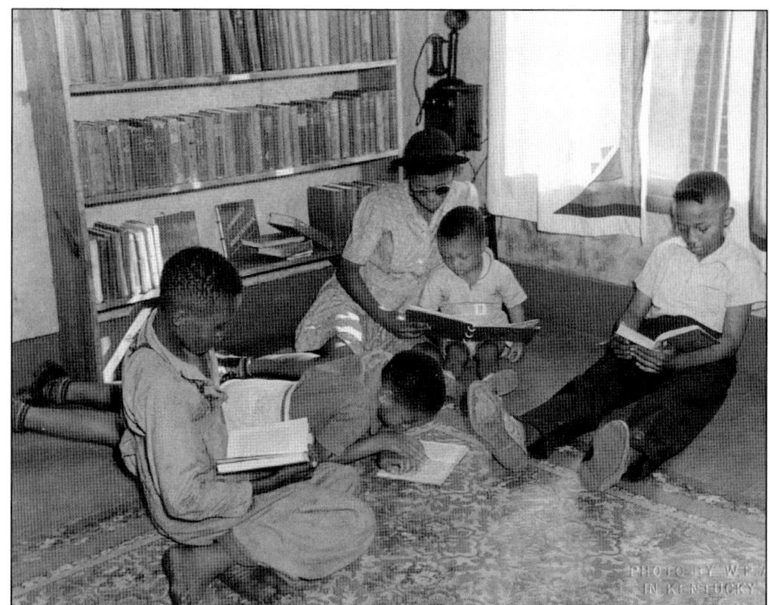

The librarian also served walk-in patrons who lived close enough to visit the central library in person. The patrons were welcome to browse the collection and curl up together to read and enjoy their new treasures. (Courtesy of WPA collection, Archives and Records Management Division, Kentucky Department for Libraries and Archives.)

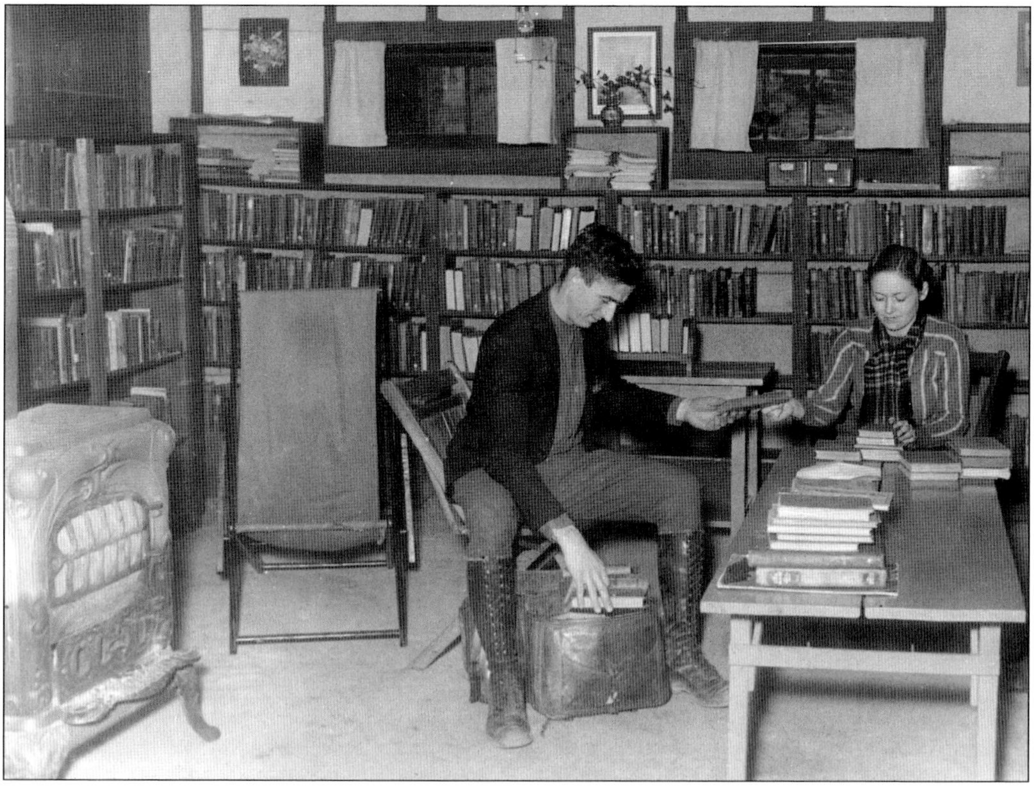

Books and reading materials rotated between library locations and were chosen based on patrons preferences. Packhorse librarians visited the central library about twice a month. If they needed to trade out books in between time, they made stops at stations along their routes where books were stored. (Courtesy of WPA collection, Archives and Records Management Division, Kentucky Department for Libraries and Archives.)

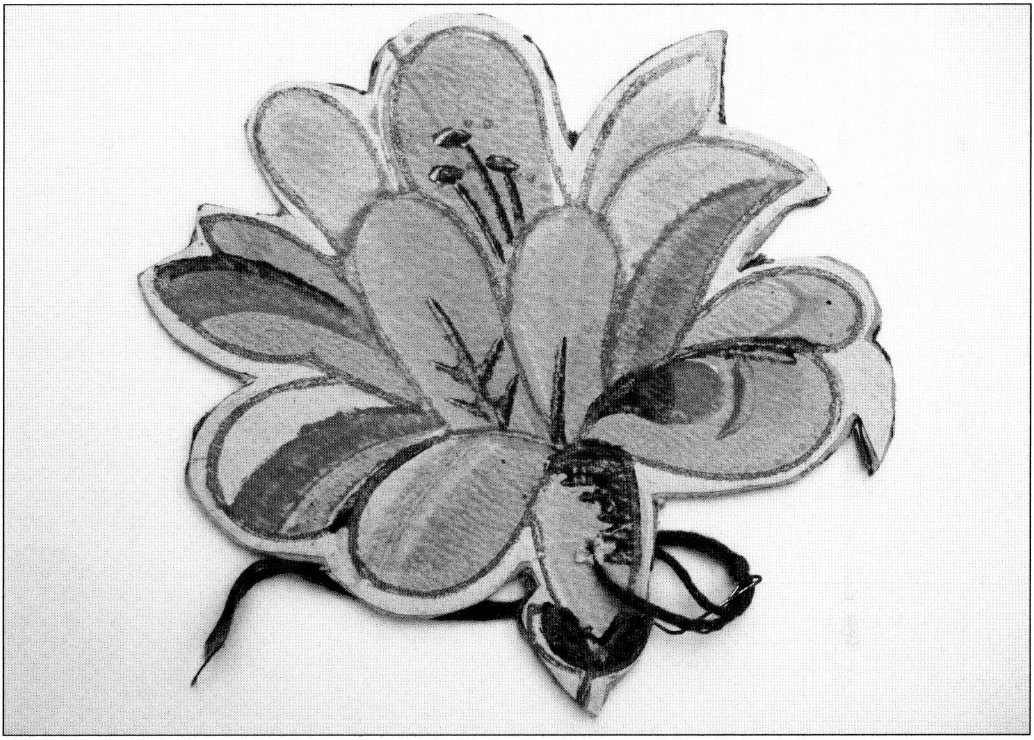

"This is your bookmark, please don't loose me" was written in cursive on the back of the flower bookmark. Librarians made bookmarks from wallpaper swatches, old flower catalogs, and old Christmas cards, so patrons could keep their place in the book without dog-earing corners. This kept the reading materials in better condition so they could remain in circulation longer. Other resourceful tricks included repurposing cheese boxes into card catalog files, license plates bent to make bookends, painted prune boxes for bookshelves, and bent broom handles for racks. (Above, photograph by Prof. Jason Vance of Middle Tennessee State University; courtesy of the Franklin D. Roosevelt Presidential Library; below, courtesy of Mallie Cody Turner Collection [MS049-1993], Morehead State University Special Collections and Archives.)

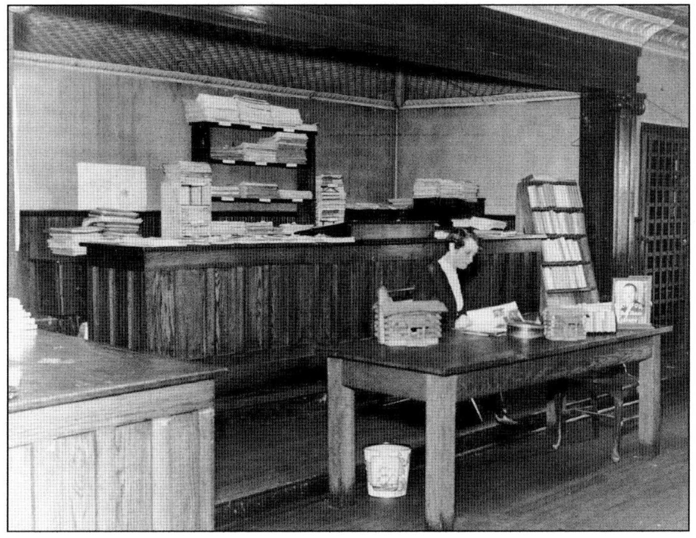

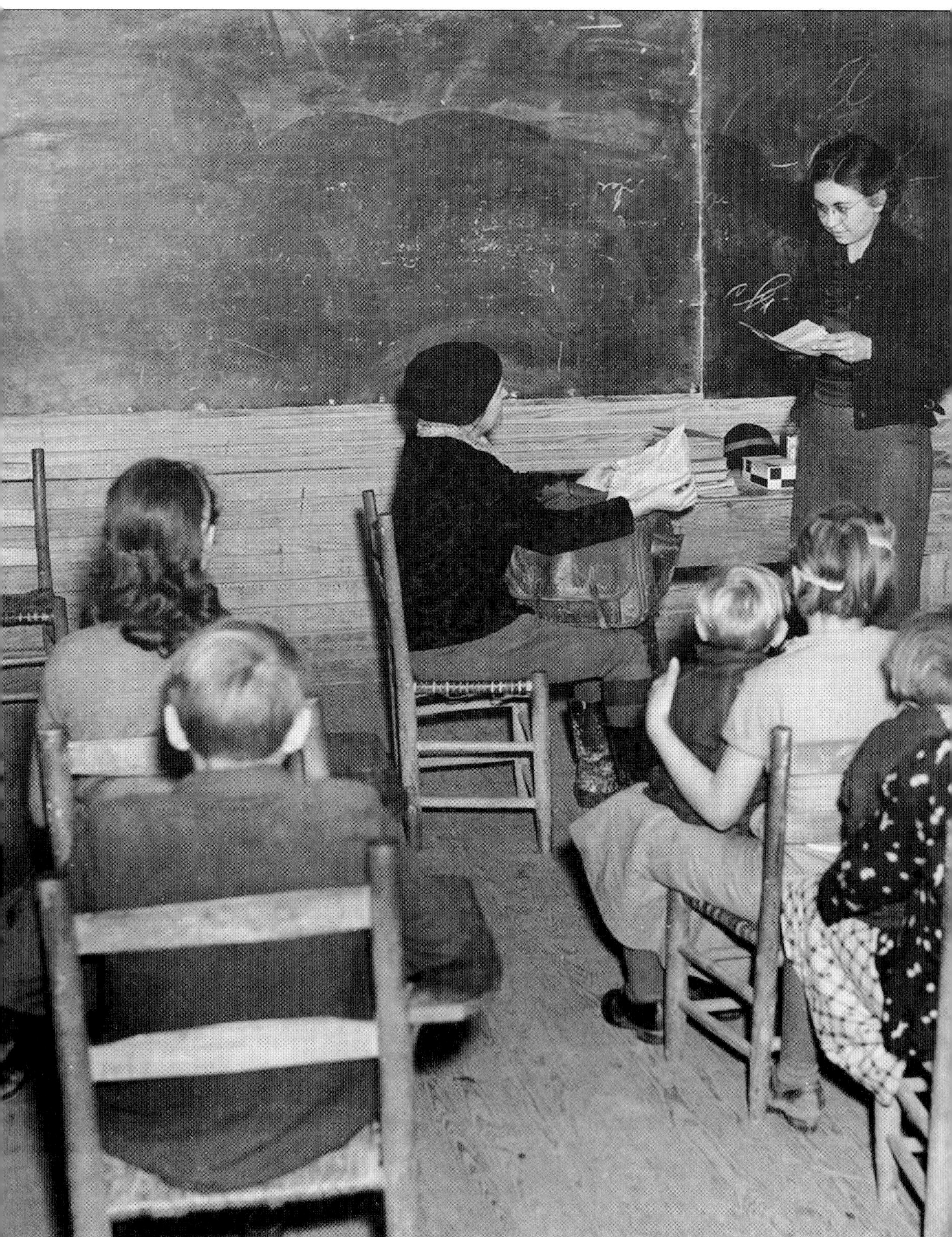

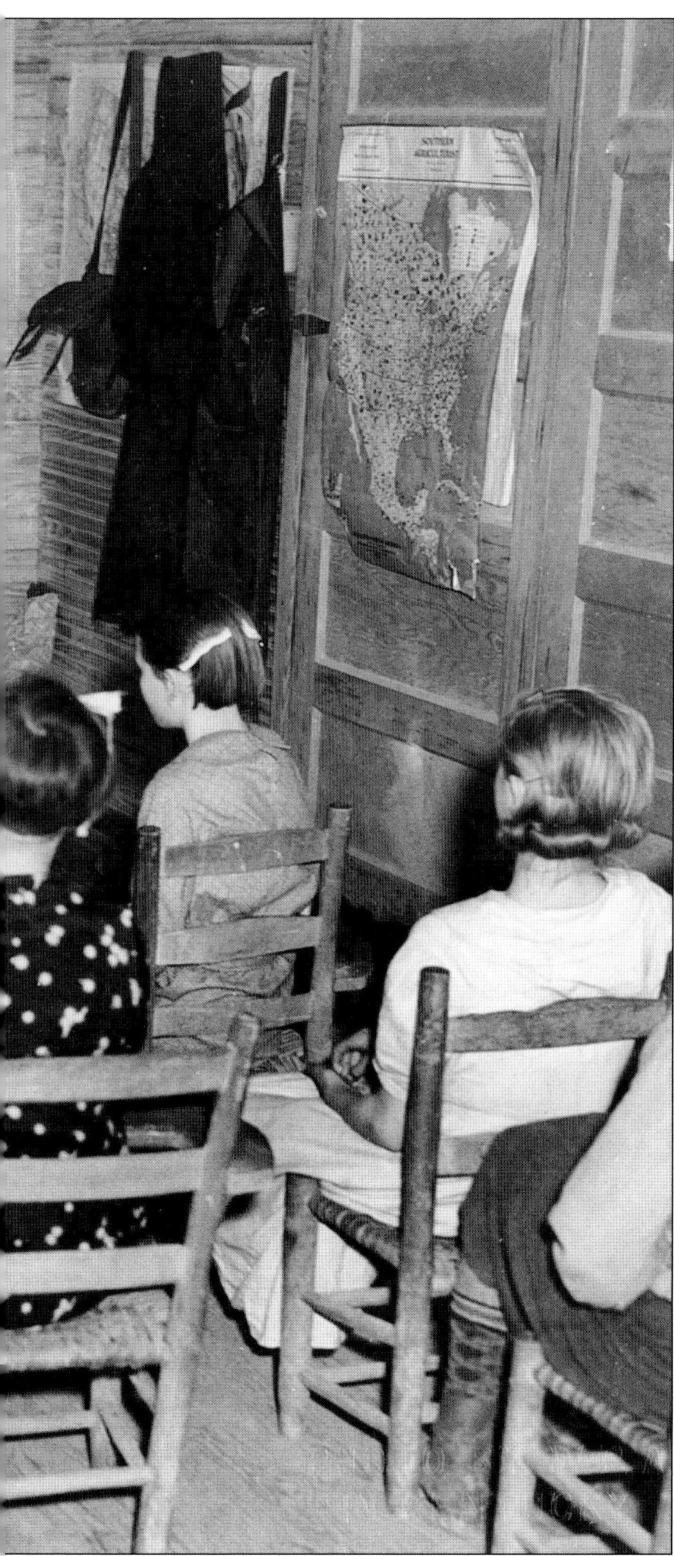

The teacher and class anticipated the treasures the packhorse librarian brought in her bag. All ages and grade levels met in one-room schoolhouses. Some had up to 45 students in one class. The little ones sat on the laps of the older kids who were allowed to attend school instead of working to make money for the family. Schools only had a few textbooks, so the students would share among them. The teachers and classes welcomed the librarians who brought books, maps, and other materials for them to use in the classroom. (Courtesy of WPA collection, Archives and Records Management Division, Kentucky Department for Libraries and Archives.)

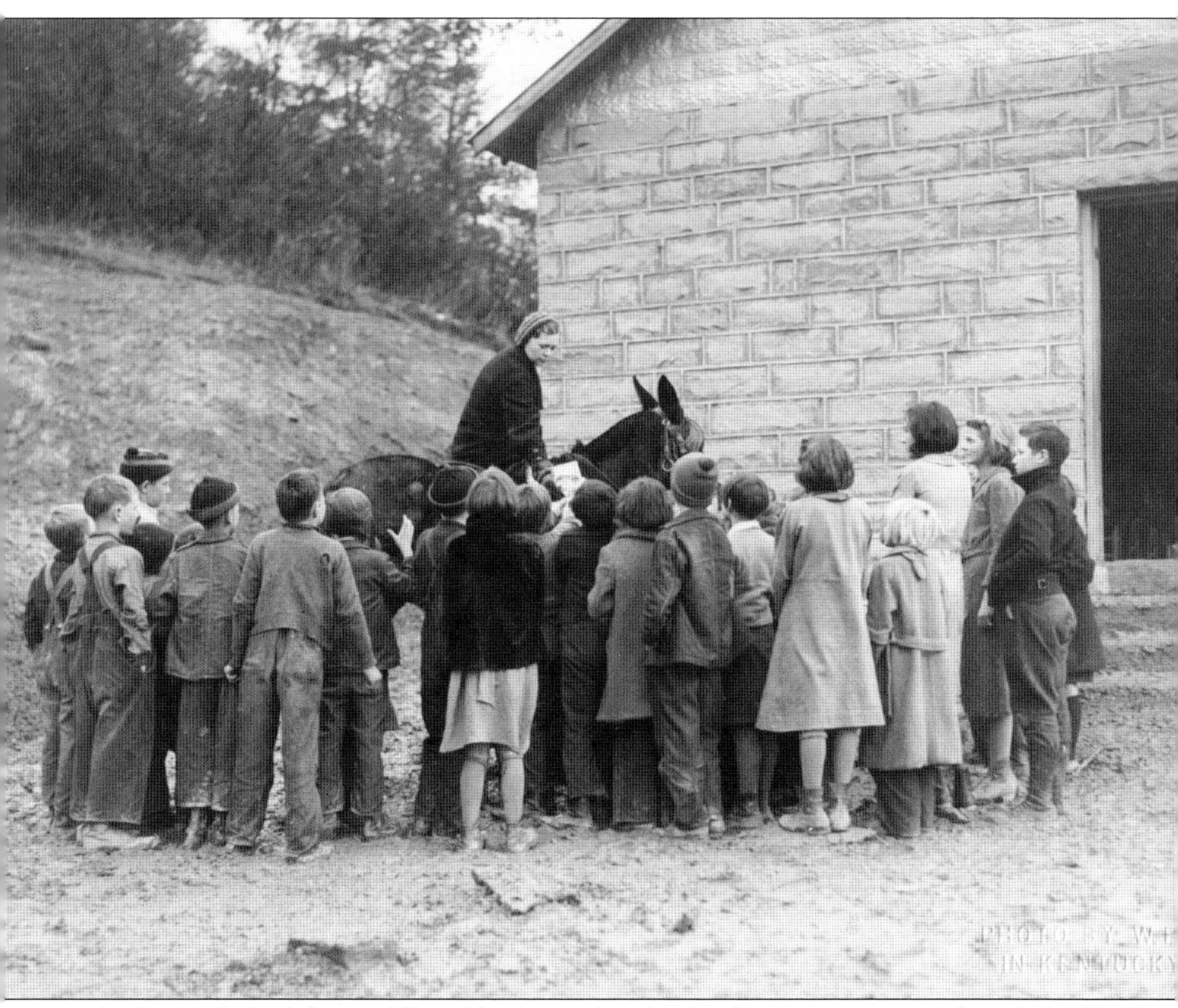

Students welcomed their packhorse librarian in the schoolyard and were encouraged to take books home. Even when the schools were closed, children continued the habit and met their carrier at the schoolhouse. Most children had never checked out a book prior to the packhorse librarians. During the years of the Packhorse Library Project, there were frequent reports of better schoolwork due to the books supplied by the librarians. (Courtesy of WPA collection, Archives and Records Management Division, Kentucky Department for Libraries and Archives.)

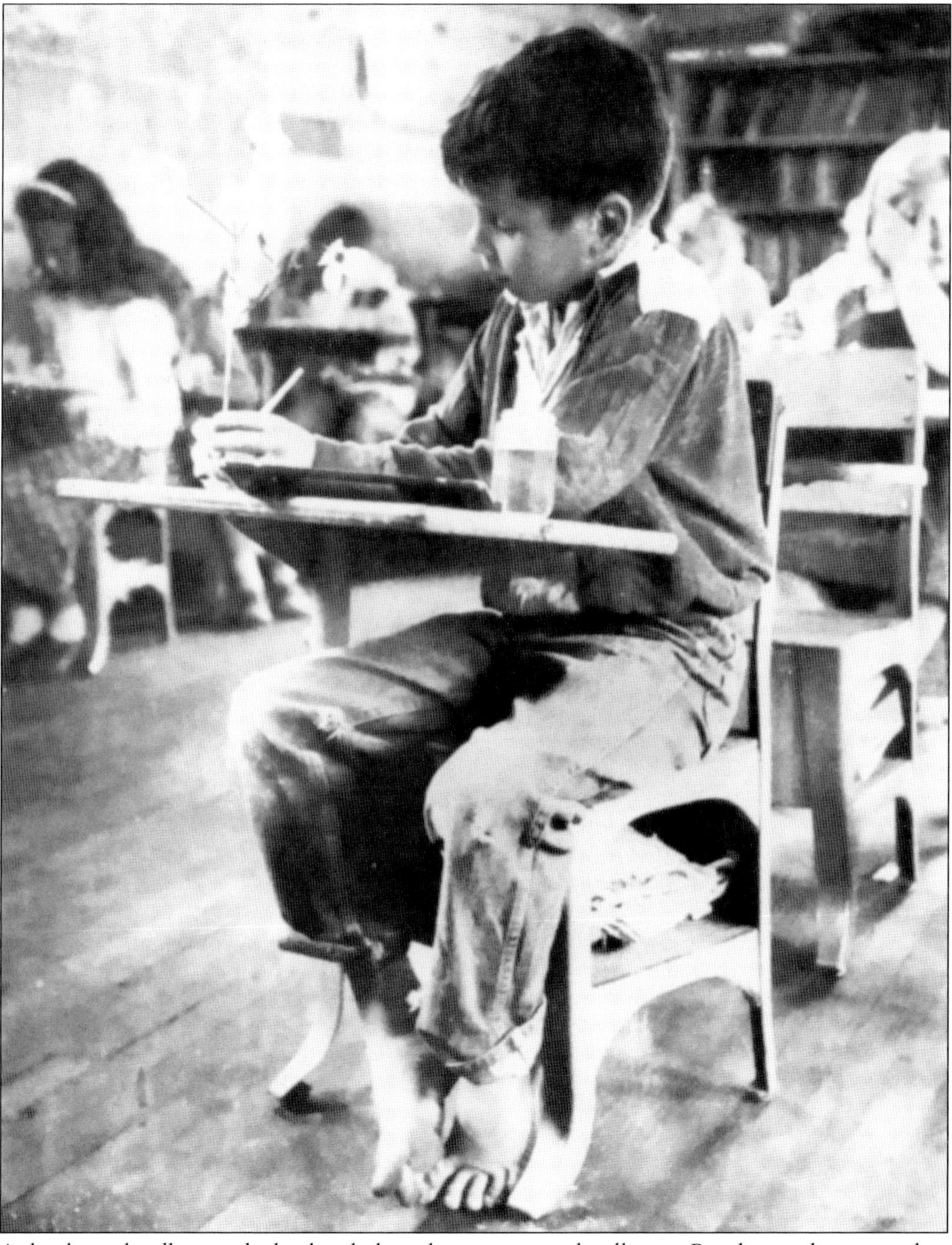

A shoeless schoolboy worked at his desk in the one-room schoolhouse. Besides needing to work, a common reason children did not attend school was due to clothing. Not all families could afford enough clothes or shoes. Not only were they especially necessary in the winter months, but the rocky terrain when traveling from home to school warranted footwear. Some households only had one pair of pants or shoes, and the kids took turns wearing them so they could attend school. (Courtesy of the 1955 Bookmobile Project Collection of the Louisa St. Clair Archive, the Hindman Settlement School.)

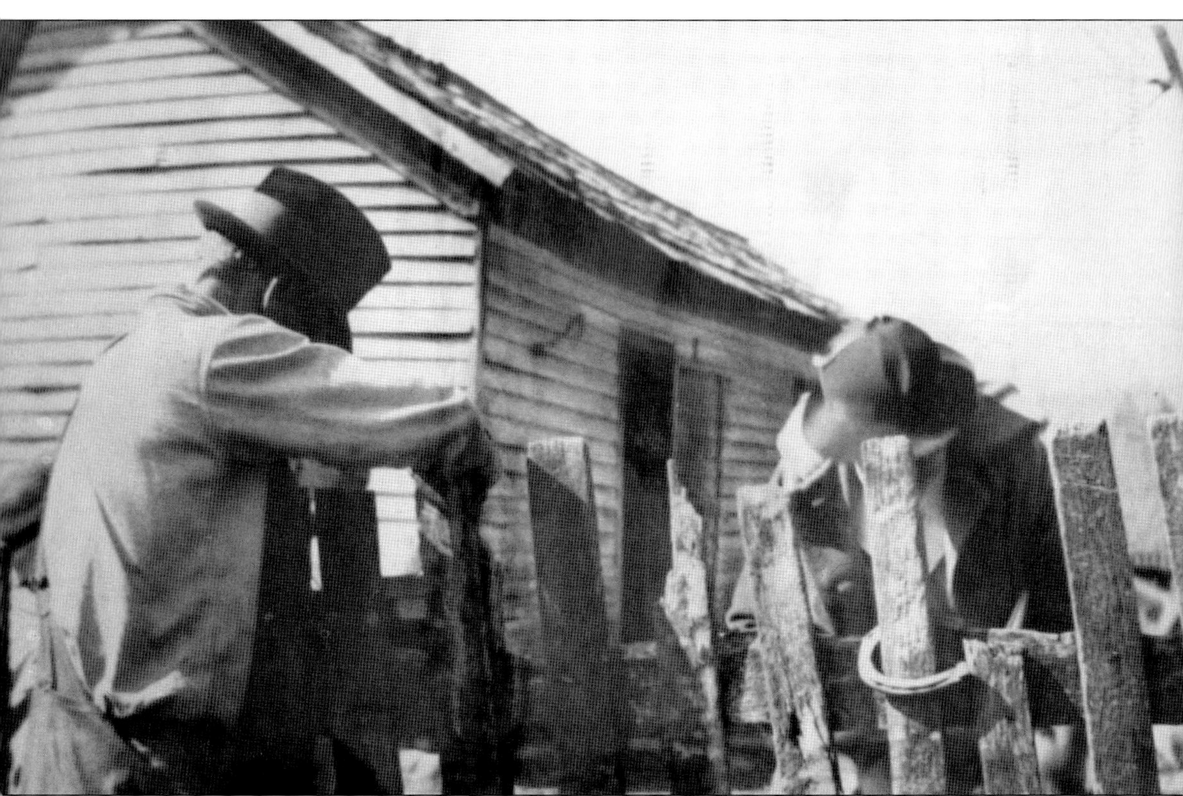

A patron was fixing his fence at his cabin home when the packhorse librarian made her routine stop. She exchanged books with readers who had finished the materials brought to them on the previous visit. Patrons could pick new choices when the librarian returned two weeks later. (Photograph by Prof. Jason Vance of Middle Tennessee State University; courtesy of the Franklin D. Roosevelt Presidential Library.)

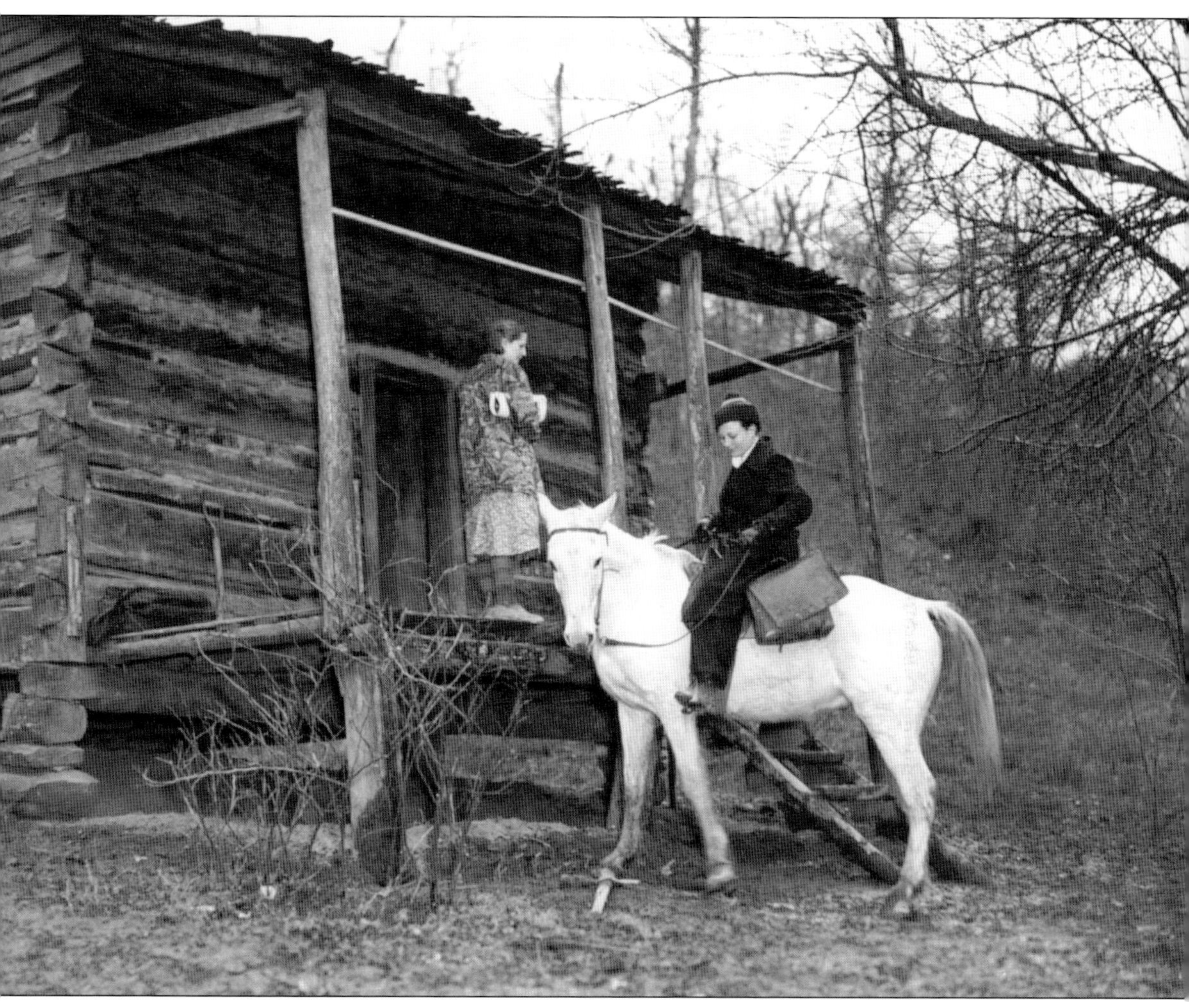

Literature was not the only thing packhorse librarians brought to patrons. They passed on news about births and deaths, sent for doctors or midwives, and relayed messages along the route to other mountain families. Patrons depended on the librarians' visits for companionship during troubling times. (Courtesy of WPA collection, Archives and Records Management Division, Kentucky Department for Libraries and Archives.)

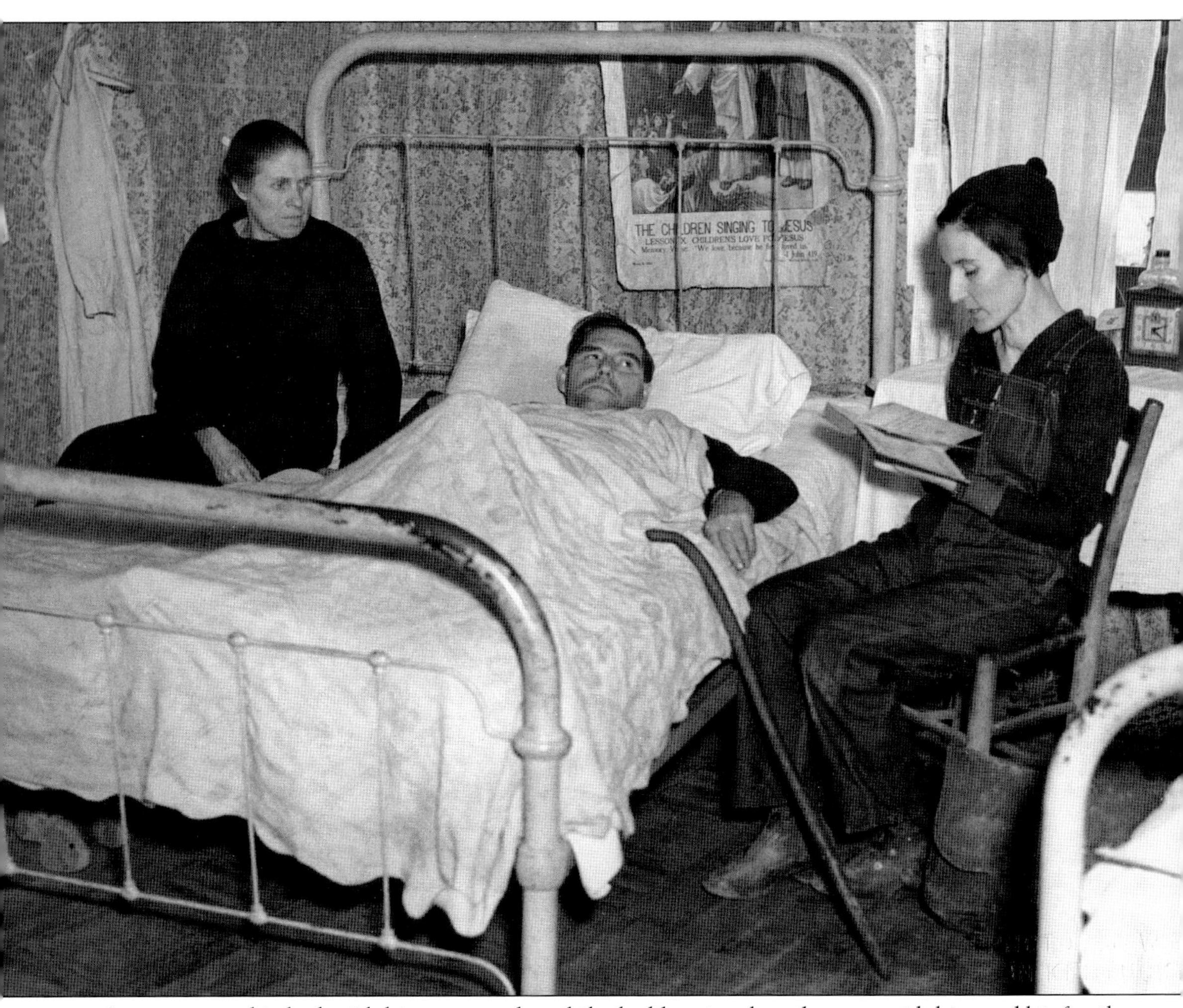

A patron rested in bed, with his cane nearby, while the librarian shared a story with him and his family member. Everyone benefitted from the books, including the elderly, disabled, and sick. Packhorse librarians read to the blind and those extremely sick to help pass the time, soothe their worries, and lighten their spirits. Children and families enjoyed stories being read aloud too. Although the librarians had many stops to make in a day, they always made time for their patrons, knowing the importance. (Courtesy of WPA collection, Archives and Records Management Division, Kentucky Department for Libraries and Archives.)

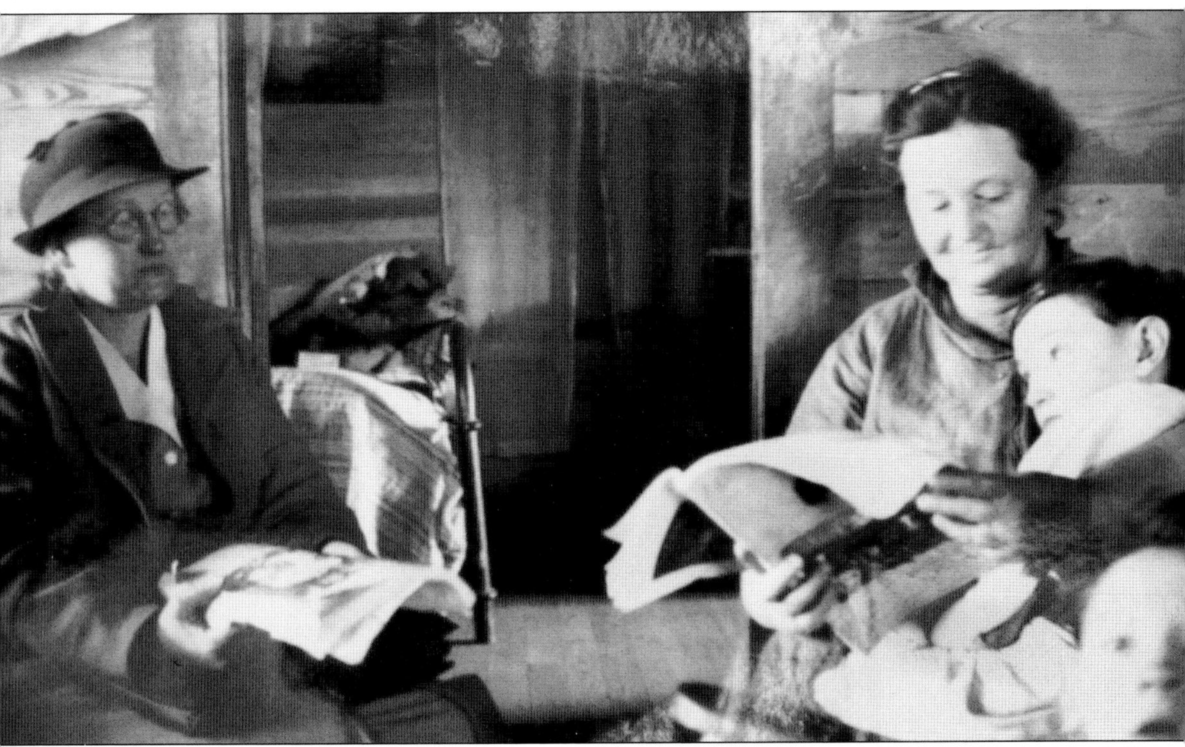

A woman leafed through a magazine or newspaper the packhorse librarian brought while cuddling with a child. Another child peeked up from the floor. Delivery of reading materials and story time were not the only jobs of the librarian. They also provided reading lessons for those who did not know how to read or were in the process of learning. Patrons prided themselves on their southern hospitality and wanted to show their thanks, even if only in a small way. They often gave the librarian food or, if they had none to spare, a special family recipe as a token of their gratitude. (Photograph by Prof. Jason Vance of Middle Tennessee State University; courtesy of the Franklin D. Roosevelt Presidential Library.)

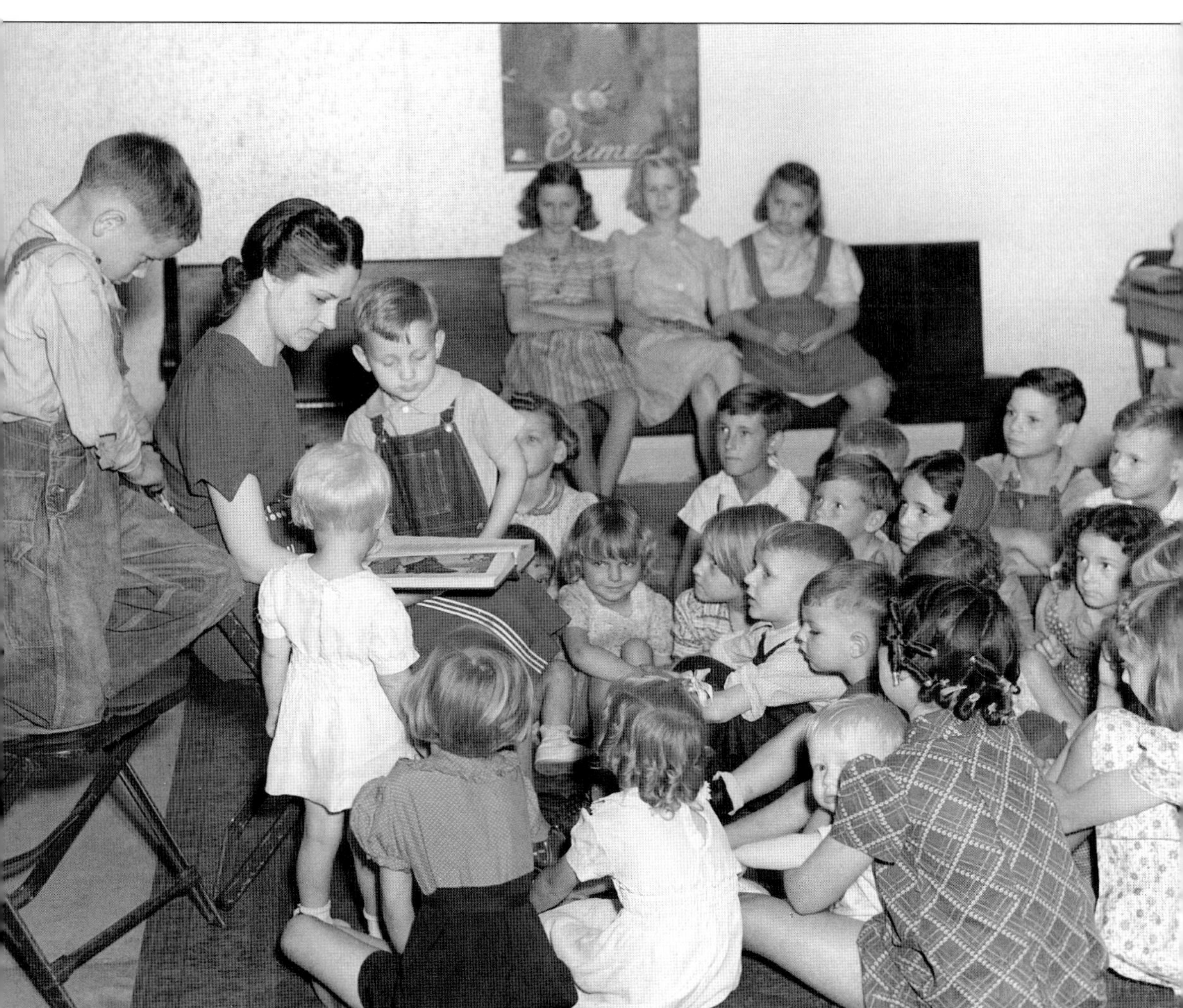

Children of all ages hovered around the librarian for story time. Main libraries and rural library centers provided a storytelling hour, which became increasingly popular among children. The weekly program gave families something to look forward to, an opportunity to get out of the house, and a way to support each other in their community during the Great Depression. (Courtesy of WPA collection, Archives and Records Management Division, Kentucky Department for Libraries and Archives.)

Five

WINDOWS TO THE WORLD

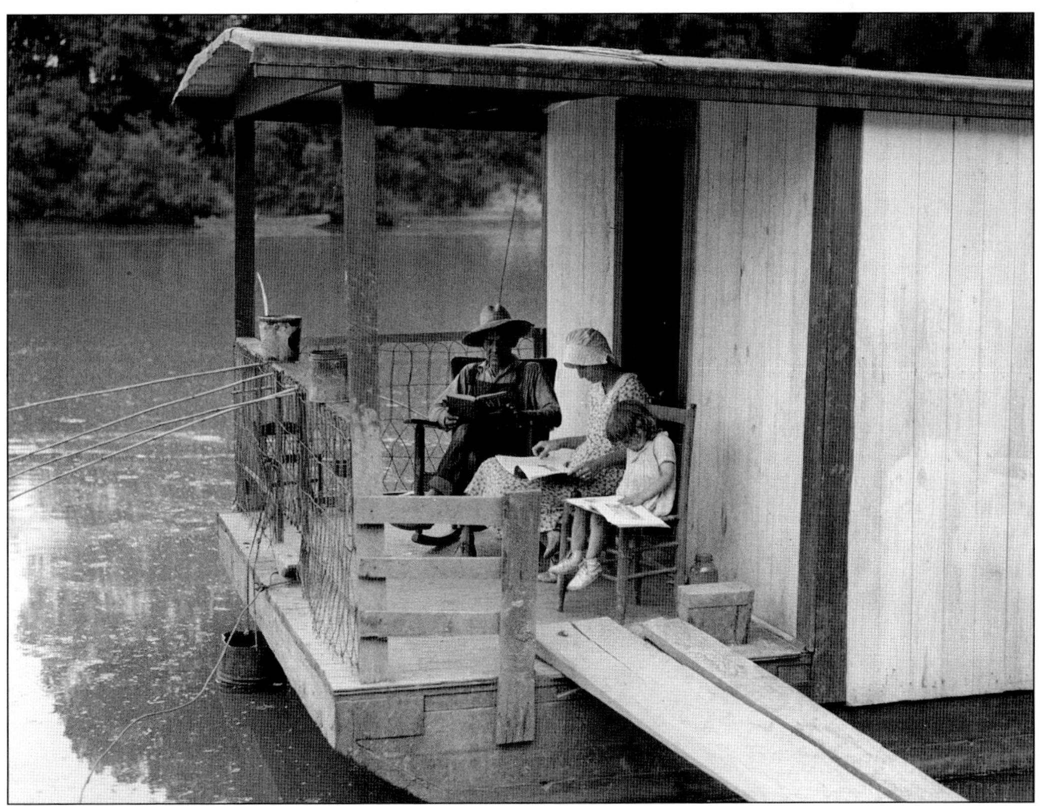

Librarians strived to meet the literary needs and wants of their patrons. A mountain family sat together devouring the librarian's latest delivery. A book for the man, magazine for the woman, and a scrapbook for the child. (Courtesy of WPA collection, Archives and Records Management Division, Kentucky Department for Libraries and Archives.)

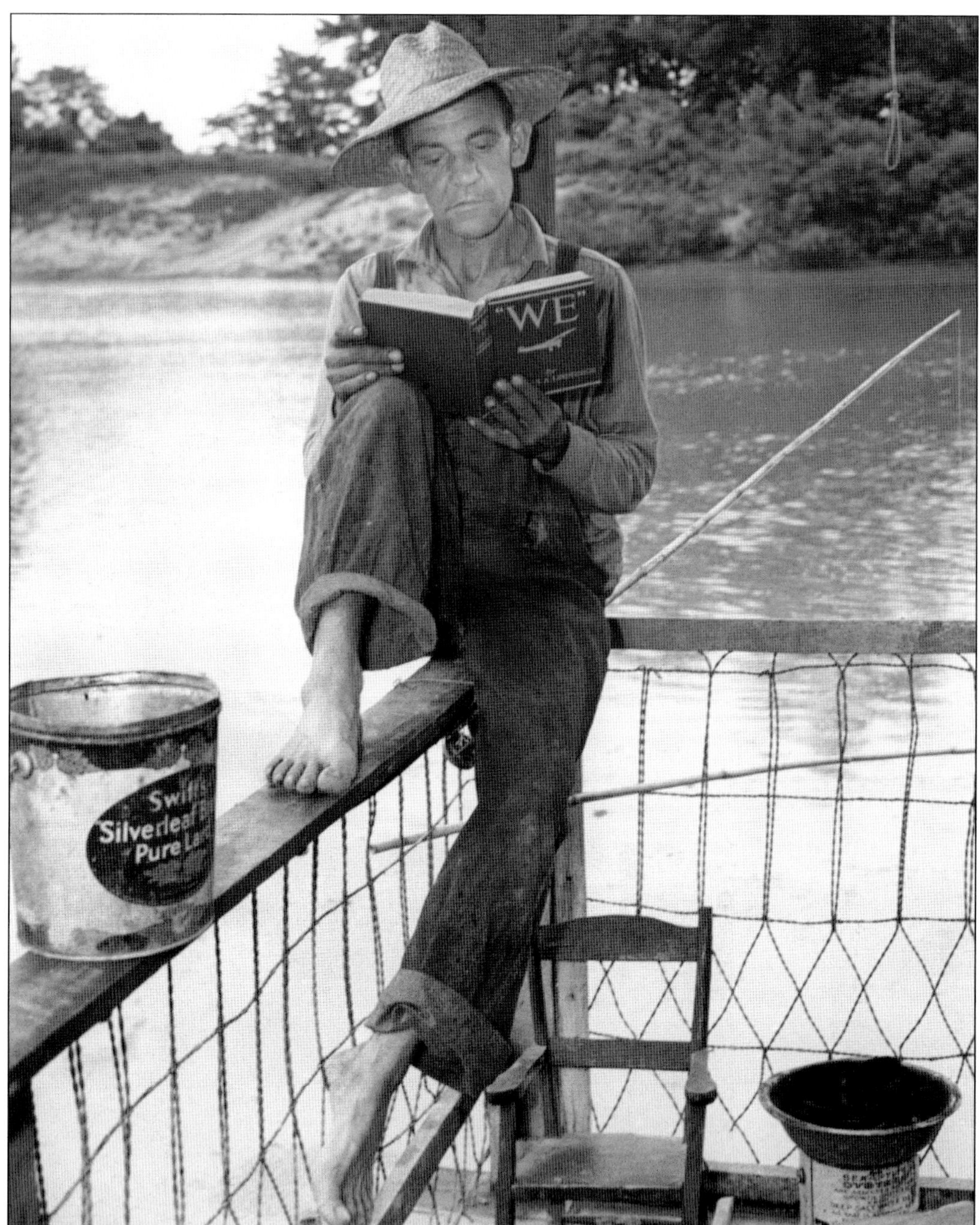

Riverboat patron Houseboat Henry passed the time immersing himself in Charles A. Lindbergh's autobiography *WE*. Not only were nonfiction titles popular, but works of fiction were in great demand. Other adult reading materials focused on current events, biographies, history, and religion. (Courtesy of WPA collection, Archives and Records Management Division, Kentucky Department for Libraries and Archives.)

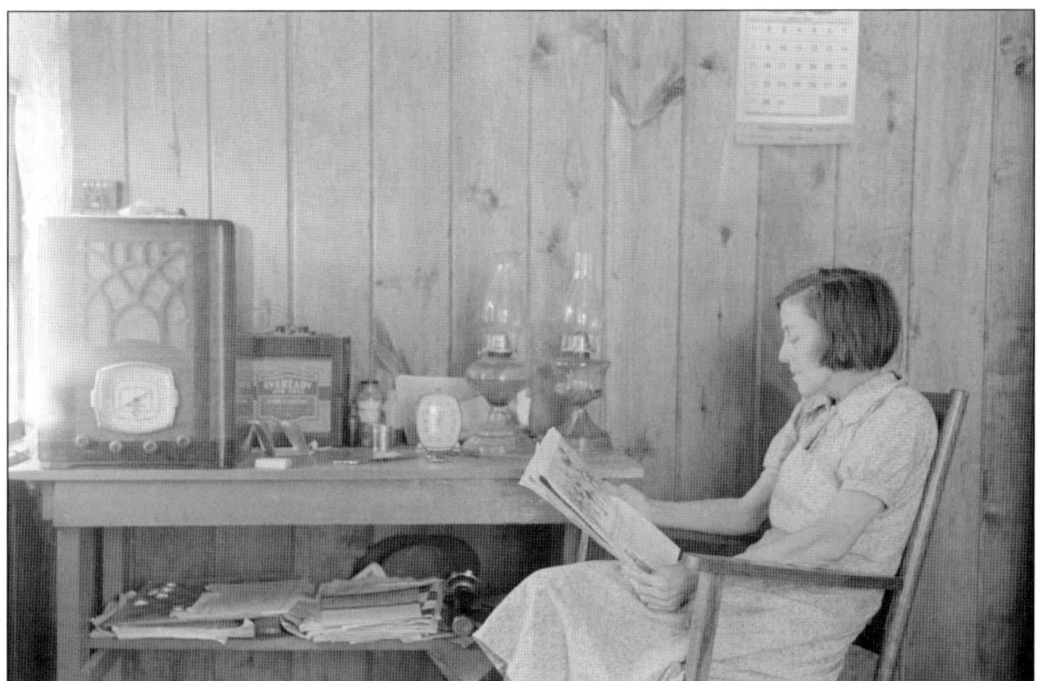

Mountain women requested instructive literature in an effort to learn new ways to take care of their families and households. Older ideas included making sure one put the baby's dress on over their feet first for the first year of life or bad luck would follow or rubbing warm, young rabbit's brains on baby's gums to help them cut their teeth. (Courtesy of the Library of Congress.)

The young cheered, "Bring me a book to read," to their packhorse librarian. Children's books were in great demand and in short supply. Illustrated books were adored because of illiterate adults and their reliance on their children to help read them. (Courtesy of WPA collection, Archives and Records Management Division, Kentucky Department for Libraries and Archives.)

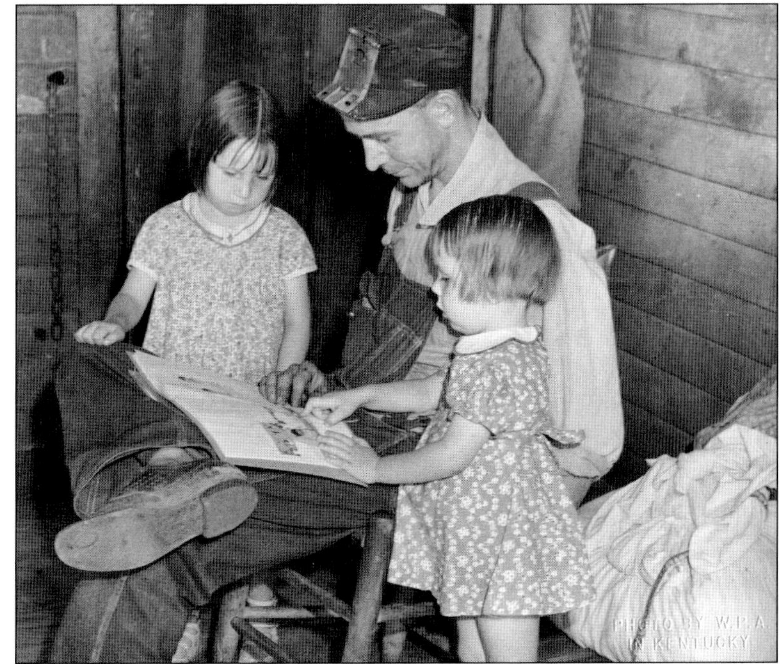

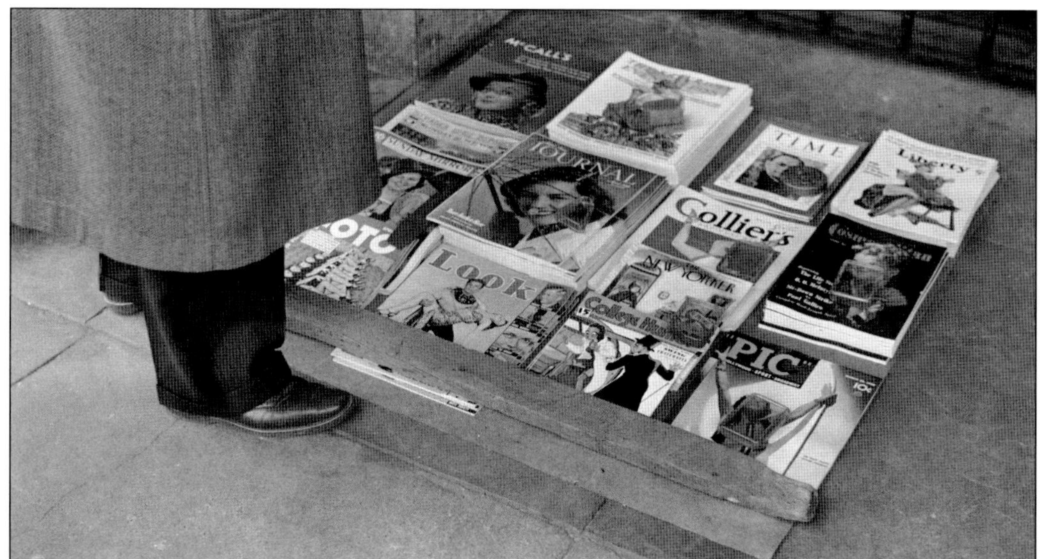

The newsstand featured popular magazines during the 1930s that were requested and enjoyed by patrons, including *Collier's, Cosmopolitan, Liberty, The New Yorker, Pic, The Saturday Evening Post, Sunday Morning,* and *Time.* Prices ranged from 5¢ to 15¢ per issue but were available for free to check out through the library. Other magazine categories included agriculture, childcare, cooking, health care, and machinery. (Courtesy of the Library of Congress.)

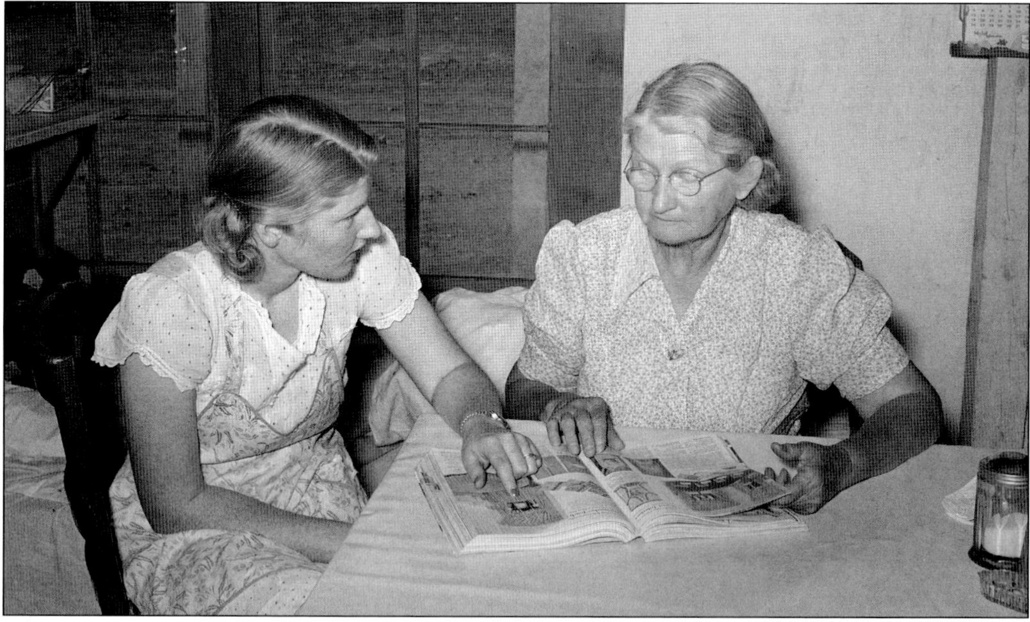

Since their mountain homes were secluded, the ladies enjoyed looking through the 1940 Sears Roebuck spring/summer catalog. They admired the selection of curtains and drapes in the home decor section of the catalog: "Priscillas, cottage set, tailored pairs, dressing table skirt and bedspread are finished with petticoat ruffles trimmed with ribbon beading." Folks loved to borrow catalogs and magazines with pictures so they could admire the goods they had never seen before. Instead of purchasing items out of the catalog, they could learn how to make the items themselves to save money. (Courtesy of the Library of Congress.)

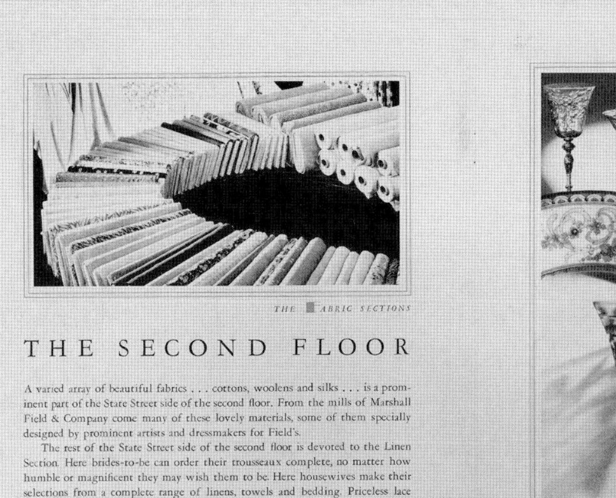

THE FABRIC SECTIONS

THE SECOND FLOOR

A varied array of beautiful fabrics . . . cottons, woolens and silks . . . is a prominent part of the State Street side of the second floor. From the mills of Marshall Field & Company come many of these lovely materials, some of them specially designed by prominent artists and dressmakers for Field's.

The rest of the State Street side of the second floor is devoted to the Linen Section. Here brides-to-be can order their trousseaux complete, no matter how humble or magnificent they may wish them to be. Here housewives make their selections from a complete range of linens, towels and bedding. Priceless lace cloths and gay peasant luncheon sets; new ensembles for bathroom and kitchen; downy, colorful blankets.

The picture on the opposite page is representative of the exquisite glass and china which, with lamps, pictures, artwares, and decorative flowers, occupy the Wabash Avenue side of the second floor.

12

CHINA AND GLASSWARE

MODERN EXAMPLES AS WELL AS ALL THE LOVELY OLD WELL-KNOWN WARES, RICH IN TRADITION AND BEAUTY, ARE TO BE FOUND ON THE SECOND FLOOR

13

Marshall Field and Company in Chicago, Illinois, displayed the merchandise from the second floor in a 1933 catalog called *The Store Book*. The left page read, "A varied array of beautiful fabrics . . . cottons, woolens and silks . . . is a prominent part of the State Street side of the second floor." The right page was representative of "the exquisite glass and china which, with lamps, pictures, artwares, and decorative flowers, occupy the Wabash Avenue side of the second floor." Marshall Field's was an upscale department store founded in the 19th century. The store became a large chain before Macy's acquired it in 2005. (Courtesy of the Library of Congress.)

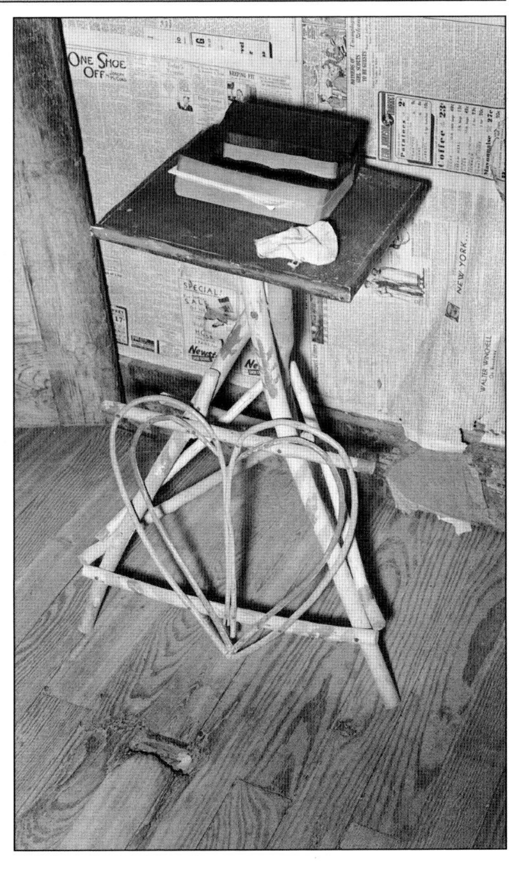

Lying on a wicker table in a farm home was one of the most requested books by the Appalachian people, the Bible. The Appalachia region has always had religious roots. Cultural traits valued by many were tied to beliefs shaped by frontier life—humility, family structure, self-sufficiency, resourcefulness, and hospitality. Due to these spiritual roots, a Bible could be found in many homes. Other adored books included works by Charles Dickens, William Shakespeare, and Mark Twain. (Courtesy of the Library of Congress.)

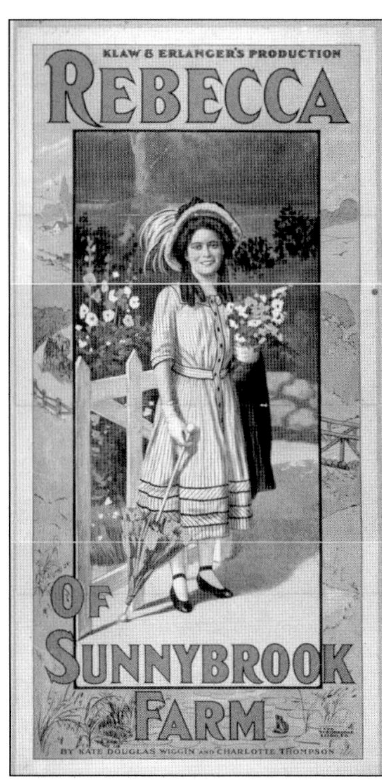

Patrons often requested books from their packhorse librarians. They eagerly anticipated their turn to devour the pages. Favorites included *Rebecca of Sunnybrook Farm* by Kate Douglas Wiggin, the story of a young girl growing up in Maine with her aunts where the unexpected seems to happen at every turn; *Robinson Crusoe* by Daniel Defoe, an adventure of an English sailor who is stranded on a deserted island for almost 30 years; and *Gulliver's Travels* by Jonathan Swift, the satire tale of a ship's surgeon and his four voyages. (Courtesy of the Library of Congress.)

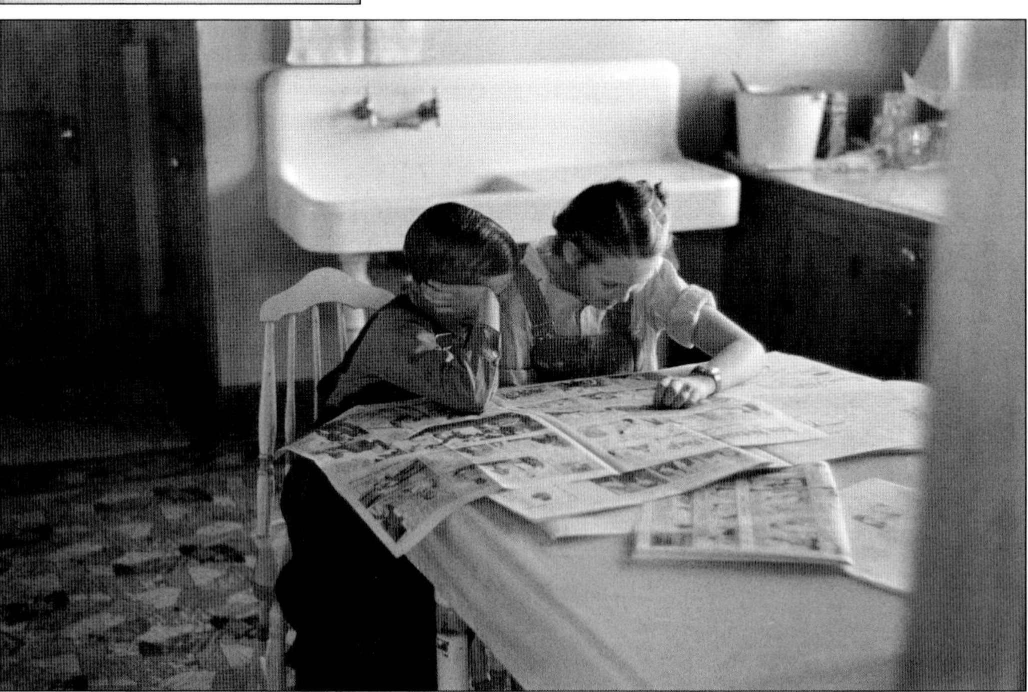

Children read the comics in the Sunday newspaper at their kitchen table. Favorites included *Dick Tracy*, *Little Orphan Annie*, *Flash Gordan*, *Nancy*, *Terry and the Pirates*, *Blondie*, and more. Although this household had the luxury of running water, many did not. People escaped in these comics because there was no depression in the funny papers. (Courtesy of the Library of Congress.)

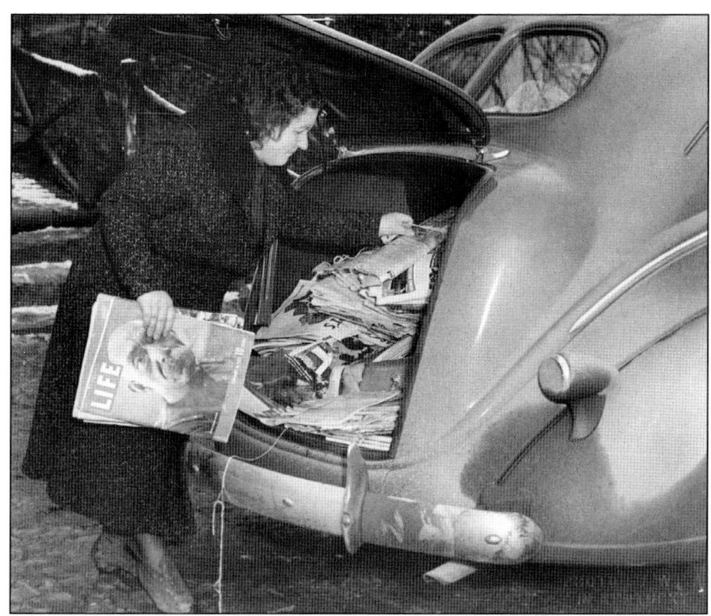

People near and far donated to the Packhorse Library Project, including schools, churches, clubs, philanthropists, academics, women's clubs, individuals, Kentucky Parents and Teachers Association, Rotary Club, and Kiwanis Club to name a few. Donations included books, magazines, readers, recipe collections, quilt patterns, and religious works. (Courtesy of WPA collection, Archives and Records Management Division, Kentucky Department for Libraries and Archives.)

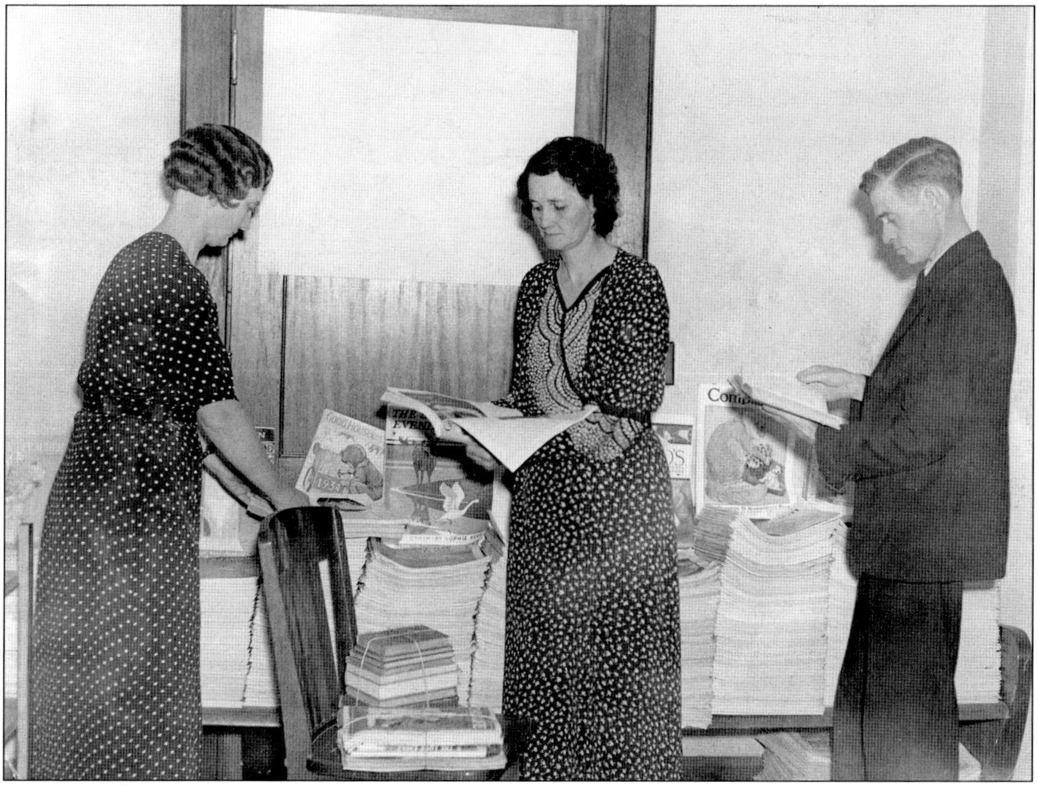

People browsed through stacks of donated magazines of multiple copies at a central library, including *Parent-Teacher, Good Housekeeping, The Saturday Evening Post,* and *Woman's Home Companion.* At the height of the program, the Kentucky Parents and Teachers Association held a "Penny Fund" program, which asked members to donate one penny toward purchasing new books. (Courtesy of Mallie Cody Turner Collection [MS049-1993], Morehead State University Special Collections and Archives.)

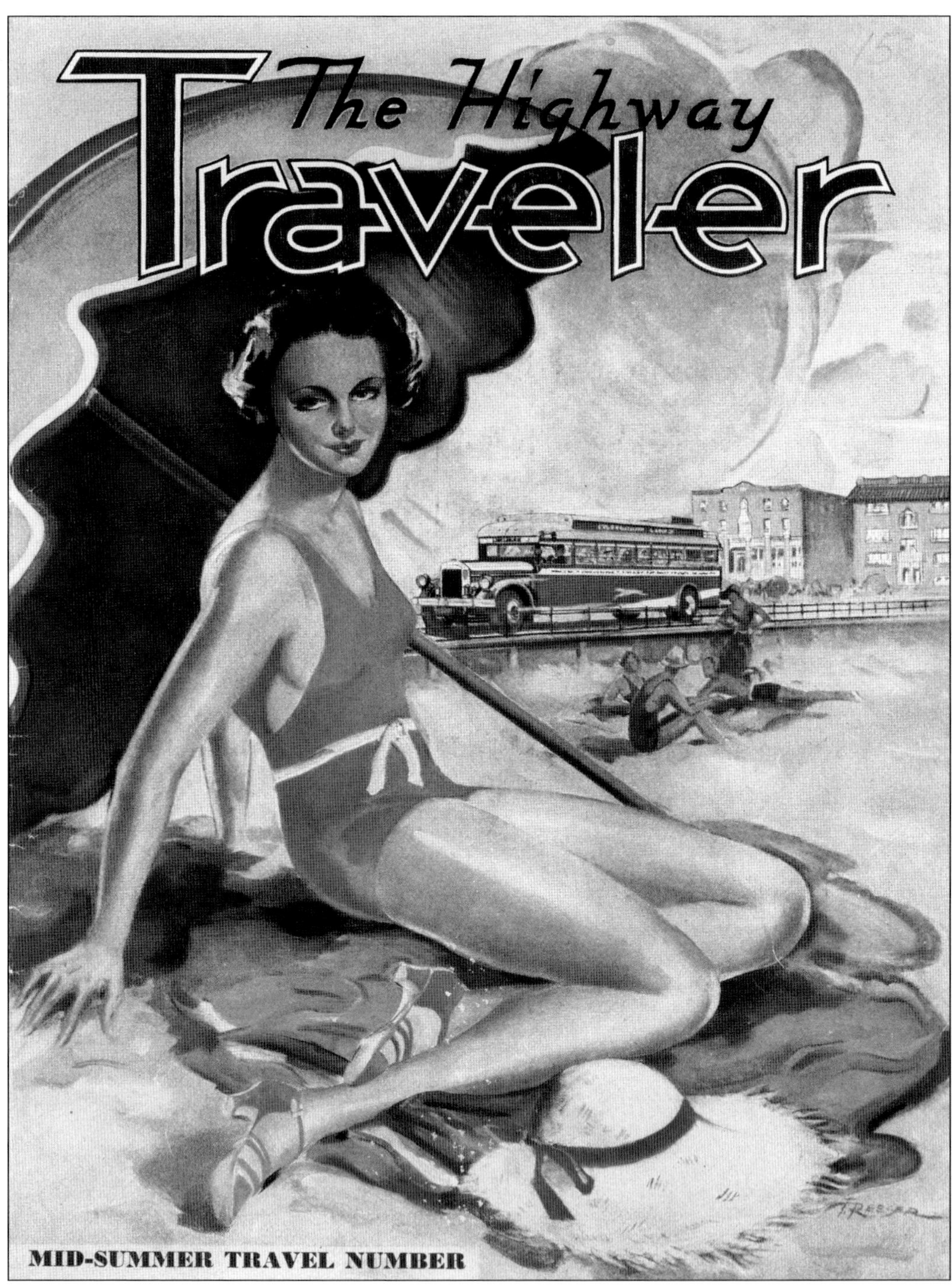

The Highway Traveler mid-summer 1933 magazine featured a woman seated on the beach with a Greyhound bus in the background. This issue would have been a delightful find as people could visit places around the world without leaving their own home. Other donations included *Western Stories*, *Life*, *McCall's*, *Pathfinder*, *Hollard Magazine*, and geography magazines. (Courtesy of the Library of Congress.)

Six

Keepsakes

Once books and reading materials became damaged beyond repair, librarians got creative. They constructed scrapbooks from the remaining pieces of books, magazines, pamphlets, drawings, and stories. The librarians made the books according to demand and tried to answer their patrons questions. These keepsakes documented the time, place, and culture of the area. (Courtesy of WPA collection, Archives and Records Management Division, Kentucky Department for Libraries and Archives.)

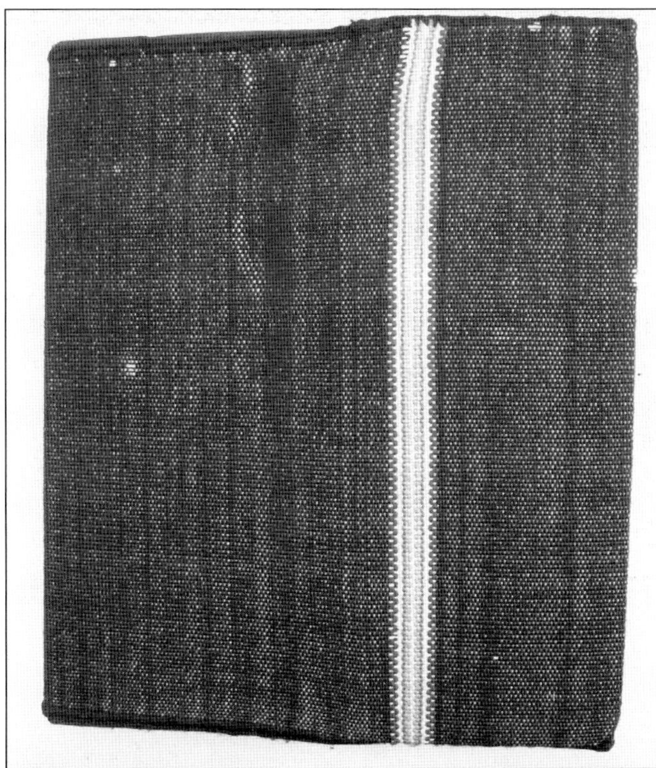

The scrapbook cover was woven on a loom at the Irvine Training Work Center in Estill County, Kentucky. The loom had only been in the workroom for six weeks. If a binder could not be found to make the scrapbook, librarians constructed their own. They made the base of the front and back cover from discarded window shades, file folders, construction paper, cardboard, wallpaper, and other materials. In 1940, more than 2,000 scrapbooks were created to help with the increasing needs of the mountain communities. (Photographs by Prof. Jason Vance of Middle Tennessee State University; courtesy of the Franklin D. Roosevelt Presidential Library.)

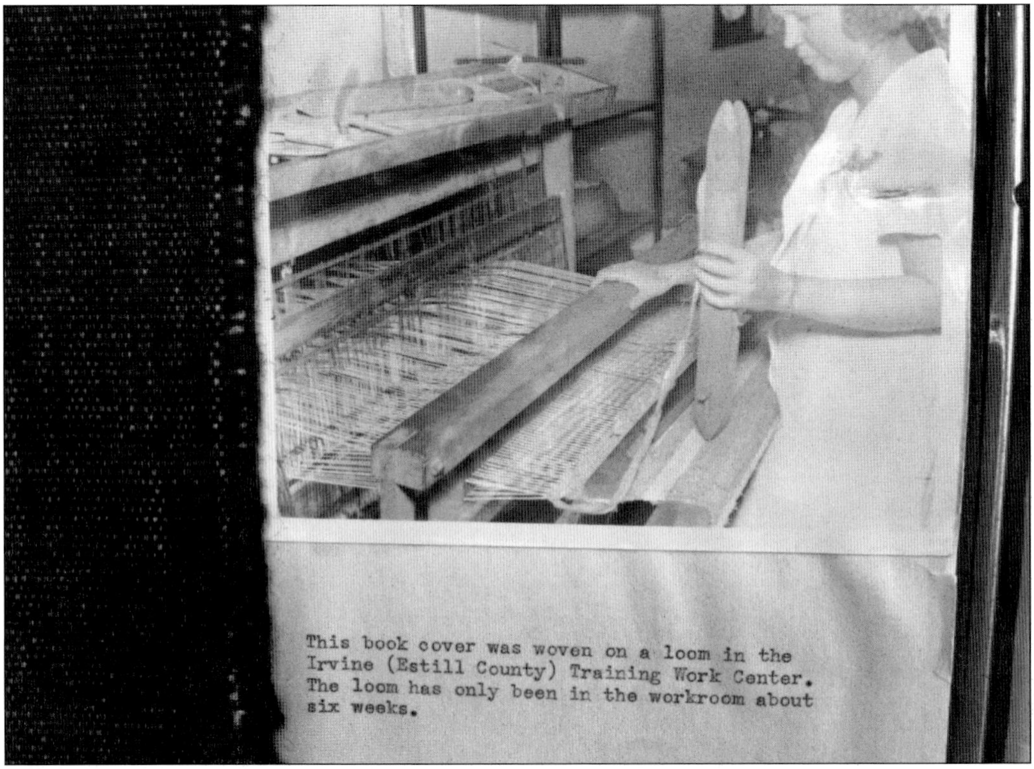

This book cover was woven on a loom in the Irvine (Estill County) Training Work Center. The loom has only been in the workroom about six weeks.

A librarian constructed a scrapbook to put into circulation. When materials became too worn or damaged or items like pamphlets, recipes, and quilt patterns were donated, a scrapbook was the perfect solution. Librarians pasted pictures, stories, and magazines into the pages of a scrapbook. Even patrons contributed their own stories and drawings to be included. (Courtesy of WPA collection, Archives and Records Management Division, Kentucky Department for Libraries and Archives.)

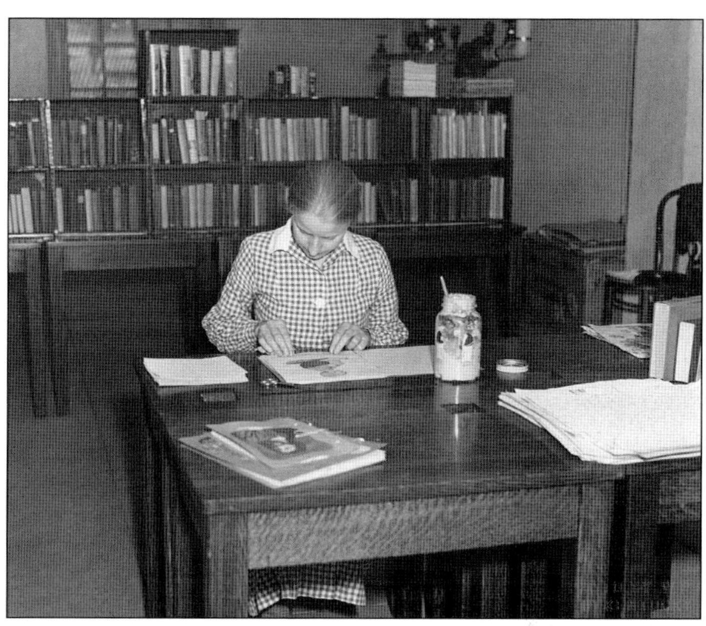

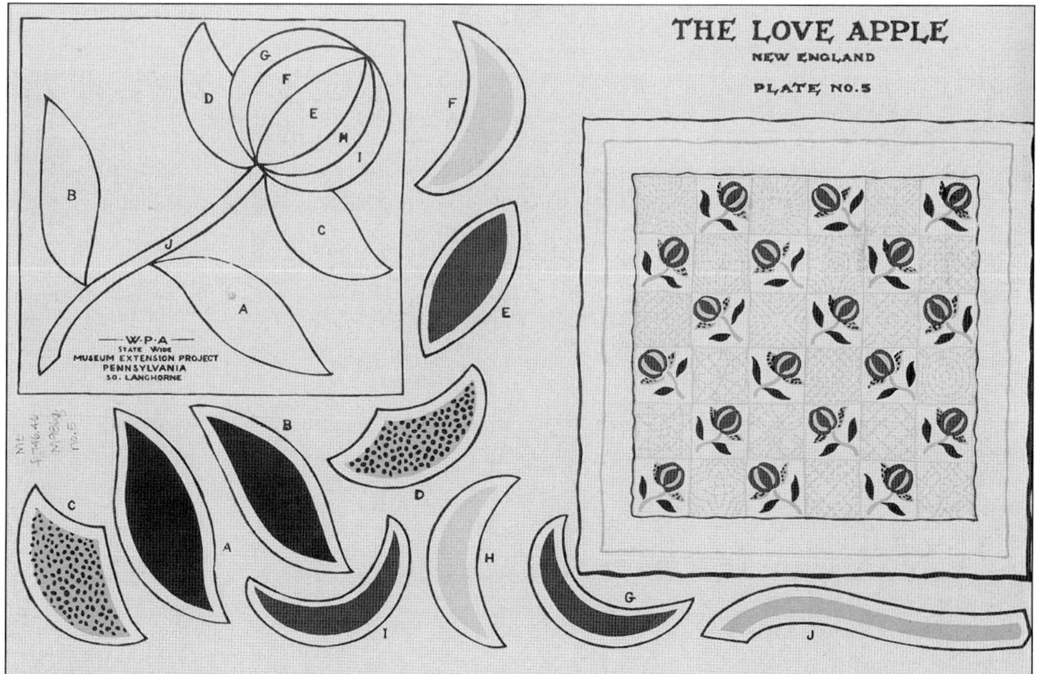

Each scrapbook had its own theme. The "Love Apple" quilt pattern would have been included in a quilt scrapbook, a favorite among patrons. Other scrapbook themes included religion, animals, local flora and fauna, recipes, stories, mountain ballads, Kentucky history, pictures, postcards, biographical sketches of famous people, and local histories. (Courtesy of Berea College Special Collections and Archives.)

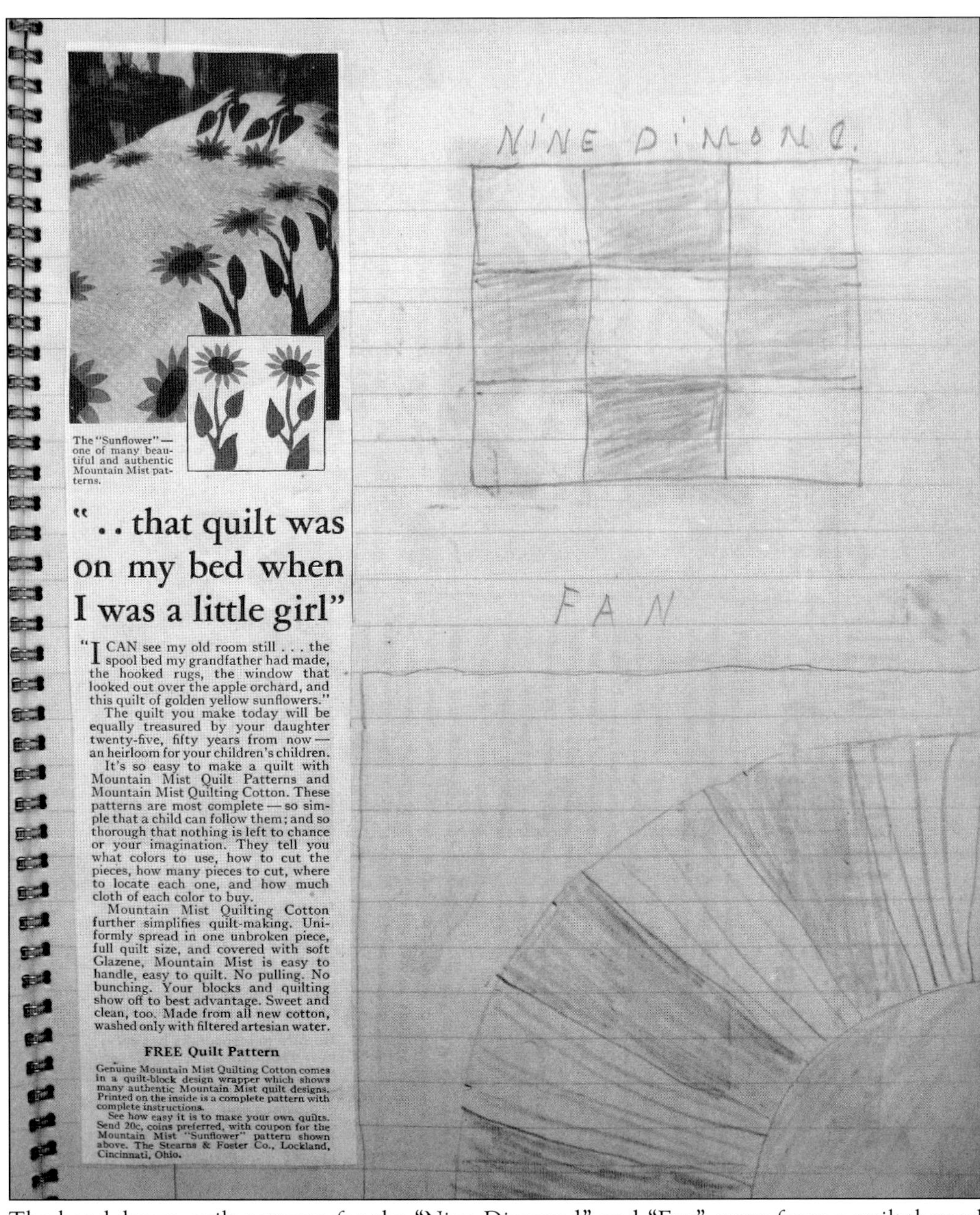

The hand-drawn quilt patterns for the "Nine Diamond" and "Fan" came from a quilt-themed scrapbook from Lee County, Kentucky. Commonly shared patterns included a star, ocean wave, flower garden, and Dutch girl. The newspaper pictured "The 'Sunflower'—one of the many beautiful and authentic Mountain Mist Quilting Cotton patterns" from the Stearns and Foster Company in Cincinnati, Ohio. The article shared the nostalgic feeling of making a quilt today will be treasured by their children and their children's children for many years. Just like stories and traditions were passed down through the generations so were the cherished handmade gifts such as a quilt. Patrons felt proud when they contributed their quilt designs for the packhorse librarian's scrapbooks for others to enjoy. (Photograph by Prof. Jason Vance of Middle Tennessee State University; courtesy of the Franklin D. Roosevelt Presidential Library.)

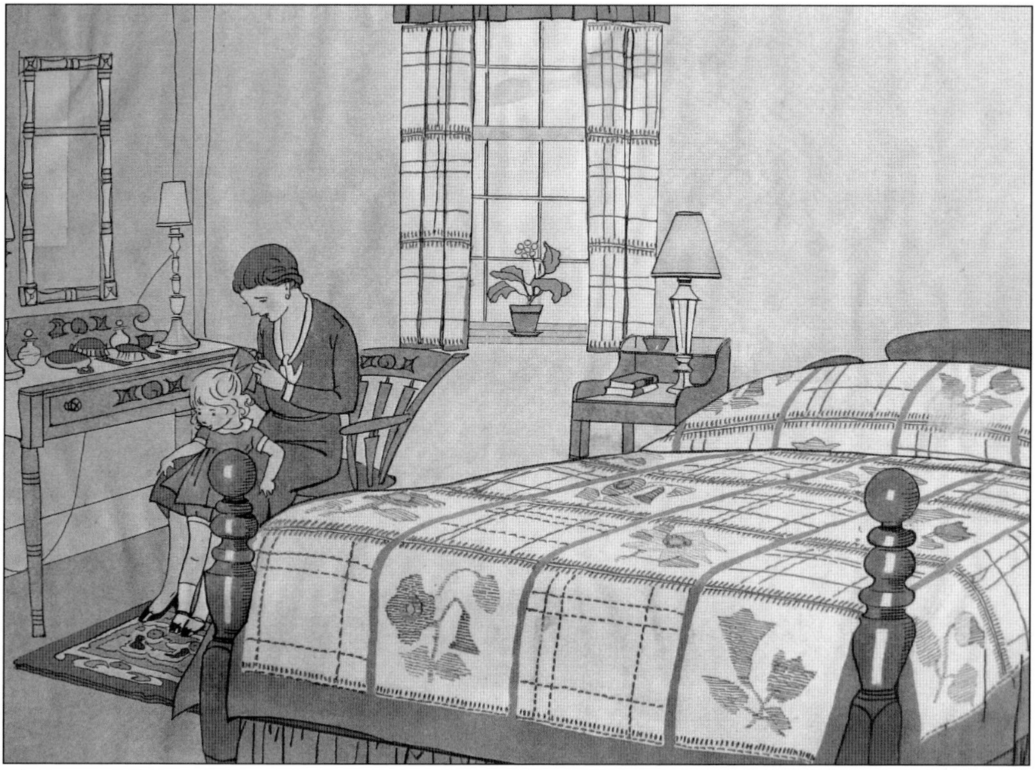

The picture showed the finished quilt designed by Katharine Peirson from *Woman's Home Companion* magazine. The description said, "An air of simple living and old-fashioned charm characterizes this early American room with its old (or new) maple or painted furniture (notice the little nighttable made out of a washstand), its rag rugs and hand-embroidered bedspread. The material for this extremely decorative spread, by the way, consists of ordinary open-mesh dishcloths and the wool embroidery is done in plain darning stitches." Prices included 10¢ each for plain squares for curtains with wool, 25¢ each for pillow squares (one stamped and one plain with wools), and $4 for 17 squares for bedspreads (17 stamped and 17 plain with wools). (Photographs by Prof. Jason Vance of Middle Tennessee State University; courtesy of the Franklin D. Roosevelt Presidential Library.)

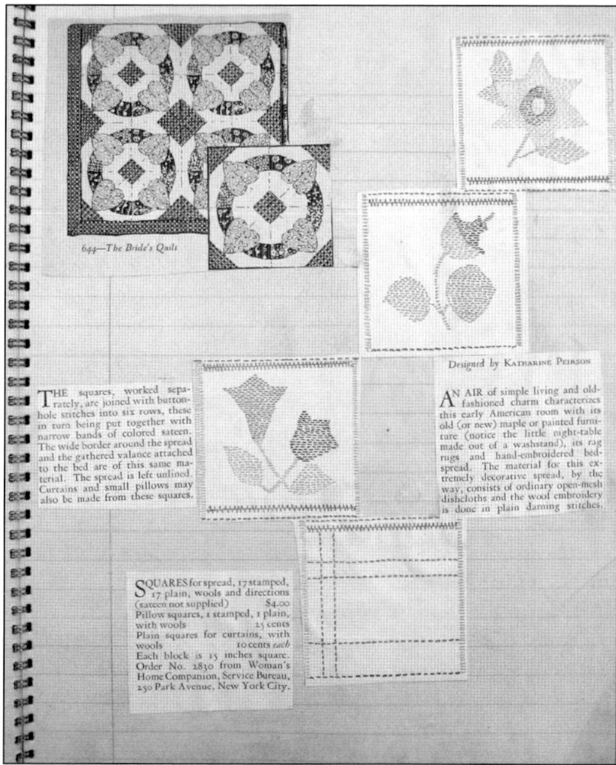

644—*The Bride's Quilt*

Designed by Katharine Peirson

AN AIR of simple living and old-fashioned charm characterizes this early American room with its old (or new) maple or painted furniture (notice the little night-table made out of a washstand), its rag rugs and hand-embroidered bedspread. The material for this extremely decorative spread, by the way, consists of ordinary open-mesh dishcloths and the wool embroidery is done in plain darning stitches.

THE squares, worked separately, are joined with buttonhole stitches into six rows, these in turn being put together with narrow bands of colored sateen. The wide border around the spread and the gathered valance attached to the bed are of this same material. The spread is left unlined. Curtains and small pillows may also be made from these squares.

SQUARES for spread, 17 stamped, 17 plain, wools and directions (sateen not supplied) $4.00
Pillow squares, 1 stamped, 1 plain, with wools 25 cents
Plain squares for curtains, with wools 10 cents *each*
Each block is 15 inches square. Order No. 2830 from Woman's Home Companion, Service Bureau, 250 Park Avenue, New York City.

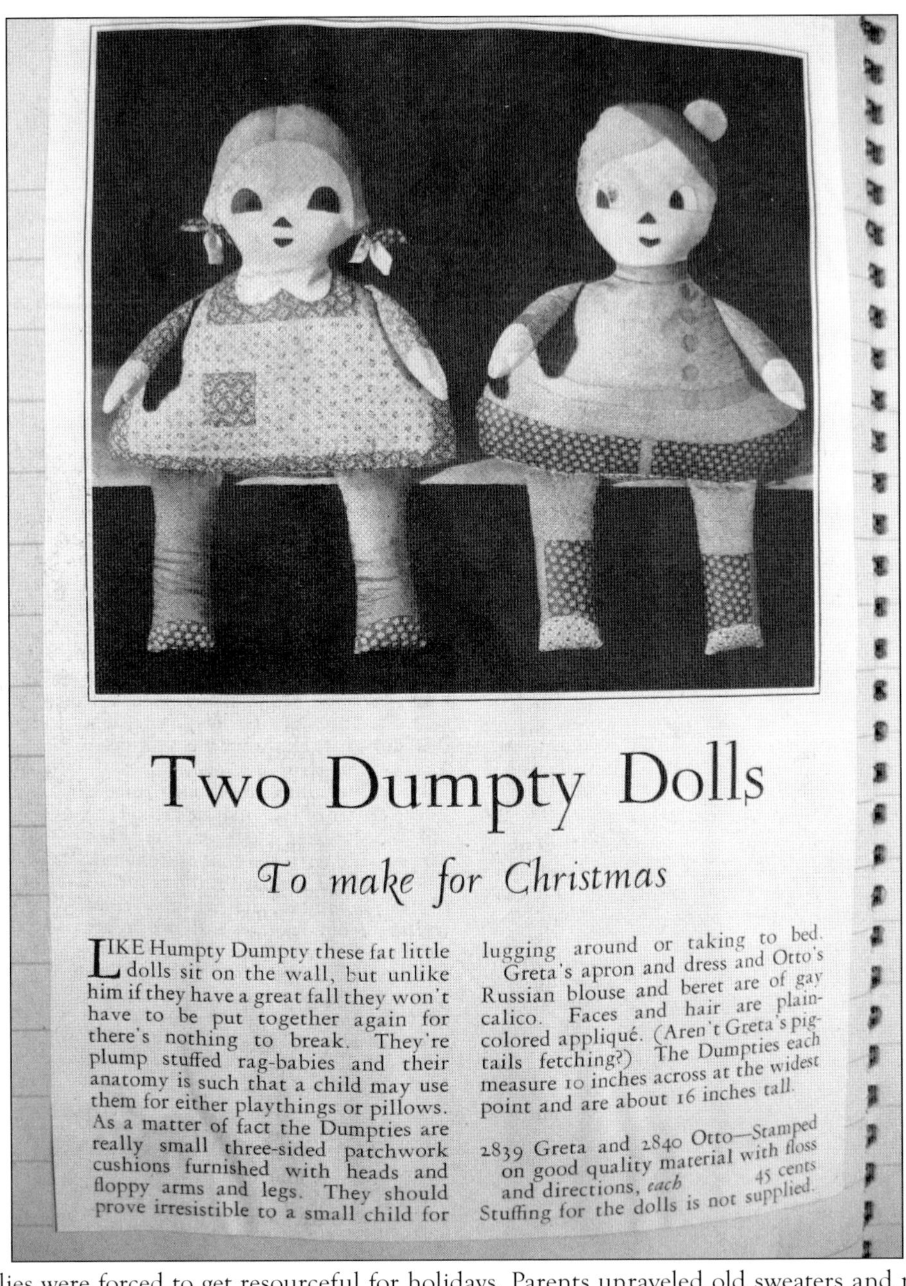

Two Dumpty Dolls

To make for Christmas

LIKE Humpty Dumpty these fat little dolls sit on the wall, but unlike him if they have a great fall they won't have to be put together again for there's nothing to break. They're plump stuffed rag-babies and their anatomy is such that a child may use them for either playthings or pillows. As a matter of fact the Dumpties are really small three-sided patchwork cushions furnished with heads and floppy arms and legs. They should prove irresistible to a small child for lugging around or taking to bed.

Greta's apron and dress and Otto's Russian blouse and beret are of gay calico. Faces and hair are plain-colored appliqué. (Aren't Greta's pig-tails fetching?) The Dumpties each measure 10 inches across at the widest point and are about 16 inches tall.

2839 Greta and 2840 Otto—Stamped on good quality material with floss and directions, *each* 45 cents
Stuffing for the dolls is not supplied.

Families were forced to get resourceful for holidays. Parents unraveled old sweaters and reused the yarn to knit new scarves and mittens. They looked through scrapbooks for ideas. Advertised in one of the scrapbooks, these "Two Dumpty Dolls" were an affordable gift for Christmas. "Like Humpty Dumpty these fat little dolls sit on the wall, but unlike him if they have a great fall, they won't have to be put together again for there's nothing to break. They're plump stuffed rag-babies, and their anatomy is such that a child may use them for either playthings or pillows." Greta and Otto's stamped material, floss, and directions were only 45¢ each (stuffing not included). "They should prove irresistible to a small child for lugging around or taking to bed." (Photograph by Prof. Jason Vance of Middle Tennessee State University; courtesy of the Franklin D. Roosevelt Presidential Library.)

A "48 State-Bird Quilt-Blocks" pattern for only $1.59 postpaid was featured in a quilt-themed scrapbook and enticed readers to purchase. The purchase included 48 nine-inch blocks and instructions. Alaska and Hawaii were not included in this pattern as they did not become states until 1959. (Photograph by Prof. Jason Vance of Middle Tennessee State University; courtesy of the Franklin D. Roosevelt Presidential Library.)

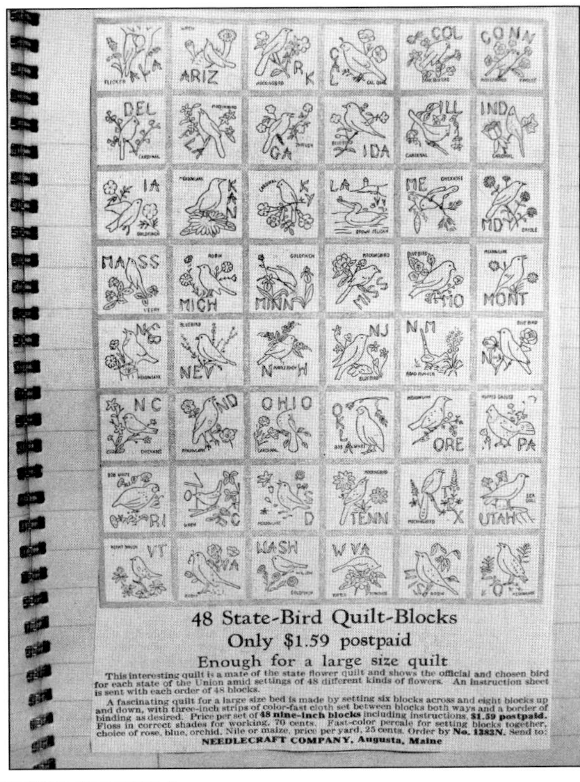

48 State-Bird Quilt-Blocks

Only $1.59 postpaid

Enough for a large size quilt

This interesting quilt is a mate of the state flower quilt and shows the official and chosen bird for each state of the Union amid settings of 48 different kinds of flowers. An instruction sheet is sent with each order of 48 blocks.

A fascinating quilt for a large size bed is made by setting six blocks across and eight blocks up and down, with three-inch strips of color-fast cloth set between blocks both ways and a border of binding as desired. Price per set of **48 nine-inch blocks** including instructions, **$1.59 postpaid.** Floss in correct shades for working, 70 cents. Fast-color percale for setting blocks together, choice of rose, blue, orchid, Nile or maize, price per yard, 25 cents. Order by **No. 1282N.** Send to:

NEEDLECRAFT COMPANY, Augusta, Maine

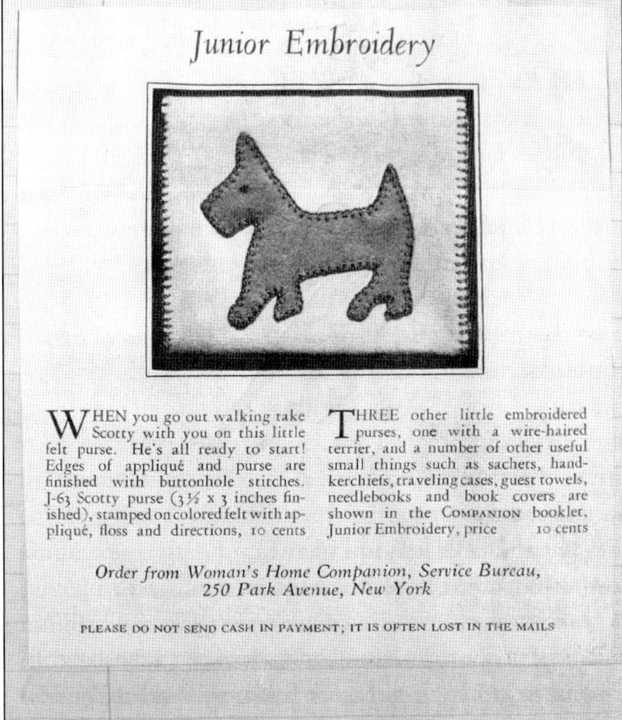

Junior Embroidery

WHEN you go out walking take Scotty with you on this little felt purse. He's all ready to start! Edges of appliqué and purse are finished with buttonhole stitches. J-63 Scotty purse (3½ x 3 inches finished), stamped on colored felt with appliqué, floss and directions, 10 cents

THREE other little embroidered purses, one with a wire-haired terrier, and a number of other useful small things such as sachets, handkerchiefs, traveling cases, guest towels, needlebooks and book covers are shown in the COMPANION booklet, Junior Embroidery, price 10 cents

Order from Woman's Home Companion, Service Bureau, 250 Park Avenue, New York

PLEASE DO NOT SEND CASH IN PAYMENT; IT IS OFTEN LOST IN THE MAILS

A perfect starter project included a junior embroidery felt purse pattern from *Woman's Home Companion* magazine displayed in a scrapbook. Many girls learned needlework and enjoyed this project. "When you go out walking take Scotty with you on this little felt purse. He's all ready to start," read the article. (Photograph by Prof. Jason Vance of Middle Tennessee State University; courtesy of the Franklin D. Roosevelt Presidential Library.)

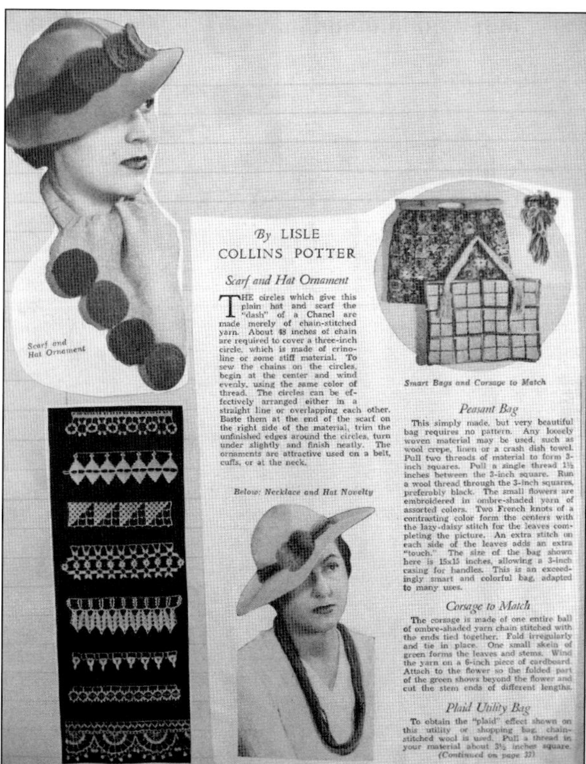

By LISLE COLLINS POTTER

Scarf and Hat Ornament

THE circles which give this plain hat and scarf the "dash" of a Chanel are made merely of chain-stitched yarn. About 48 inches of chain are required to cover a three-inch circle, which is made of crinoline or some stiff material. To sew the chains on the circles, begin at the center and wind evenly, using the same color of thread. The circles can be effectively arranged either in a straight line or overlapping each other. Baste them at the end of the scarf on the right side of the material, trim the unfinished edges around the circles, turn under slightly and finish neatly. The ornaments are attractive used on a belt, cuffs, or at the neck.

Scarf and Hat Ornament

Below: Necklace and Hat Novelty

Smart Bags and Corsage to Match

Peasant Bag

This simply made, but very beautiful bag requires no pattern. Any loosely woven material may be used, such as wool crepe, linen or a crash dish towel. Pull two threads of material to form 3-inch squares. Pull a single thread 1½ inches between the 3-inch square. Run a wool thread through the 3-inch squares, preferably black. The small flowers are embroidered in ombre-shaded yarn of assorted colors. Two French knots of a contrasting color form the centers with the lazy-daisy stitch for the leaves completing the picture. An extra stitch on each side of the leaves adds an extra "touch." The size of the bag shown here is 15x15 inches, allowing a 3-inch casing for handles. This is an exceedingly smart and colorful bag, adapted to many uses.

Corsage to Match

The corsage is made of one entire ball of ombre-shaded yarn chain stitched with the ends tied together. Fold irregularly and tie in place. One small skein of green forms the leaves and stems. Wind the yarn on a 6-inch piece of cardboard. Attach to the flower so the folded part of the green shows beyond the flower and cut the stem ends of different lengths.

Plaid Utility Bag

To obtain the "plaid" effect shown on this utility or shopping bag, chain-stitched wool is used. Pull a thread in your material about 3½ inches square.

(Continued on page 33)

The scarf and hat ornament by Lisle Collins Potter boasted "the circles which give this plain hat and scarf the 'dash' of a Chanel are made merely of chain-stitched yarn." Other shared styles included a necklace and hat novelty, peasant bag, matching corsage, and plaid utility bag. (Photograph by Prof. Jason Vance of Middle Tennessee State University; courtesy of the Franklin D. Roosevelt Presidential Library.)

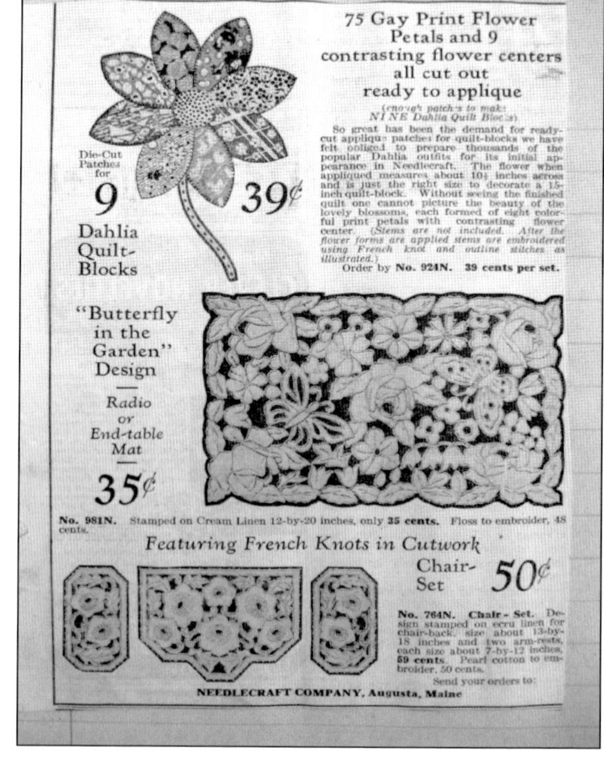

75 Gay Print Flower Petals and 9 contrasting flower centers all cut out ready to applique

(enough patches to make NINE Dahlia Quilt Blocks)

So great has been the demand for ready-cut applique patches for quilt-blocks we have felt obliged to prepare thousands of the popular Dahlia outfits for its initial appearance in Needlecraft. The flower when appliqued measures about 10½ inches across and is just the right size to decorate a 15-inch quilt-block. Without seeing the finished quilt one cannot picture the beauty of the lovely blossoms, each formed of eight colorful print petals with contrasting flower center. *(Stems are not included. After the flower forms are applied stems are embroidered using French knot and outline stitches as illustrated.)*

Order by **No. 924N.** **39 cents per set.**

Die-Cut Patches for 9 Dahlia Quilt-Blocks 39¢

"Butterfly in the Garden" Design

Radio or End-table Mat

35¢

No. 981N. Stamped on Cream Linen 12-by-20 inches, only **35 cents.** Floss to embroider, 48 cents.

Featuring French Knots in Cutwork

Chair-Set 50¢

No. 764N. Chair-Set. Design stamped on ecru linen for chair-back, size about 13-by-18 inches and two arm-rests, each size about 7-by-12 inches, **59 cents.** Pearl cotton to embroider, 50 cents.

Send your orders to:

NEEDLECRAFT COMPANY, Augusta, Maine

A "Butterfly in the Garden" pattern for a radio or end table mat advertised for only 35¢ from the Needlecraft Company in Augusta, Maine, and adorned this scrapbook page. The matching chair set that featured French knots in cutwork was 50¢. Lastly, die-cut patches to make nine "Dahlia Quilt Blocks" were available for 39¢ per set. (Photograph by Prof. Jason Vance of Middle Tennessee State University; courtesy of the Franklin D. Roosevelt Presidential Library.)

A variety of crocheted home goods included instructions with an abbreviations key. People spruced up their home without spending money on patterns or instructions. Projects included a table mat, book cover, "checko" mat, and popcorn lampshade. (Photograph by Prof. Jason Vance of Middle Tennessee State University; courtesy of the Franklin D. Roosevelt Presidential Library.)

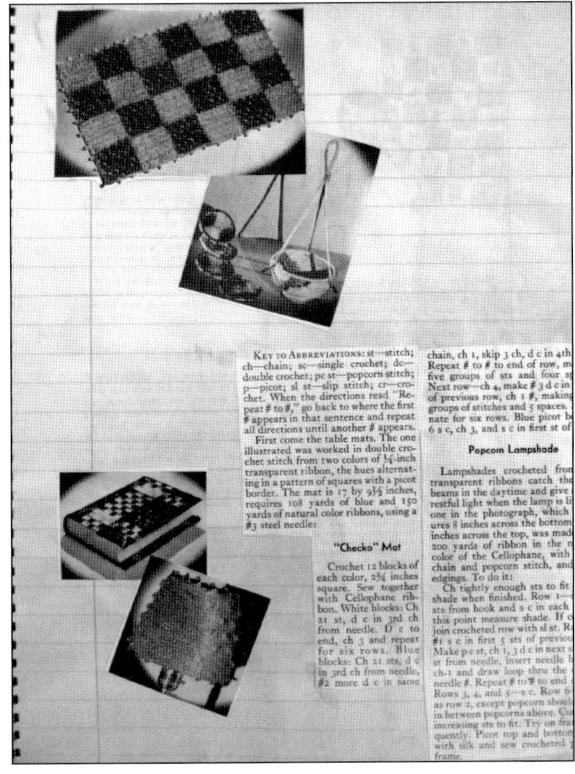

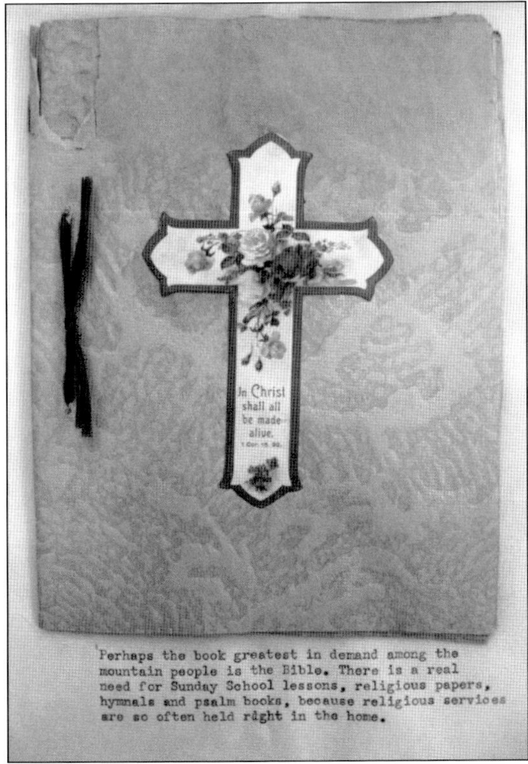

During the 1930s and 1940s, religion played an important role in the lives of rural Appalachia. Since religious services were often held in the home during this time, the need for religious-themed scrapbooks was useful. They included lessons, hymnals, Psalms, and scripture. (Photograph by Prof. Jason Vance of Middle Tennessee State University; courtesy of the Franklin D. Roosevelt Presidential Library.)

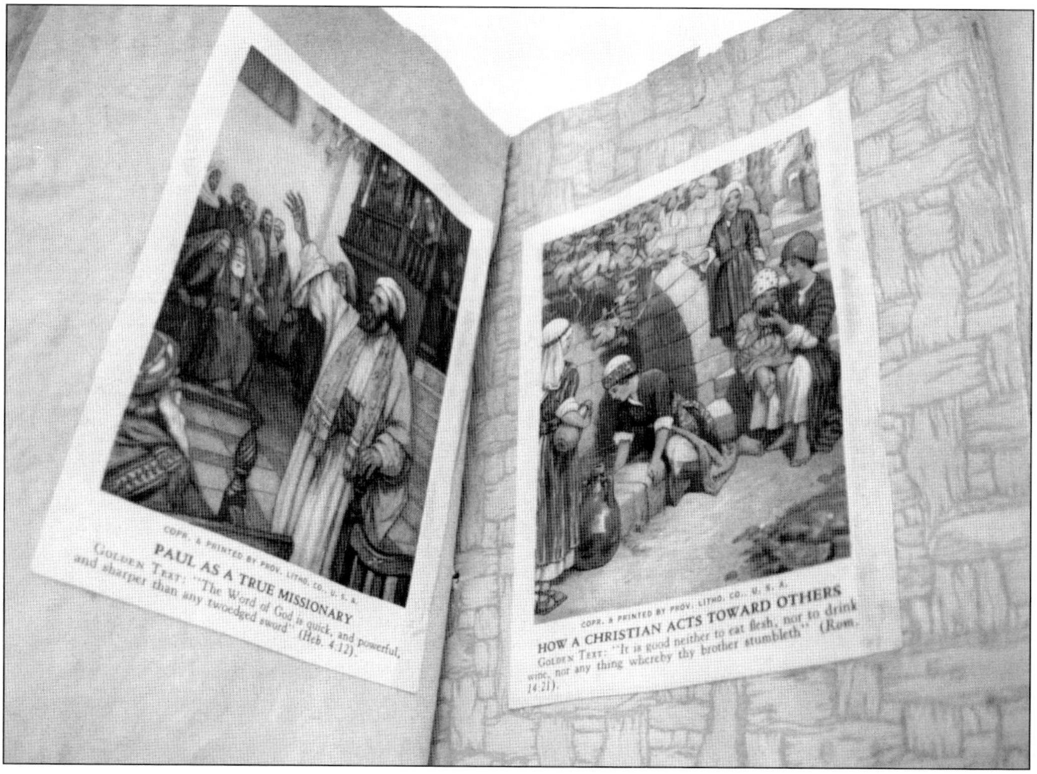

Within the religious-themed scrapbooks, Biblical cards with verses and illustrations were included. The illustrations helped folks who were illiterate or beginner readers. The cards shared Paul as a missionary and how a Christian should act toward others with the accompanying verses, Hebrews 4:12 and Romans 14:21. (Photograph by Prof. Jason Vance of Middle Tennessee State University; courtesy of the Franklin D. Roosevelt Presidential Library.)

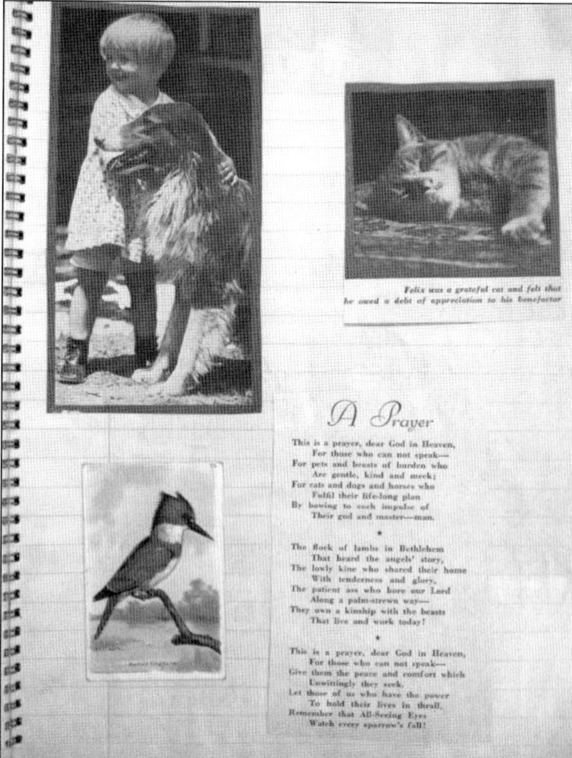

Photographs of people and their pets cuddled up reflected the relationship between people and animals. A belted kingfisher bird perched on a branch for the birdwatchers in the community. A rhyming prayer is included for "those who can not speak—for pets and beasts of burden who are gentle, kind and meek." (Photograph by Prof. Jason Vance of Middle Tennessee State University; courtesy of the Franklin D. Roosevelt Presidential Library.)

Angelo Patri, an Italian American educator, shared his thoughts on boys and dogs in this newspaper clipping. Patri believed boys must have a dog(s) as part of their upbringing. The two boys "have been entrusted with a pointer, and the pointer has entrusted himself to them." (Photograph by Prof. Jason Vance of Middle Tennessee State University; courtesy of the Franklin D. Roosevelt Presidential Library.)

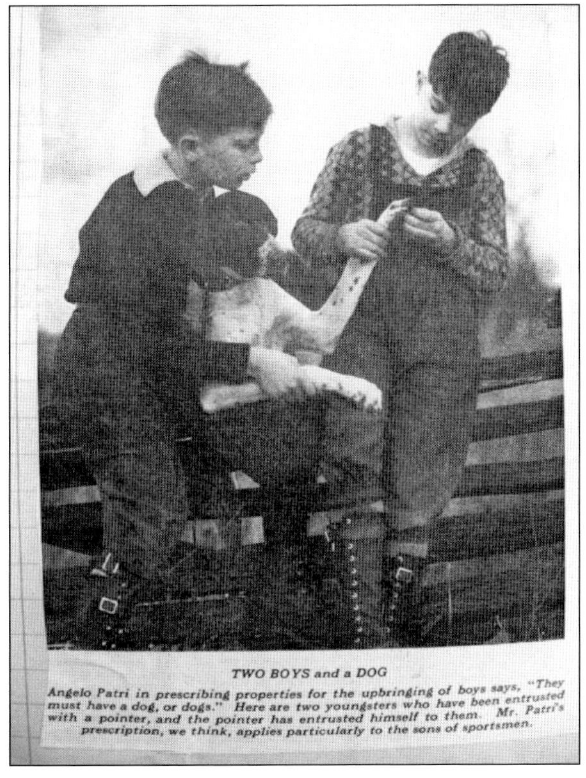

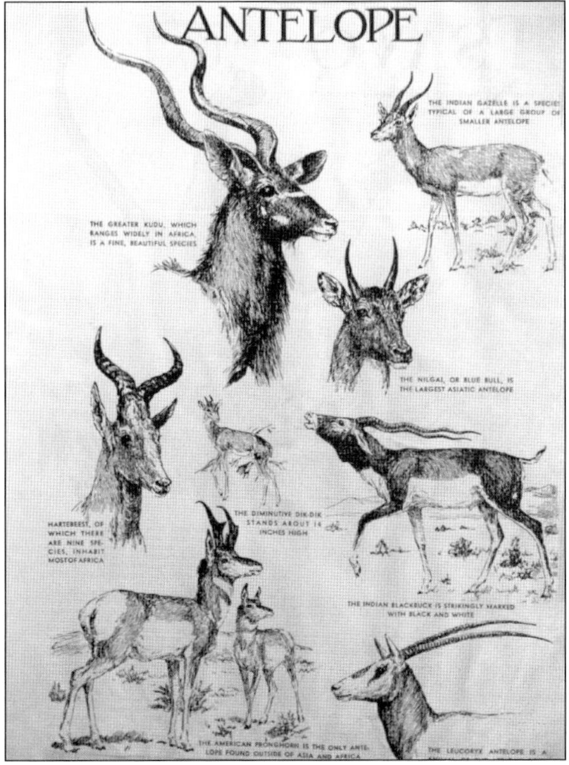

Some scrapbooks were pictorial and featured nature scenes, animals, and flowers. Many images were clipped from a *National Geographic Society* magazine. Howard L. Hastings's drawings of antelopes around the globe invited illiterate patrons to experience the world beyond their walls. Family members and neighbors could join them and read the descriptions together. (Photograph by Prof. Jason Vance of Middle Tennessee State University; courtesy of the Franklin D. Roosevelt Presidential Library.)

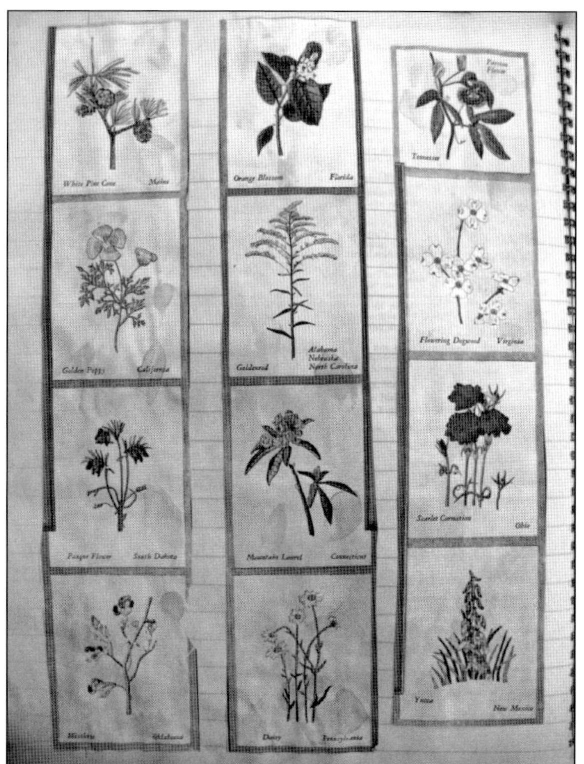

Twelve beautiful flowers from different states were pasted on a scrapbook page. Since many could not travel to California, New Mexico, or Maine, they got a glimpse of the flowers native to those parts of the country. (Photograph by Prof. Jason Vance of Middle Tennessee State University; courtesy of the Franklin D. Roosevelt Presidential Library.)

Breathtaking blossoms in Brussels covered this scrapbook's page. "Laeken Visitors Walk Through A Bower of Bloom 500 Yards Long" was taken from a *National Geographic Society* magazine. Patrons glimpsed the Royal Palace in Belgium and its azaleas in the month of May. (Photograph by Prof. Jason Vance of Middle Tennessee State University; courtesy of the Franklin D. Roosevelt Presidential Library.)

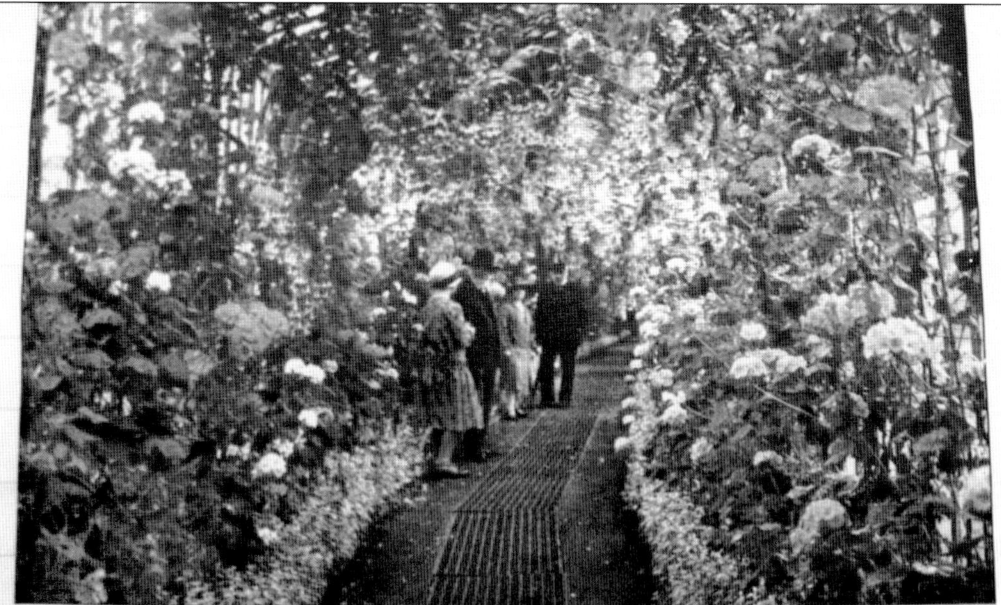

This scrapbook page invited readers to draw tulips with colored chalk or pastels. Simple instructions with examples were provided. Arts and crafts were encouraged through the WPA programs and were important in Appalachia culture. Other highlighted birds included a pine grosbeak and black-capped chickadee. (Photograph by Prof. Jason Vance of Middle Tennessee State University; courtesy of the Franklin D. Roosevelt Presidential Library.)

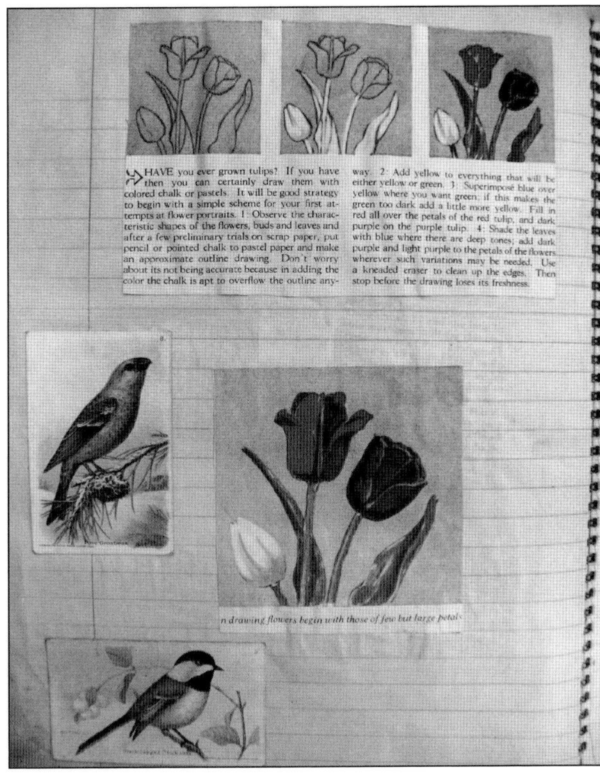

BAKED O'POSSUM

First dress the O'possum and stew until tender. Then place small twigs or limbs of spice wood in pan with O'possum to flavor; add pepper, lard and salt and bake.

BAKED GROUNDHOG

Par-boil until tender. Get spice wood switches and lay under and over and place in oven and bake.

DRIED PUMPKIN

Break up into small pieces and wash with warm water and add a piece of bacon to season and sweeten with molasses. Cook until real tender.

PICKLED BEANS

String beans, break them between every bean, cook until tender, then put them into a stone jar. Make salt water and pour over the beans. Break a stone to fit the jar to weight the beans down so the water will stand over them. Tie a cloth over the top of the jar.

PICKLED CORN

Gather the corn from the field while it is tender, take off the shuck and silks. Make a very strong salt water and place the corn in it. Weight down with a stone. Tie a strong cloth over the top.

HOMINY

Put about $2\frac{1}{2}$ gallons of wood ashed in a churn and pour water over them and let stand for 2 or 3 days to make a lye. Boil about 2 gallon of corn in this lye till it is skinned and boil in fresh waterm wash 3 or 4 times. Boil till tender.

SHUCK BEANS

Cook in water until about half done; then wash and place bacon and salt and pod and cook until tender.

ASH CAKES

About one quart of corn meal.
1 Teaspoon salt
1 cup sour milk.
Mix up with water(stiff) and have hot wood ashes in open fire-place, make hole in hot ashes put the round roll in and cover with hot coles of fire, bake until brown.

Appalachia folks prided themselves on their southern cooking. Naturally, a recipe scrapbook received much attention. A compilation of orally shared recipes was typed up to include with others. These recipes only needed a few ingredients and included pickled beans, ash cakes, baked o'possum, and baked groundhog. (Photograph by Prof. Jason Vance of Middle Tennessee State University; courtesy of the Franklin D. Roosevelt Presidential Library.)

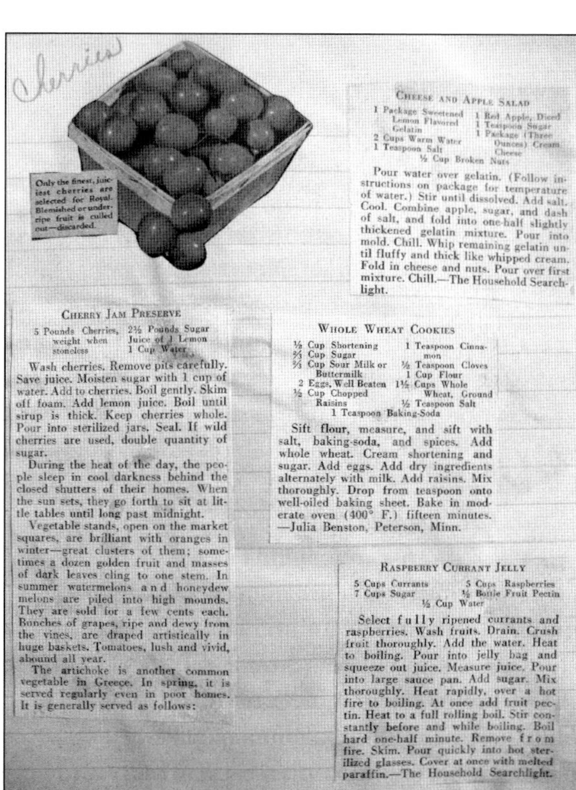

Cherries

CHEESE AND APPLE SALAD

1 Package Sweetened Lemon Flavored Gelatin
2 Cups Warm Water
1 Teaspoon Salt
1 Red Apple, Diced
1 Teaspoon Sugar
1 Package (Three Ounces) Cream Cheese
½ Cup Broken Nuts

Pour water over gelatin. (Follow instructions on package for temperature of water.) Stir until dissolved. Add salt. Cool. Combine apple, sugar, and dash of salt, and fold into one-half slightly thickened gelatin mixture. Pour into mold. Chill. Whip remaining gelatin until fluffy and thick like whipped cream. Fold in cheese and nuts. Pour over first mixture. Chill.—The Household Searchlight.

CHERRY JAM PRESERVE

5 Pounds Cherries, weight when stoneless
2½ Pounds Sugar
Juice of 1 Lemon
1 Cup Water

Wash cherries. Remove pits carefully. Save juice. Moisten sugar with 1 cup of water. Add to cherries. Boil gently. Skim off foam. Add lemon juice. Boil until sirup is thick. Keep cherries whole. Pour into sterilized jars. Seal. If wild cherries are used, double quantity of sugar.

During the heat of the day, the people sleep in cool darkness behind the closed shutters of their homes. When the sun sets, they go forth to sit at little tables until long past midnight.

Vegetable stands, open on the market squares, are brilliant with oranges in winter—great clusters of them; sometimes a dozen golden fruit and masses of dark leaves cling to one stem. In summer watermelons and honeydew melons are piled into high mounds. They are sold for a few cents each. Bunches of grapes, ripe and dewy from the vines, are draped artistically in huge baskets. Tomatoes, lush and vivid, abound all year.

The artichoke is another common vegetable in Greece. In spring, it is served regularly even in poor homes. It is generally served as follows:

WHOLE WHEAT COOKIES

½ Cup Shortening
⅔ Cup Sugar
⅔ Cup Sour Milk or Buttermilk
2 Eggs, Well Beaten
½ Cup Chopped Raisins
1 Teaspoon Cinnamon
½ Teaspoon Cloves
1 Cup Flour
1½ Cups Whole Wheat, Ground
½ Teaspoon Salt
1 Teaspoon Baking-Soda

Sift flour, measure, and sift with salt, baking-soda, and spices. Add whole wheat. Cream shortening and sugar. Add eggs. Add dry ingredients alternately with milk. Add raisins. Mix thoroughly. Drop from teaspoon onto well-oiled baking sheet. Bake in moderate oven (400° F.) fifteen minutes. —Julia Benston, Peterson, Minn.

RASPBERRY CURRANT JELLY

5 Cups Currants
7 Cups Sugar
5 Cups Raspberries
½ Bottle Fruit Pectin
½ Cup Water

Select fully ripened currants and raspberries. Wash fruits. Drain. Crush fruit thoroughly. Add the water. Heat to boiling. Pour into jelly bag and squeeze out juice. Measure juice. Pour into large sauce pan. Add sugar. Mix thoroughly. Heat rapidly, over a hot fire to boiling. At once add fruit pectin. Heat to a full rolling boil. Stir constantly before and while boiling. Boil hard one-half minute. Remove from fire. Skim. Pour quickly into hot sterilized glasses. Cover at once with melted paraffin.—The Household Searchlight.

Not only would patrons share recipes to be added to the community scrapbook, but they would pay their gratitude to the packhorse librarians by gifting them their family's favorite recipe. Cherries and other fruits were the main ingredients for the desserts shown here. (Photograph by Prof. Jason Vance of Middle Tennessee State University; courtesy of the Franklin D. Roosevelt Presidential Library.)

Some recipes highlighted brand names like Heinz Tomato Juice with the advertisement's slogan "One of the 57" because its product line included 57 different items. Other name brands included in recipes were All-Bran, Crisco, Campbell's condensed soup, and Eagle Brand condensed milk. (Photograph by Prof. Jason Vance of Middle Tennessee State University; courtesy of the Franklin D. Roosevelt Presidential Library.)

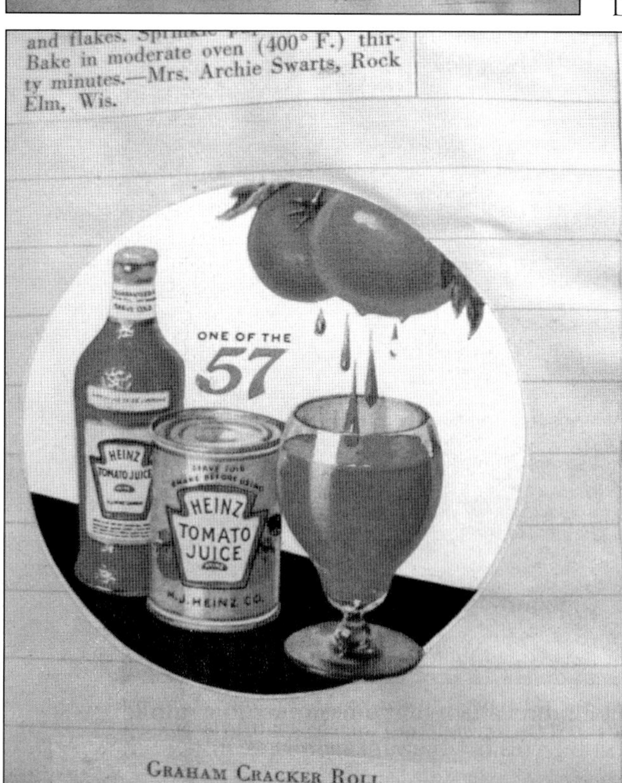

and flakes. ... Bake in moderate oven (400° F.) thirty minutes.—Mrs. Archie Swarts, Rock Elm, Wis.

GRAHAM CRACKER ROLL

ISLAND MEAT BALLS

4 Cups Ground Meat
¼ Cup Bread Crumbs
1 Small Onion, Chopped
1 Teaspoon Mixed Herbs
Salt and Pepper
1 Tablespoon Grated Cheese
1 Egg White, Well Beaten
Olive Oil

Combine ingredients. Season to taste. Form into small balls. Fry until golden brown in pure olive oil.

Chopped meat in grape-vine or cabbage leaves is another favorite dish here. In summer use the grape leaf; in winter cabbage.

ARTICHOKES

10 Artichokes
6 Ounces Olive Oil
1 Chopped Onion, Medium Size
10 Tiny Spring Onions
10 Carrots, Small
1 Teaspoon Flour
1 Teaspoon Mixed Herbs
Juice 1 Lemon
2 Cups Water

Cut off hard outer leaves and spiky tops of artichokes. Wash and scrape stalks. Rub with lemon. Soak in slightly salted water to prevent blackening. Put olive oil and chopped onion on stove. Do not allow to brown. Add flour. Add vegetables, herbs, and lemon juice. Add seasoning. Add water to cover.

Kraft Cheese marketed the nutritious value and cookability of its product through recipes. "You know milk is Nature's most nearly perfect food. Think how marvelously nutritious Kraft Cheese is . . . with more than a gallon of rich milk used to make a single pound!" and "They cook perfectly . . . these Kraft Cheeses." (Photograph by Prof. Jason Vance of Middle Tennessee State University; courtesy of the Franklin D. Roosevelt Presidential Library.)

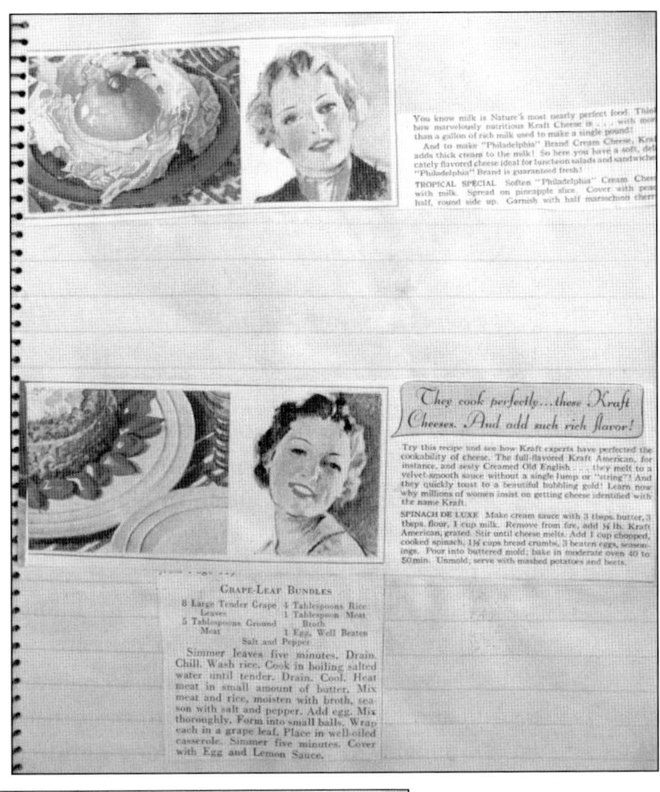

You know milk is Nature's most nearly perfect food. Thin how marvelously nutritious Kraft Cheese is . . . with mor than a gallon of rich milk used to make a single pound!

And to make "Philadelphia" Brand Cream Cheese, Kra adds thick cream to the milk! So here you have a soft, del cately flavored cheese ideal for luncheon salads and sandwiche "Philadelphia" Brand is guaranteed fresh!

TROPICAL SPECIAL Soften "Philadelphia" Cream Chee with milk. Spread on pineapple slice. Cover with pea half, round side up. Garnish with half maraschino cherr

They cook perfectly...these Kraft Cheeses. And add such rich flavor!

Try this recipe and see how Kraft experts have perfected the cookability of cheese. The full-flavored Kraft American, for instance, and zesty Creamed Old English . . . they melt to a velvet-smooth sauce without a single lump or "string"! And they quickly toast to a beautiful bubbling gold! Learn now why millions of women insist on getting cheese identified with the name Kraft.

SPINACH DE LUXE Make cream sauce with 3 tbsps. butter, 3 tbsps. flour, 1 cup milk. Remove from fire, add ¼ lb. Kraft American, grated. Stir until cheese melts. Add 1 cup chopped, cooked spinach, 1½ cups bread crumbs, 3 beaten eggs, seasonings. Pour into buttered mold; bake in moderate oven 40 to 50 min. Unmold; serve with mashed potatoes and beets.

GRAPE-LEAF BUNDLES

8 Large Tender Grape Leaves
5 Tablespoons Ground Meat
4 Tablespoons Rice
1 Tablespoon Meat Broth
1 Egg, Well Beaten
Salt and Pepper

Simmer leaves five minutes. Drain. Chill. Wash rice. Cook in boiling salted water until tender. Drain. Cool. Heat meat in small amount of butter. Mix meat and rice, moisten with broth, season with salt and pepper. Add egg. Mix thoroughly. Form into small balls. Wrap each in a grape leaf. Place in well-oiled casserole. Simmer five minutes. Cover with Egg and Lemon Sauce.

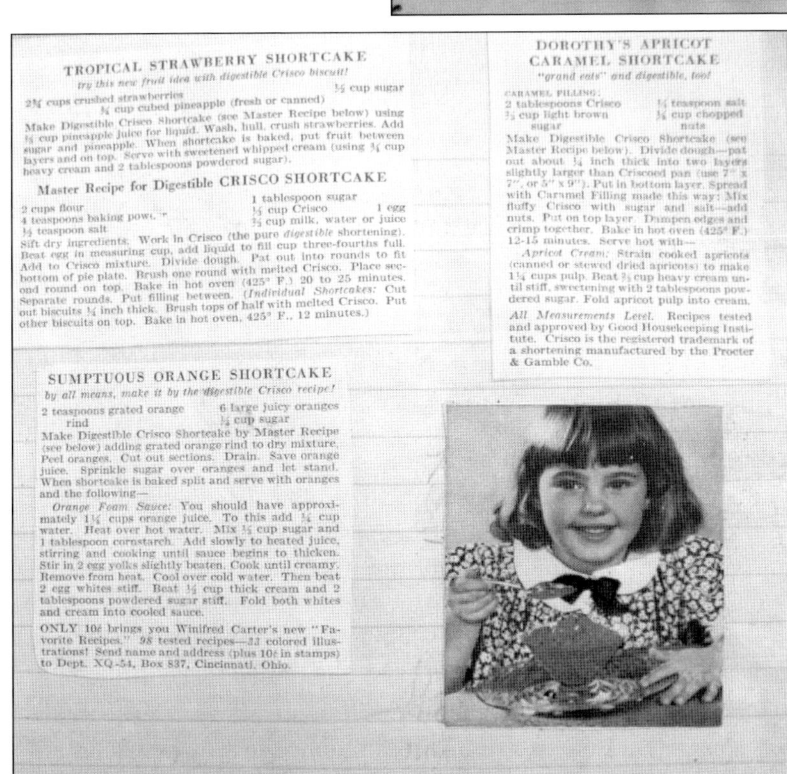

TROPICAL STRAWBERRY SHORTCAKE

try this new fruit idea with digestible Crisco biscuit!

½ cup sugar
2¾ cups crushed strawberries
¾ cup cubed pineapple (fresh or canned)

Make Digestible Crisco Shortcake (see Master Recipe below) using ⅓ cup pineapple juice for liquid. Wash, hull, crush strawberries. Add sugar and pineapple. When shortcake is baked, put fruit between layers and on top. Serve with sweetened whipped cream (using ¾ cup heavy cream and 2 tablespoons powdered sugar).

Master Recipe for Digestible CRISCO SHORTCAKE

2 cups flour
4 teaspoons baking powder
½ teaspoon salt
1 tablespoon sugar
⅓ cup Crisco
1 egg
⅔ cup milk, water or juice

Sift dry ingredients. Work in Crisco (the pure *digestible* shortening). Beat egg in measuring cup, add liquid to fill cup three-fourths full. Add to Crisco mixture. Divide dough. Pat out into rounds to fit bottom of pie plate. Brush one round with melted Crisco. Place second round on top. Bake in hot oven (425° F.) 20 to 25 minutes. Separate rounds. Put filling between. (*Individual Shortcakes:* Cut out biscuits ¼ inch thick. Brush tops of half with melted Crisco. Put other biscuits on top. Bake in hot oven, 425° F., 12 minutes.)

DOROTHY'S APRICOT CARAMEL SHORTCAKE

"grand eats" and digestible, too!

CARAMEL FILLING:
2 tablespoons Crisco
⅔ cup light brown sugar
¼ teaspoon salt
½ cup chopped nuts

Make Digestible Crisco Shortcake (see Master Recipe below). Divide dough—pat out about ¼ inch thick into two layers slightly larger than Criscoed pan (use 7" x 7", or 5" x 9"). Put in bottom layer. Spread with Caramel Filling made this way: Mix fluffy Crisco with sugar and salt—add nuts. Put on top layer. Dampen edges and crimp together. Bake in hot oven (425° F.) 12-15 minutes. Serve hot with—

Apricot Cream: Strain cooked apricots (canned or stewed dried apricots) to make 1¼ cups pulp. Beat ⅔ cup heavy cream until stiff, sweetening with 2 tablespoons powdered sugar. Fold apricot pulp into cream.

All Measurements Level. Recipes tested and approved by Good Housekeeping Institute. Crisco is the registered trademark of a shortening manufactured by the Procter & Gamble Co.

SUMPTUOUS ORANGE SHORTCAKE

by all means, make it by the digestible Crisco recipe!

2 teaspoons grated orange rind
6 large juicy oranges
½ cup sugar

Make Digestible Crisco Shortcake by Master Recipe (see below) adding grated orange rind to dry mixture. Peel oranges. Cut out sections. Drain. Save orange juice. Sprinkle sugar over oranges and let stand. When shortcake is baked split and serve with oranges and the following—

Orange Foam Sauce: You should have approximately 1¼ cups orange juice. To this add ¼ cup water. Heat over hot water. Mix ⅓ cup sugar and 1 tablespoon cornstarch. Add slowly to heated juice, stirring and cooking until sauce begins to thicken. Stir in 2 egg yolks slightly beaten. Cook until creamy. Remove from heat. Cool over cold water. Then beat 2 egg whites stiff. Beat ½ cup thick cream and 2 tablespoons powdered sugar stiff. Fold both whites and cream into cooled sauce.

ONLY 10¢ brings you Winifred Carter's new "Favorite Recipes." 98 tested recipes—33 colored illustrations! Send name and address (plus 10¢ in stamps) to Dept. XQ-54, Box 837, Cincinnati, Ohio.

For those with a sweet tooth, these shortcake recipes were perfect for their kitchen. Types of shortcakes included tropical strawberry, sumptuous orange, and Dorothy's apricot caramel. These recipes claimed to be "grand eats and digestible too" with the ingredient of Crisco, the pure shortening. (Photograph by Prof. Jason Vance of Middle Tennessee State University; courtesy of the Franklin D. Roosevelt Presidential Library.)

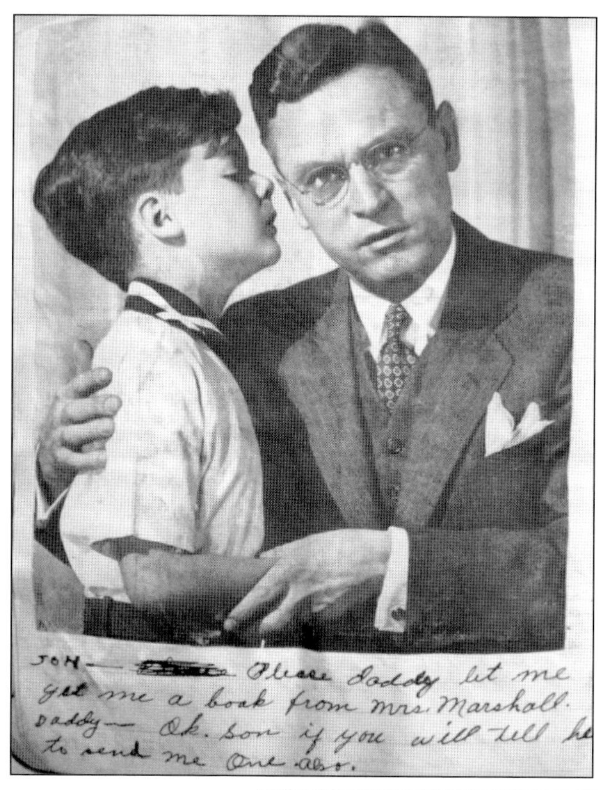

Librarians or patrons cut out pictures in newspapers, magazines, and catalogs then pasted them into scrapbooks. The patrons wrote captions and stories to be shared with others in the community. Jon whispered, "Please daddy let me get me a book from Mrs. Marshall." Daddy replied, "Ok son if you will tell her to send me one also." (Photograph by Prof. Jason Vance of Middle Tennessee State University; courtesy of the Franklin D. Roosevelt Presidential Library.)

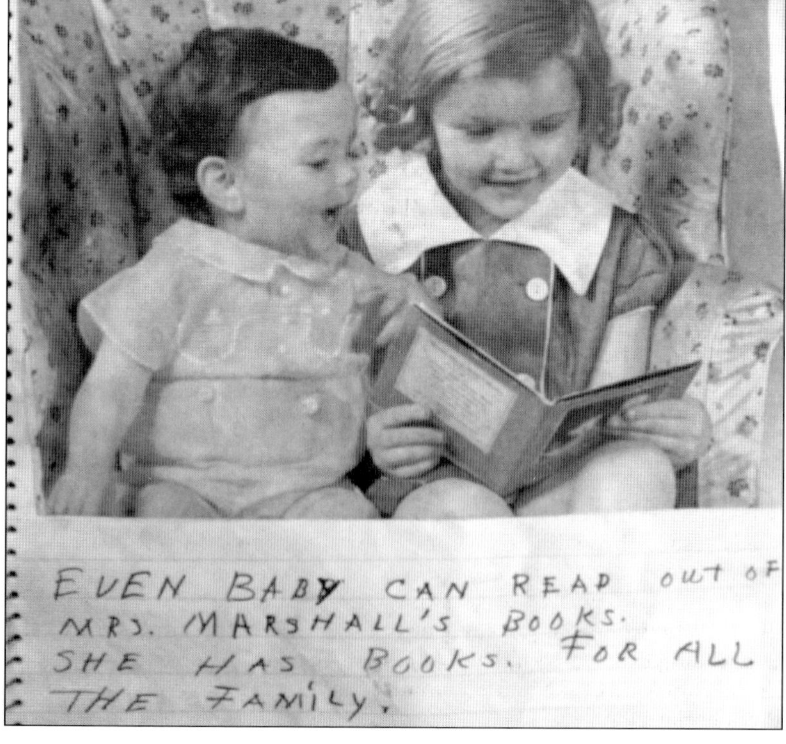

A little girl and baby curled up on a chair with a book. The caption read, "Even baby can read out of Mrs. Marshall's books. She has books for all the family." (Photograph by Prof. Jason Vance of Middle Tennessee State University; courtesy of the Franklin D. Roosevelt Presidential Library.)

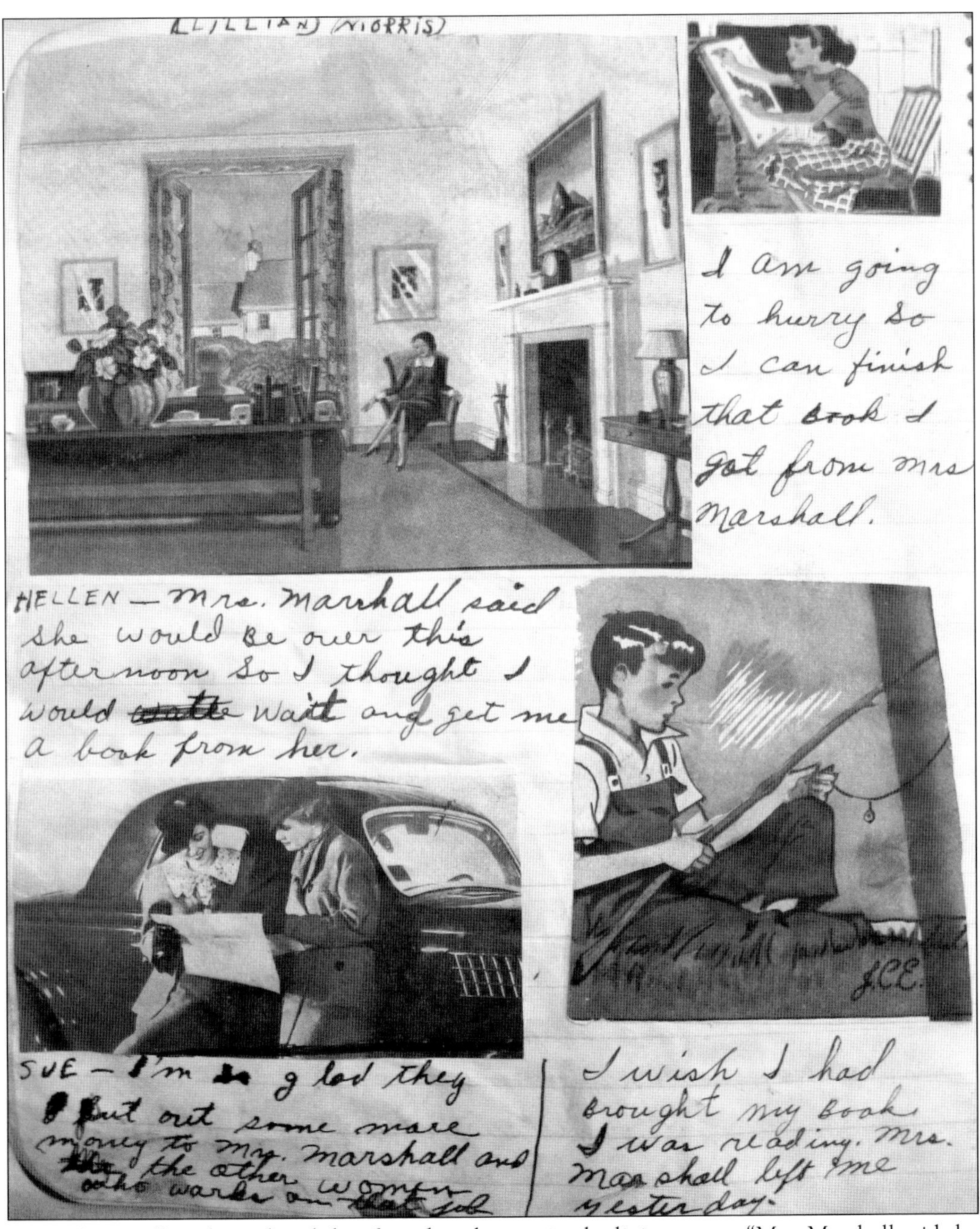

At top left, Hellen chatted with her friend as they sat in the living room. "Mrs. Marshall said she would be over this afternoon. So, I thought I would wait and get me a book from her." At top right, a lady rushed through her painting thinking, "I am going to hurry so I can finish that book I got from Mrs. Marshall." At bottom left, Sue and her friend leaned against the car reading a newspaper on an autumn day. "I'm so glad they put out some more money to Mrs. Marshall and the other women who work that job." At bottom right, the boy fishing wished he had brought his book he was reading that Mrs. Marshall left him yesterday as he looked at his empty line. (Photograph by Prof. Jason Vance of Middle Tennessee State University; courtesy of the Franklin D. Roosevelt Presidential Library.)

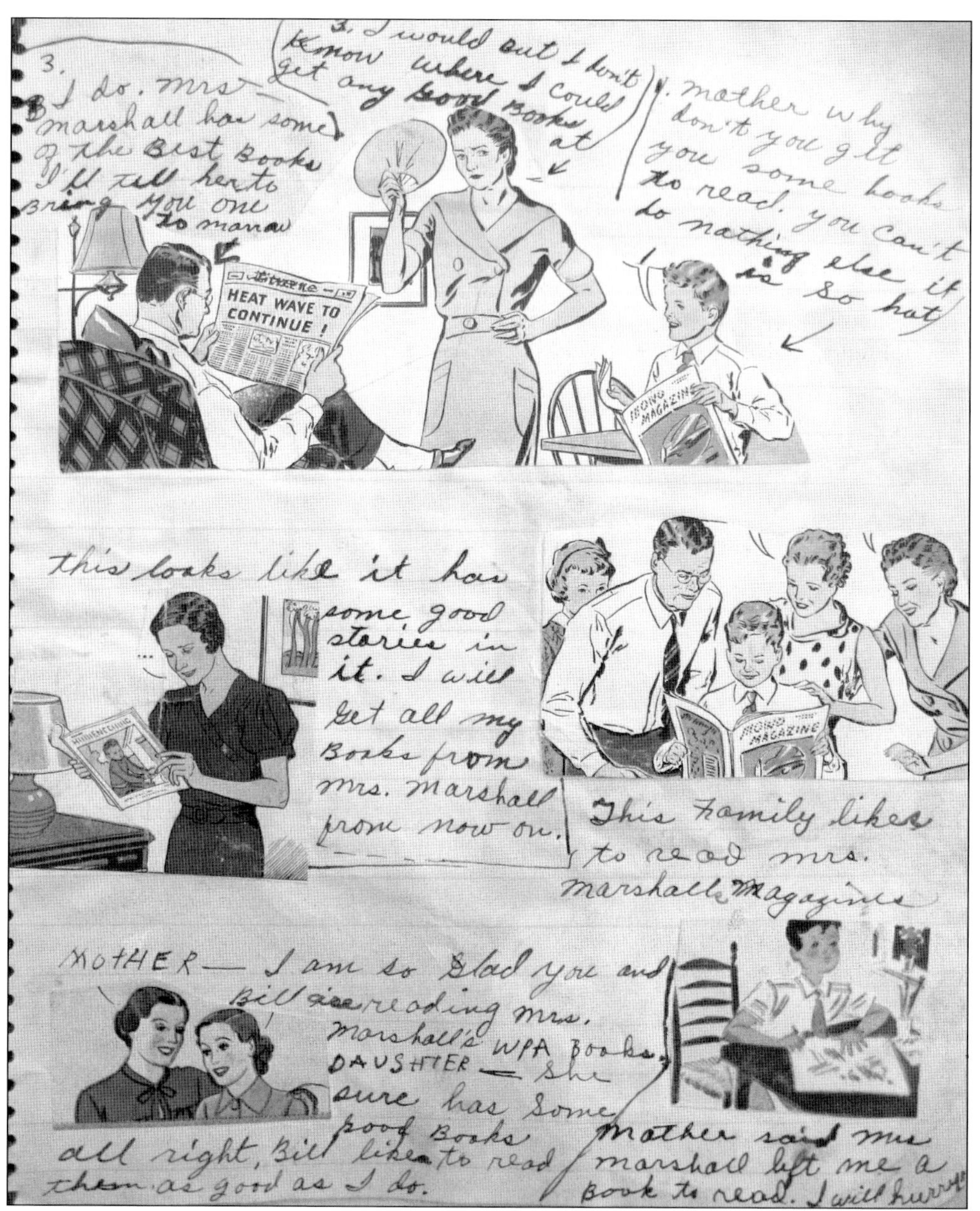

An array of clipped magazine photographs encouraged patrons to use their imagination with writing dialogue. At the top, a son asks, "Mother, why don't you get you some books to read. You can't do nothing else it's so hot." She responded waving her fan, "I would but I don't know where I could get any good books at." As Father read his newspaper, he said, "I do. Mrs. Marshall has some of the best books. I'll tell her to bring you some tomorrow." At center left, a woman flipped through a book. "This looks like it has some good stories in it. I will get my books from Mrs. Marshall from now on." At center right, this family likes to read Mrs. Marshall's magazines. At the bottom, Mother said, "I am so glad you and Bill are reading Mrs. Marshall's WPA books." Her daughter replied, "She sure has some good books all right. Bill likes to read them as good as I do." (Photograph by Prof. Jason Vance of Middle Tennessee State University; courtesy of the Franklin D. Roosevelt Presidential Library.)

The eagerness to read was reflected in the caption. “I wish I hadn’t come. I would rather stay at home and read that book I got from Mrs. Marshall,” said John. June agreed, “I was just thinking I am going back just as soon as we get through eating.” (Photograph by Prof. Jason Vance of Middle Tennessee State University; courtesy of the Franklin D. Roosevelt Presidential Library.)

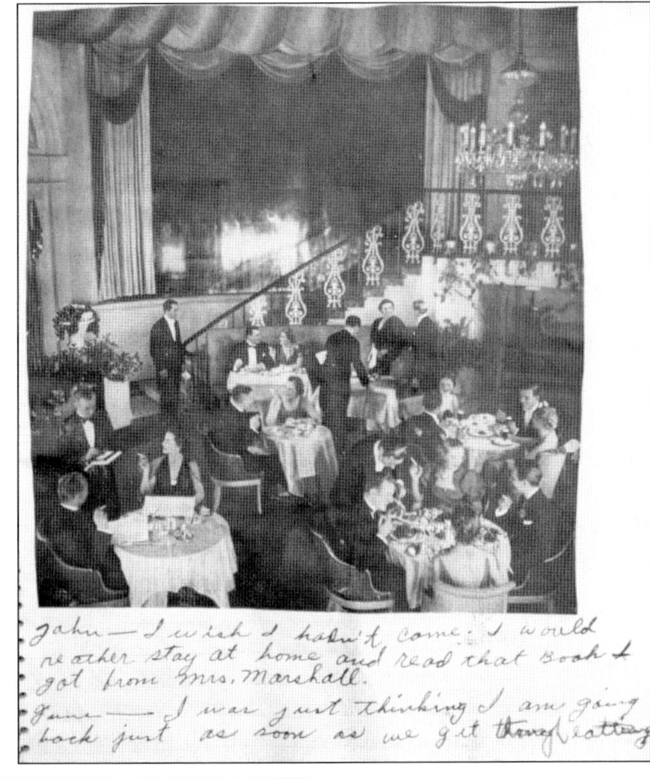

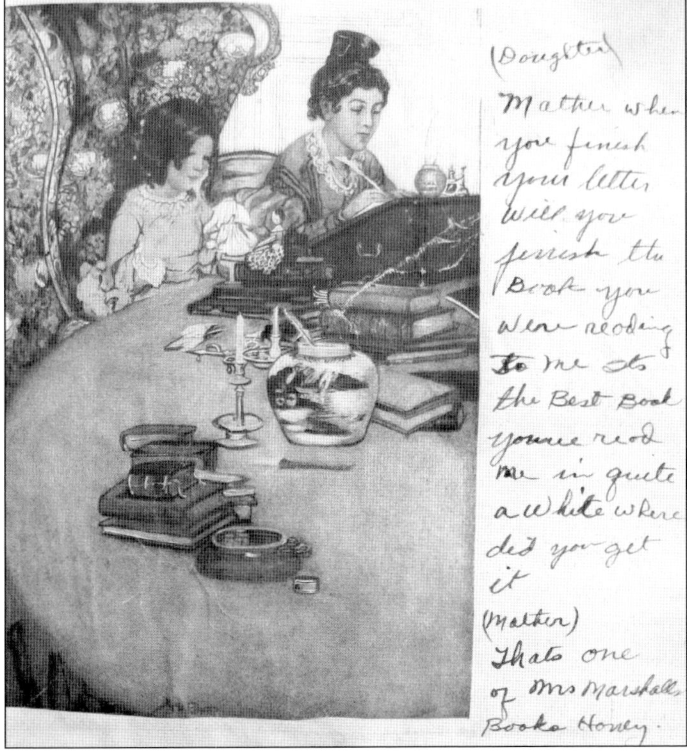

A daughter attempted to be patient sitting next to her mother. “Mother when you finish your letter will you finish the book you were reading me. It’s the best book you’ve read me in quite a while. Where did you get it?” the daughter asked. “That’s one of Mrs. Marshall’s books, honey,” her mother replied. (Photograph by Prof. Jason Vance of Middle Tennessee State University; courtesy of the Franklin D. Roosevelt Presidential Library.)

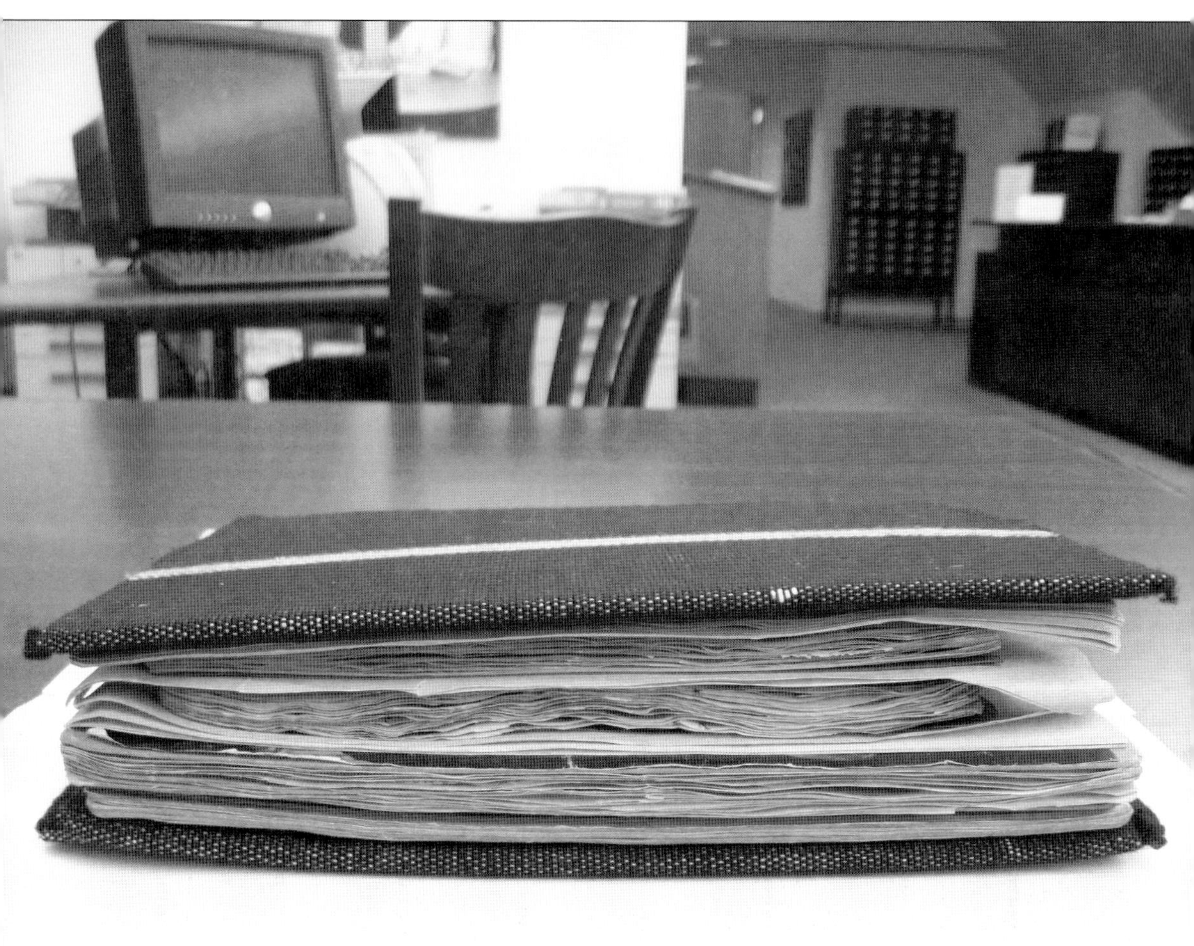

The width of this packhorse librarian scrapbook was three inches wide. More than 2,000 scrapbooks made and donated by librarians and patrons were created during the Packhorse Library Project. An April 1940 report showed 2,653 treasured scrapbooks in circulation. (Photograph by Prof. Jason Vance of Middle Tennessee State University; courtesy of the Franklin D. Roosevelt Presidential Library.)

Seven

Trials and Tribulations

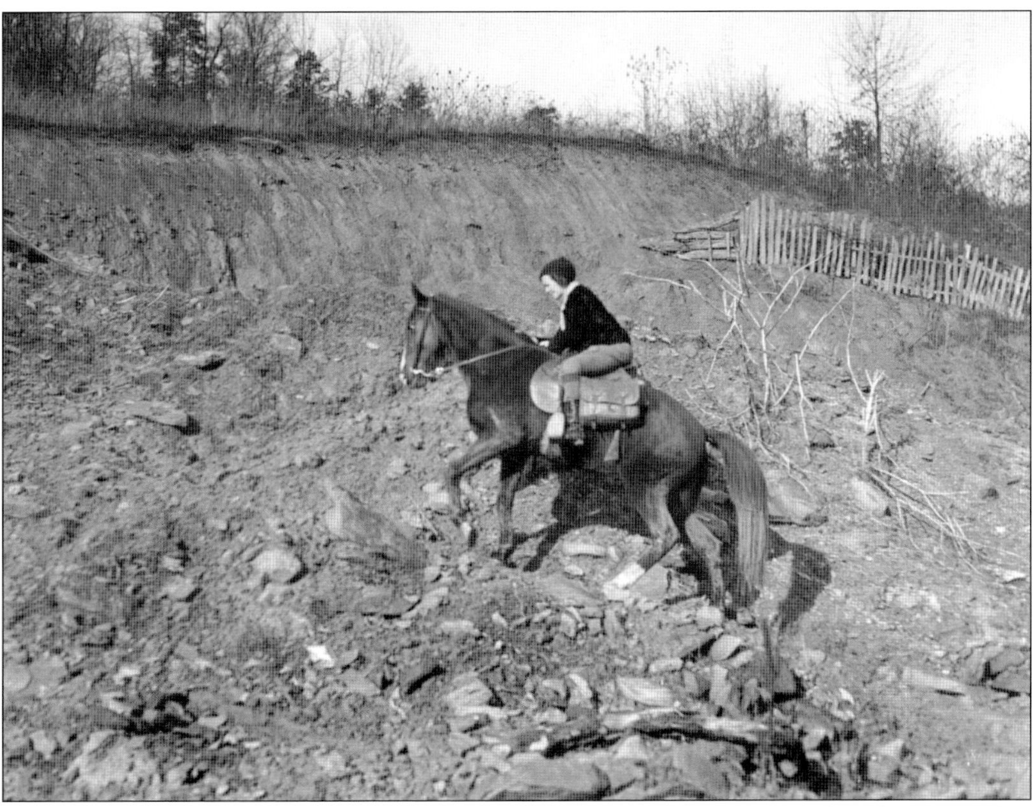

Packhorse librarians cherished their jobs; however, they were not without obstacles. Since they only visited homes and schools twice a month, they maintained schedules so readers were not disappointed. Therefore, bookwomen and their mounts took the shortest route to their patrons. Although the distance might take less time, the rocky terrain proved challenging for horses and riders. (Courtesy of WPA collection, Archives and Records Management Division, Kentucky Department for Libraries and Archives.)

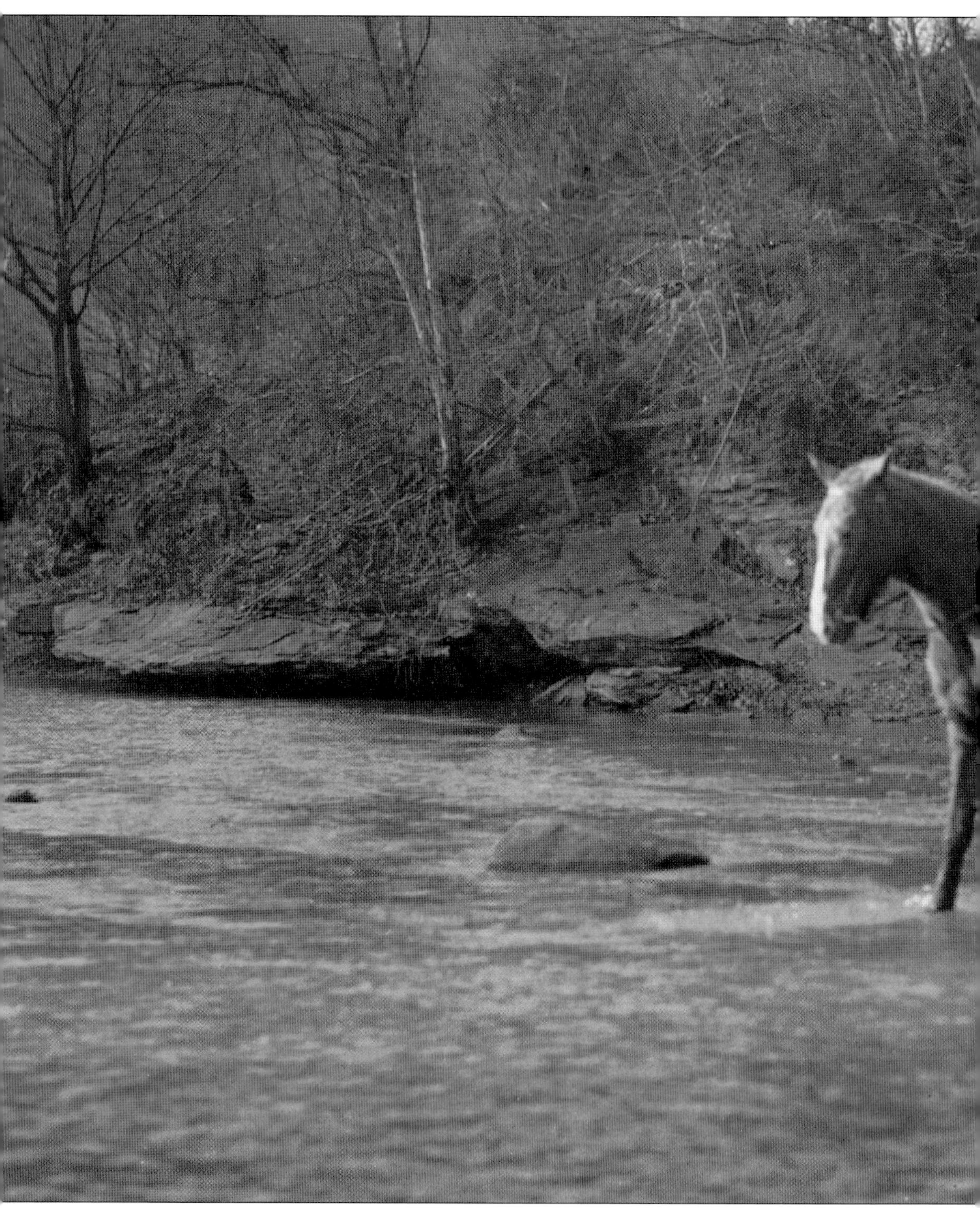

Impassable roads due to mountains or weather conditions left them with no other alternative than the creeks. However, if the creek waters rose too high, not only would the horse's belly get wet, but the librarian's feet too. Their boots froze to the stirrups in freezing temperatures. (Courtesy of

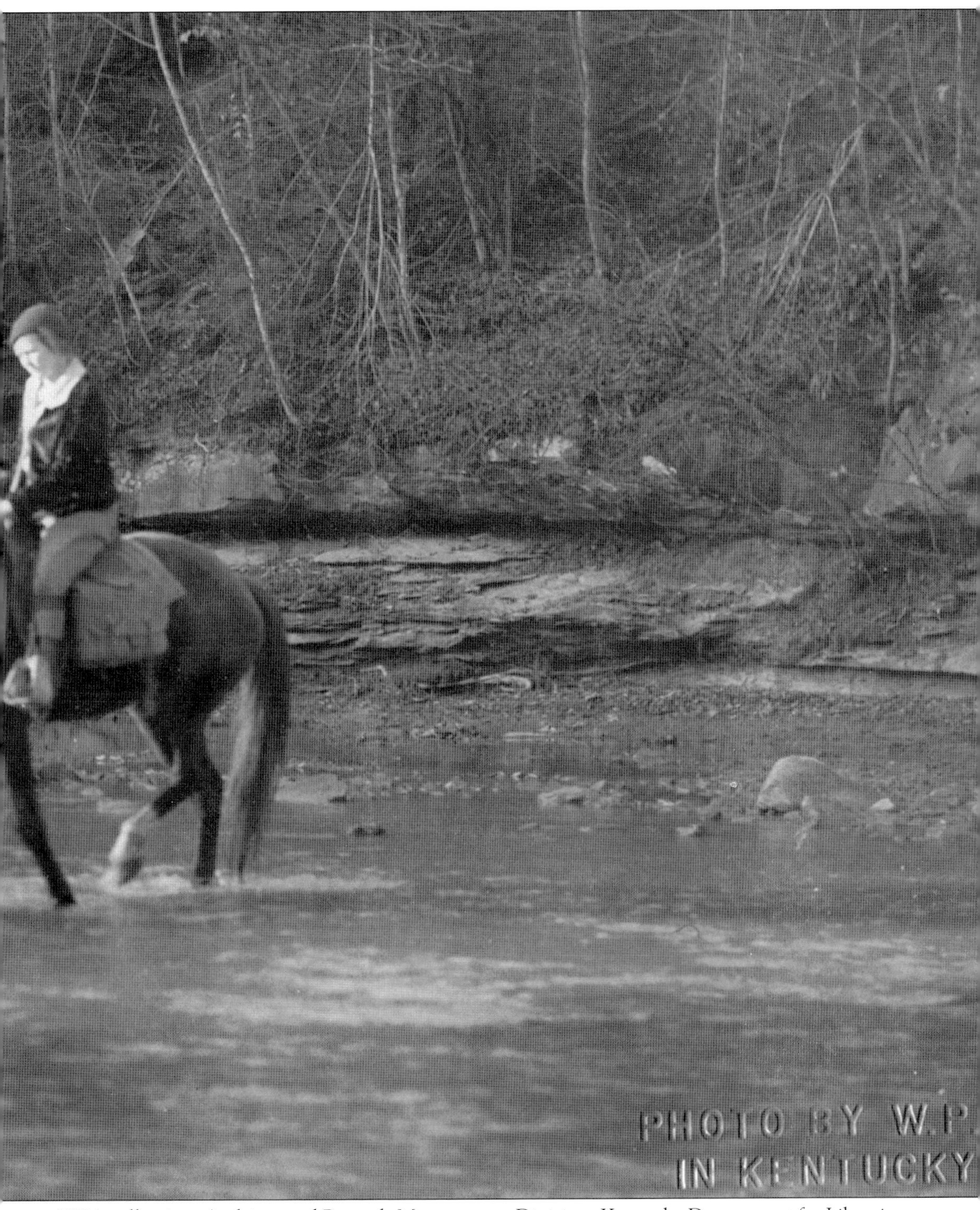

WPA collection, Archives and Records Management Division, Kentucky Department for Libraries and Archives.)

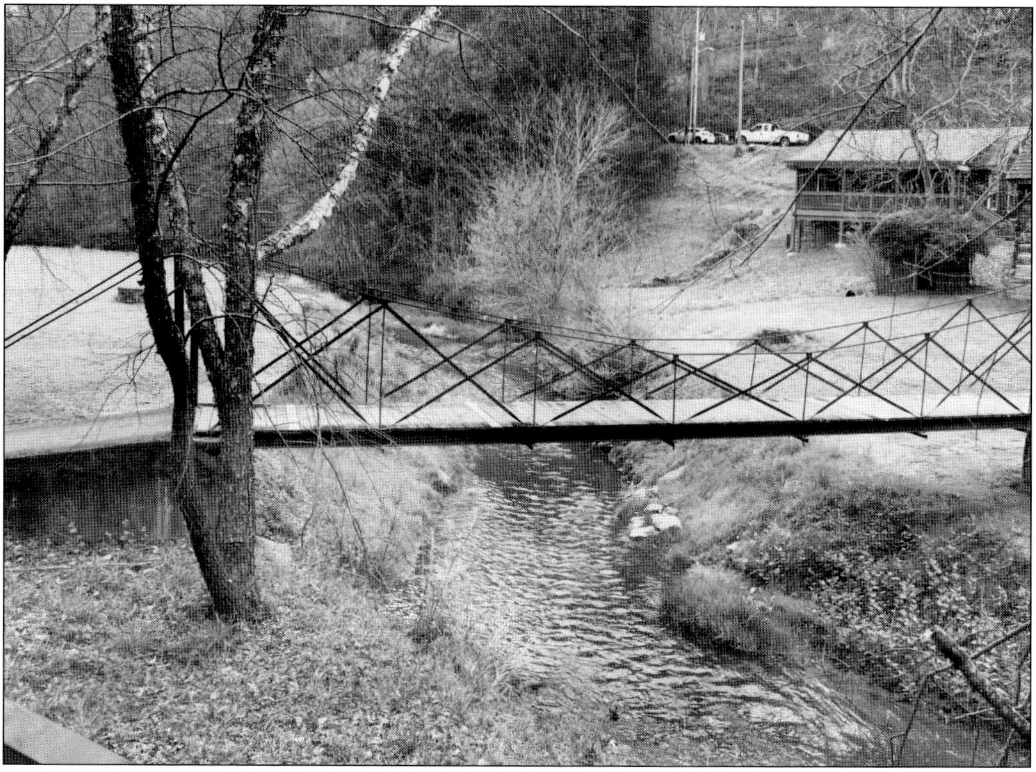

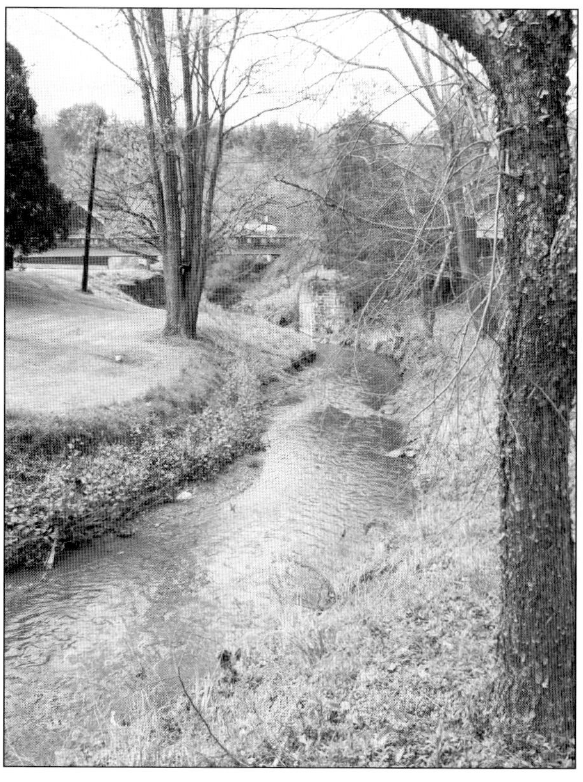

Troublesome Creek streamed through the Hindman Settlement School campus in Hindman, Kentucky. A fork of the North Fork Kentucky River, Troublesome Creek is over 40 miles long and runs through Breathitt, Perry, and Knott Counties. Kentucky is home to other unique creek names due to their treacherous nature. Cutshin Creek is located in the town of Cutshin in Leslie County. Hell for Certain, or Hell-for-Sartin, is also the name of a creek and town in Leslie County. These creeks were the roadways for the packhorse librarians on their book routes. (Photographs by Nicki Jacobsmeyer; courtesy of the Hindman Settlement School.)

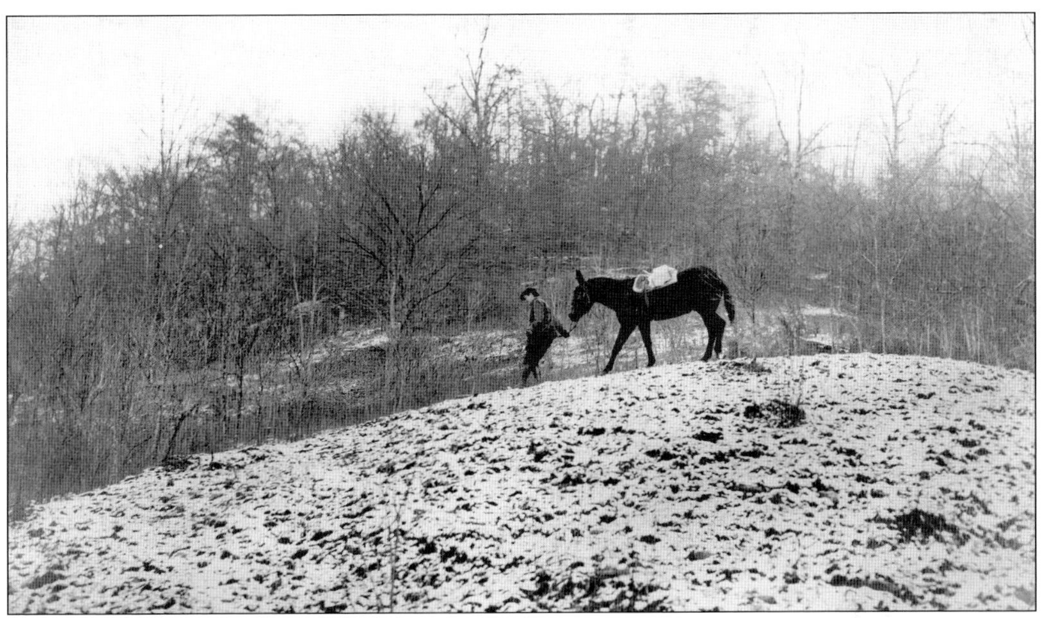

Packhorse librarians never knew for certain what weather awaited them on their routes and in the mountains. Therefore, they prepared for the worst and hoped for the best. Appalachian winters could be long and cold. Depending on the snowy or icy weather and the mount's condition, sometimes the packhorse librarians picked their way on foot along the hillsides. One librarian hiked an 18-mile route on foot after their mule died. (Above, courtesy of Mallie Cody Turner Collection [MS049-1993], Morehead State University Special Collections and Archives; below, courtesy of WPA collection, Archives and Records Management Division, Kentucky Department for Libraries and Archives.)

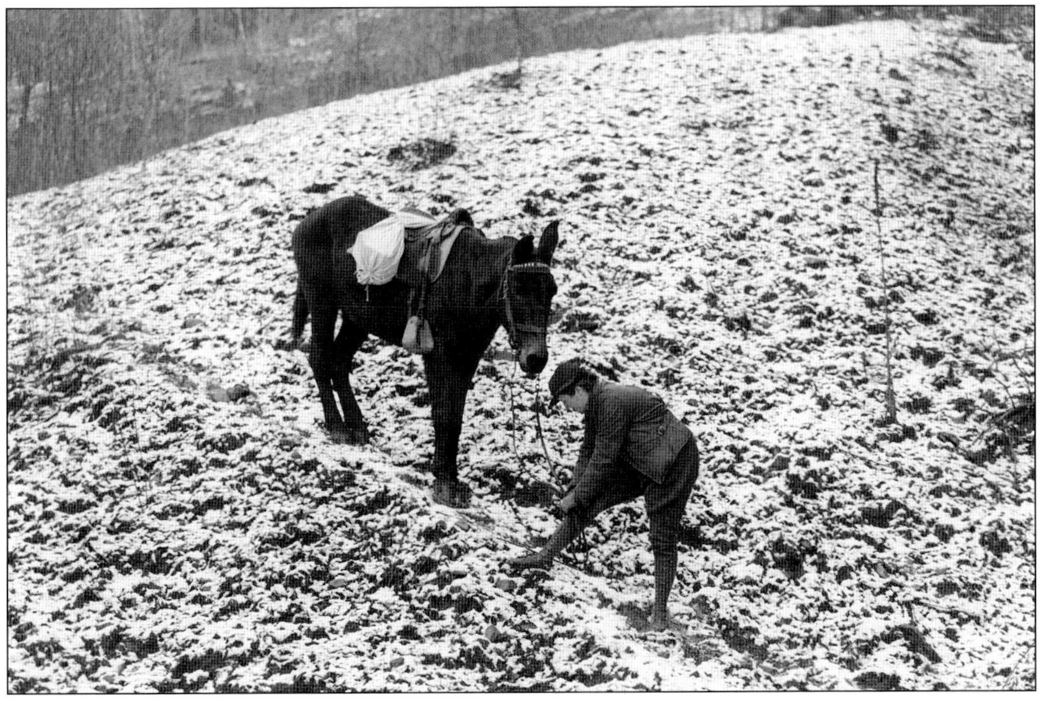

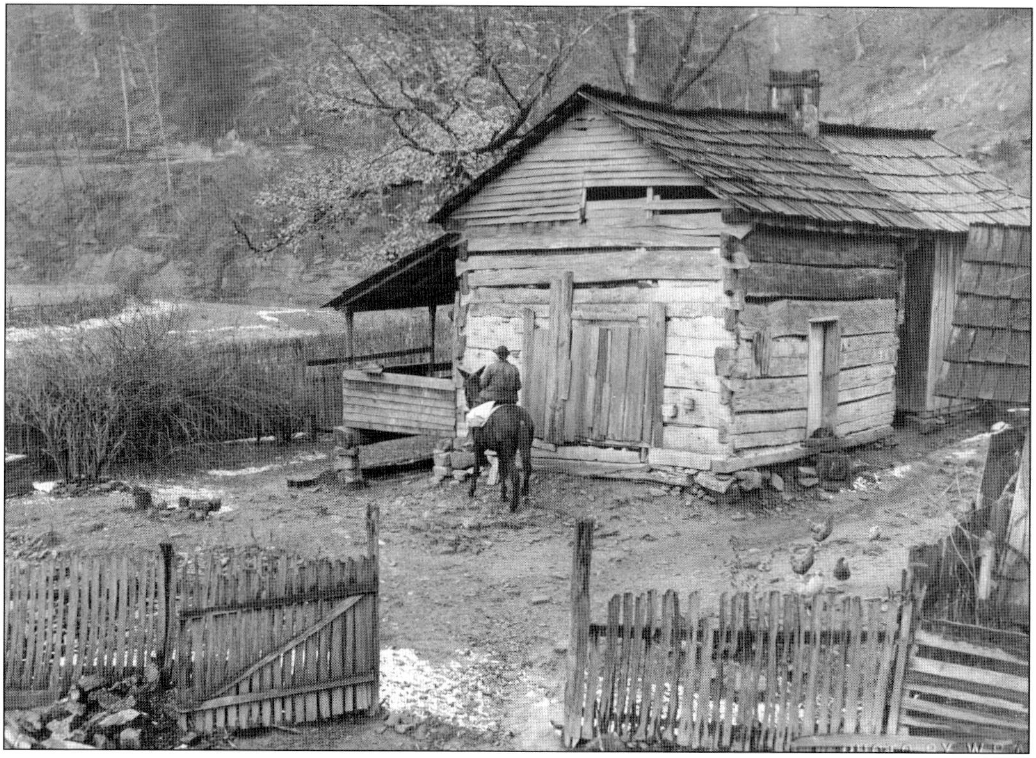

Patrons of the Packhorse Library Project had challenges as well. Some folks were suspicious of the government sending librarian's into homes and wondered about their motives. They would turn the bookwomen away, not wanting any charity. (Courtesy of WPA collection, Archives and Records Management Division, Kentucky Department for Libraries and Archives.)

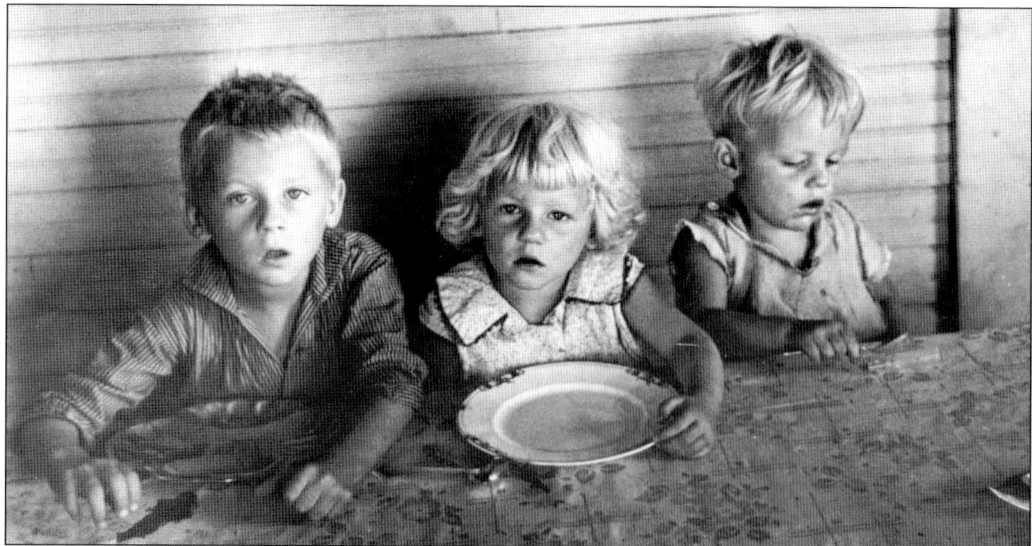

People took pride in their southern hospitality and wanted to show their packhorse librarian gratitude for the visit and books. Even though they did not have enough food for their family, they sacrificed some of their supper for a bookwoman. Librarians had a hard time refusing their gracious gift. (Courtesy of the Library of Congress.)

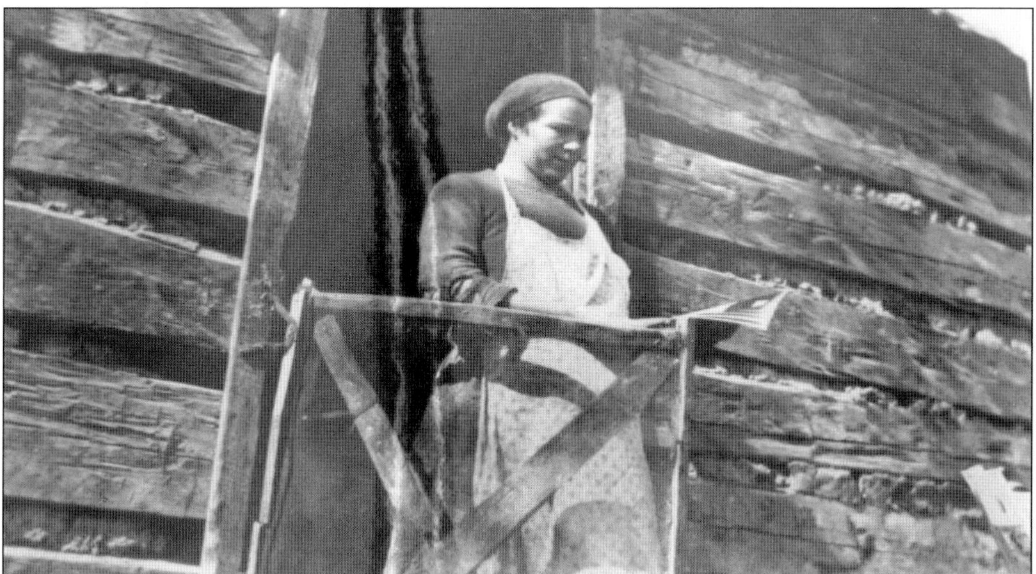

The Packhorse Library Project took donations of all genres to offer to their patrons. However, some patrons did not appreciate all the packhorse librarians had to offer. Some mountain folks were offended by the "taboo" subjects and were turned off by the reading materials and program. (Photograph by Prof. Jason Vance of Middle Tennessee State University; courtesy of the Franklin D. Roosevelt Presidential Library.)

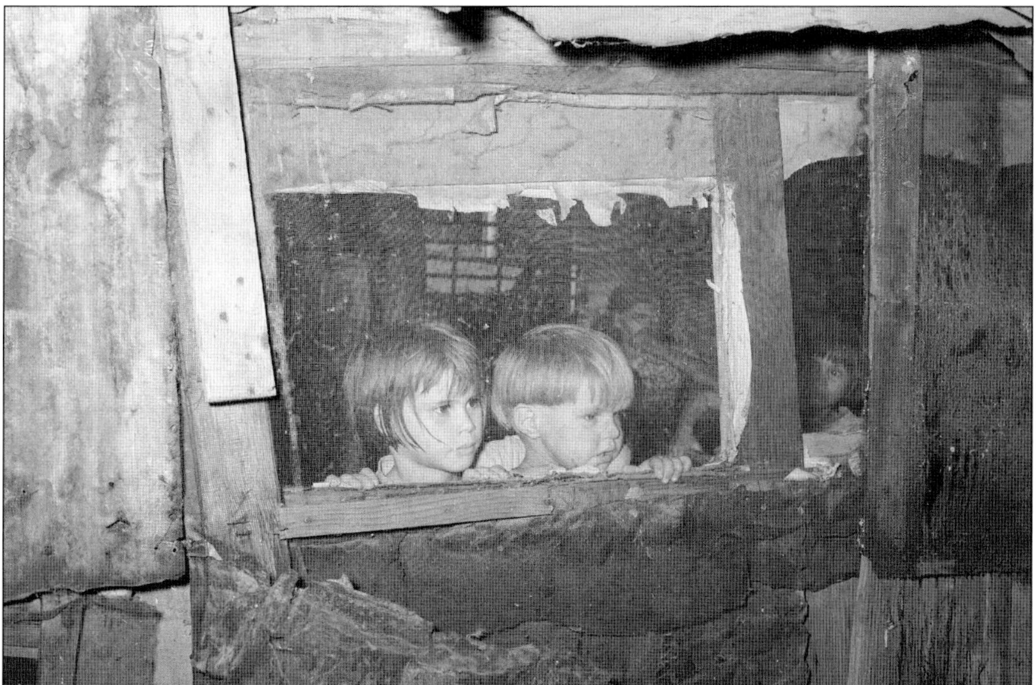

Without the convenience of utilities and appliances during the Great Depression, the list of household jobs seemed endless. When families received a visit from their packhorse librarian, the books beckoned to be read. Children only wanted to sit and read and not complete their chores. Adults found this to be an unwanted distraction. (Courtesy of the Library of Congress.)

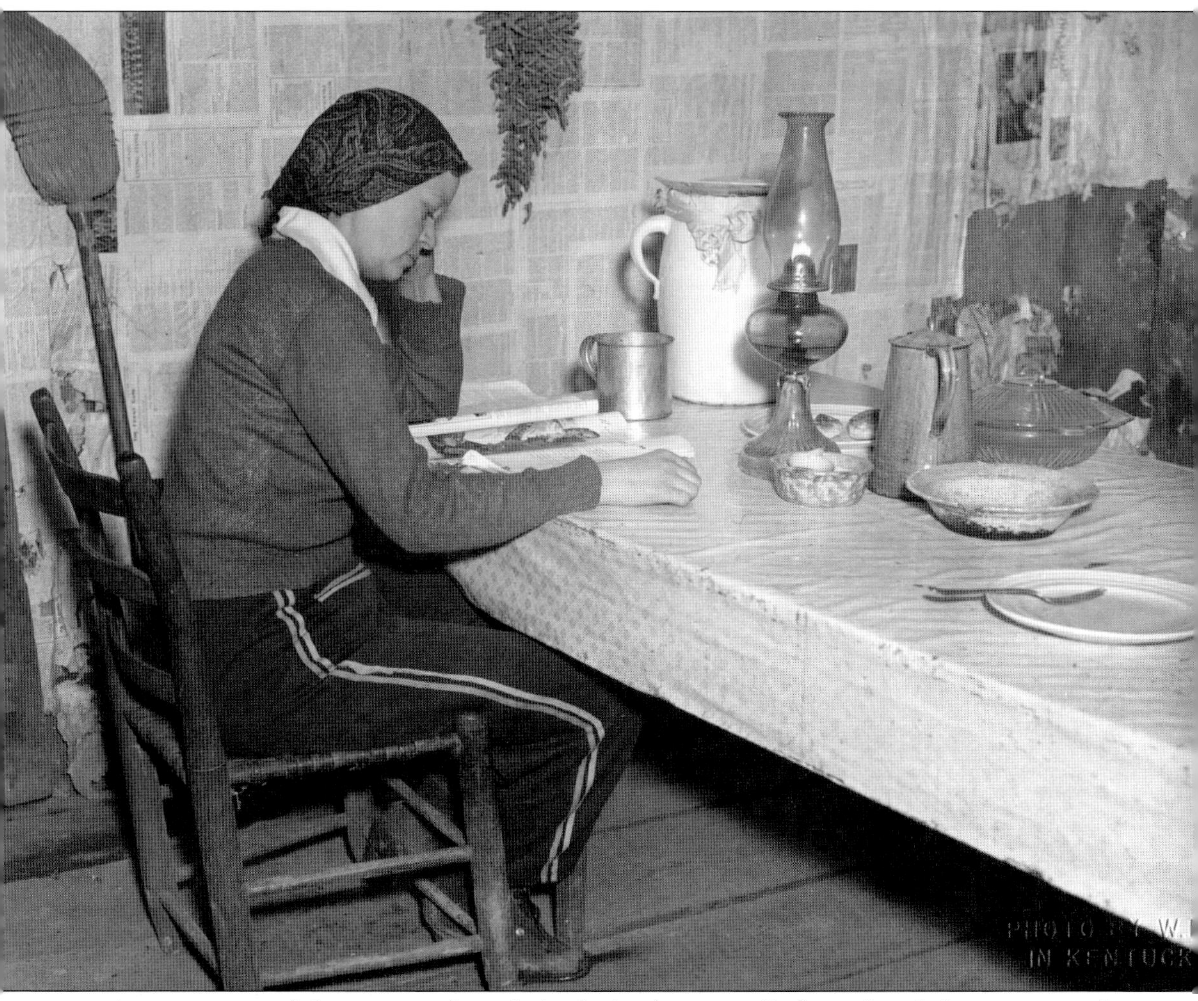

A woman enjoyed the magazine brought by the bookwoman. Daily work and chores were vital to survival, so some folks saved their reading until the evenings. They lit the oil lamp so they could enjoy their book. However, nightly reading habits resulted in needing to buy more lamp oil, and money was hard to come by. (Courtesy of WPA collection, Archives and Records Management Division, Kentucky Department for Libraries and Archives.)

Eight

Routes of Change

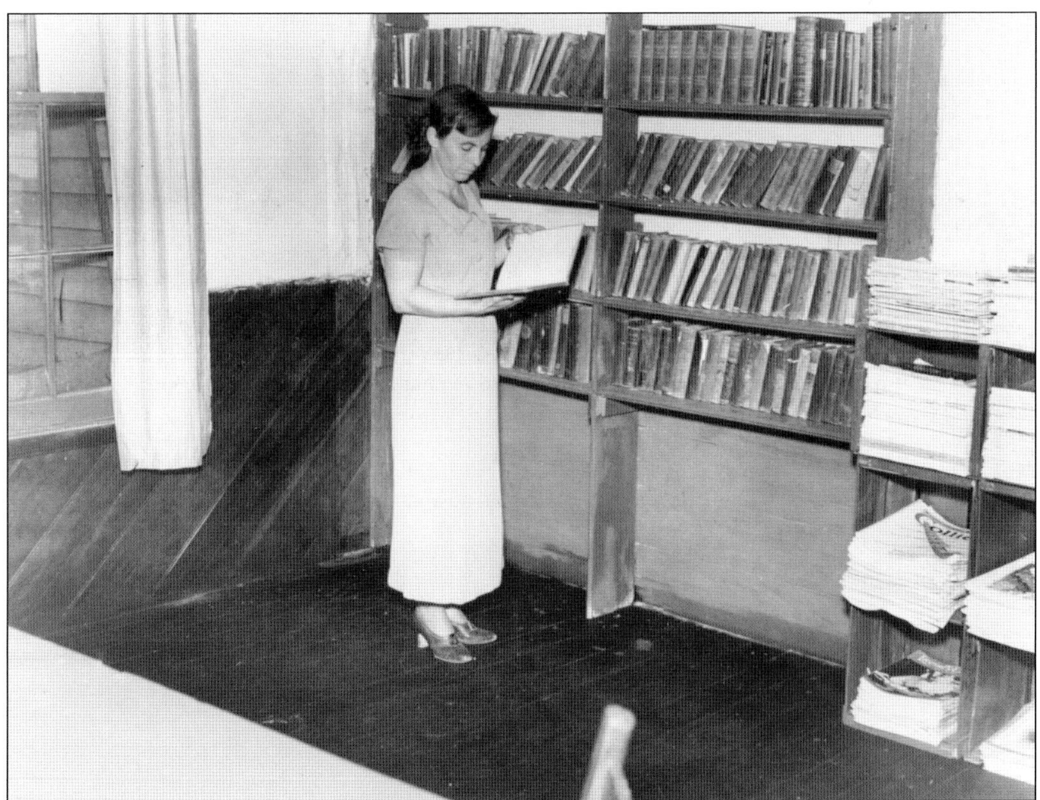

The Packhorse Library Project ended in 1943 when the WPA stopped funding. Projects tapered off when the United States became involved in World War II and a wartime economy was putting Americans back to work and reducing unemployment. (Courtesy of Mallie Cody Turner Collection [MS049-1993], Morehead State University Special Collections and Archives.)

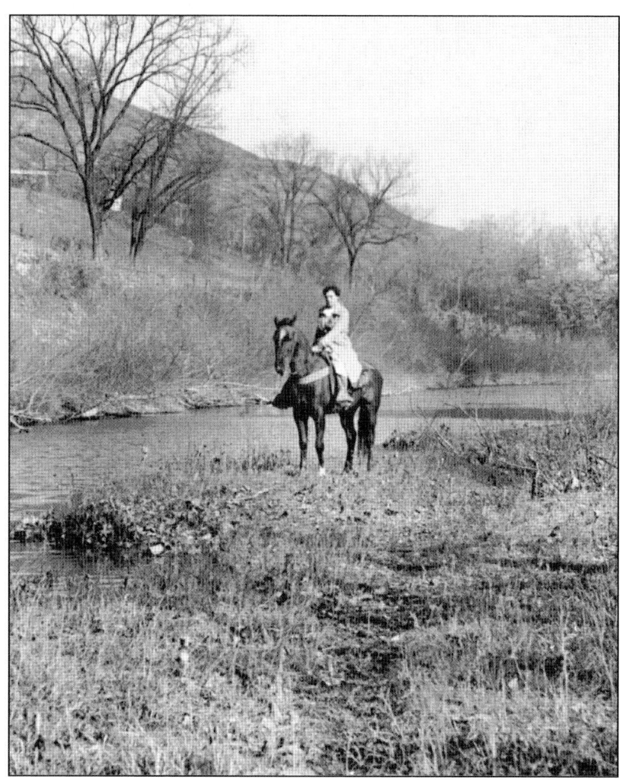

By 1943, nearly 1,000 packhorse librarians had served 105 million patrons in 48 Kentucky counties. During the Great Depression, in which folks stumbled on hard times, the librarians brought hope on horseback for an uncertain future. (Courtesy of Mallie Cody Turner Collection [MS049-1993], Morehead State University Special Collections and Archives.)

After the Packhorse Library Project ended, the packhorse librarians retired from their book routes and looked to new futures themselves. Most returned to their family farms or became schoolteachers. With World War II underway, women on the home front were critical to the war effort as well. (Courtesy of the Library of Congress.)

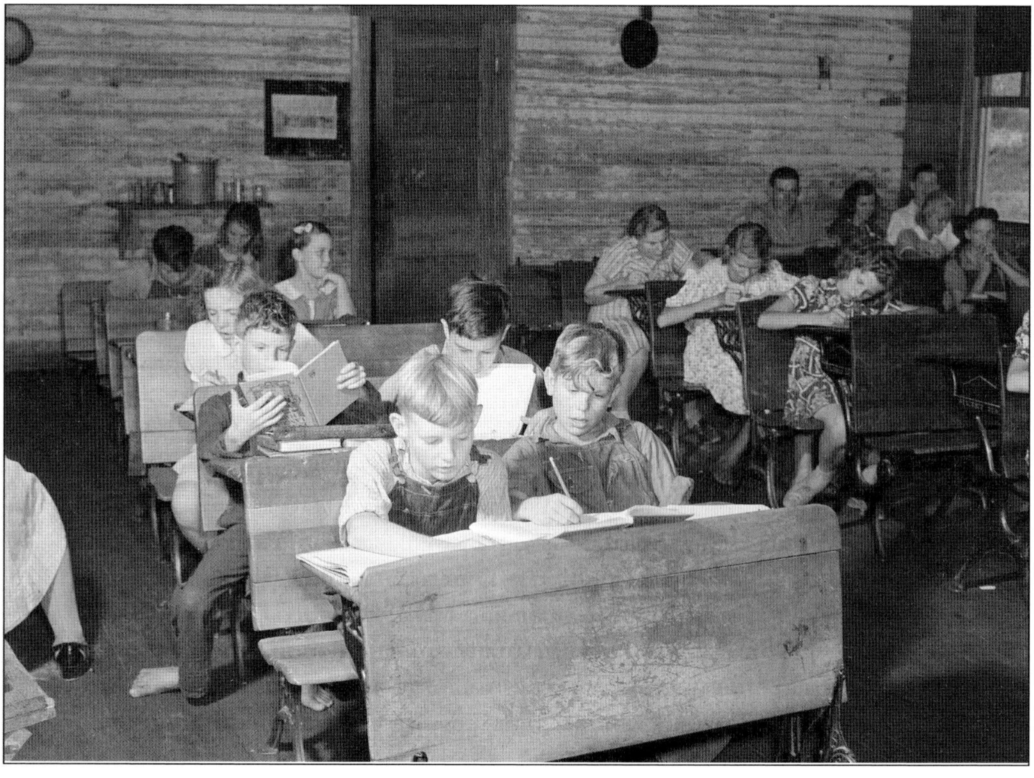

Not until the 1950s did these remote, rural communities have access to bookmobiles. A Kentucky Bookmobile Project newsletter (Issue No. 4) from Louisville, Kentucky, on October 27, 1953, disclosed a progress report. One page shared the needs of farmers (better crops, stocks, houses, recreation, home life, and community living) and how bookmobiles made this possible. (Both, courtesy of Kentucky Bookmobile Project Newsletter, October 27, 1953, in the Bookmobile Project of Friends of Kentucky Libraries [Printed Matter No. 1] vertical file, Louisville Free Public Library Special Collections, Louisville, Kentucky and Libraries, Bookmobile Project of Friends of Kentucky Libraries [Printed Matter No. 2] vertical file, Louisville Free Public Library Special Collections, Louisville, Kentucky.)

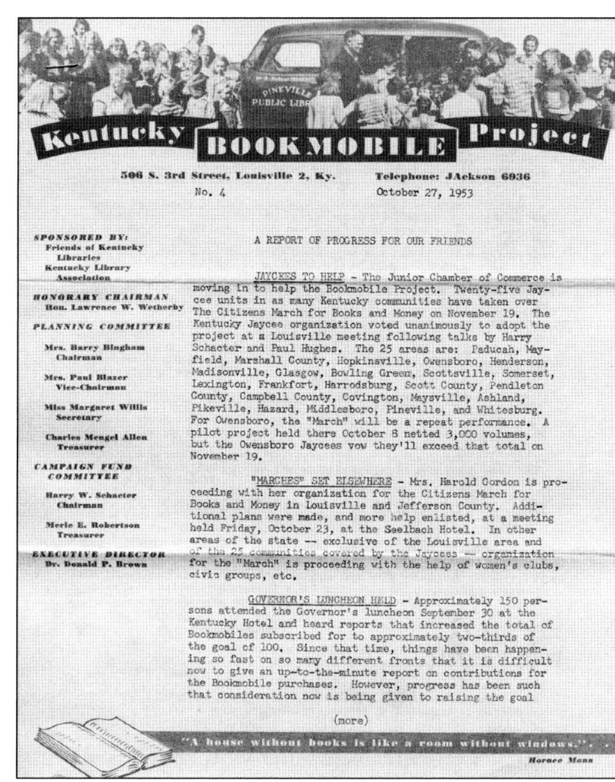

Kentucky BOOKMOBILE Project

506 S. 3rd Street, Louisville 2, Ky. Telephone: JAckson 6936

No. 4 October 27, 1953

SPONSORED BY:
Friends of Kentucky Libraries
Kentucky Library Association

HONORARY CHAIRMAN
Hon. Lawrence W. Wetherby

PLANNING COMMITTEE

Mrs. Barry Bingham
Chairman

Mrs. Paul Blazer
Vice-Chairman

Miss Margaret Willis
Secretary

Charles Mengel Allen
Treasurer

CAMPAIGN FUND COMMITTEE

Harry W. Schacter
Chairman

Merle E. Robertson
Treasurer

EXECUTIVE DIRECTOR
Dr. Donald P. Brown

A REPORT OF PROGRESS FOR OUR FRIENDS

JAYCEES TO HELP - The Junior Chamber of Commerce is moving in to help the Bookmobile Project. Twenty-five Jaycee units in as many Kentucky communities have taken over The Citizens March for Books and Money on November 19. The Kentucky Jaycee organization voted unanimously to adopt the project at a Louisville meeting following talks by Harry Schacter and Paul Hughes. The 25 areas are: Paducah, Mayfield, Marshall County, Hopkinsville, Owensboro, Henderson, Madisonville, Glasgow, Bowling Green, Scottsville, Somerset, Lexington, Frankfort, Harrodsburg, Scott County, Pendleton County, Campbell County, Covington, Maysville, Ashland, Pikeville, Hazard, Middlesboro, Pineville, and Whitesburg. For Owensboro, the "March" will be a repeat performance. A pilot project held there October 8 netted 3,000 volumes, but the Owensboro Jaycees vow they'll exceed that total on November 19.

"MARCHES" SET ELSEWHERE - Mrs. Harold Gordon is proceeding with her organization for the Citizens March for Books and Money in Louisville and Jefferson County. Additional plans were made, and more help enlisted, at a meeting held Friday, October 23, at the Seelbach Hotel. In other areas of the state -- exclusive of the Louisville area and of the 25 communities covered by the Jaycees -- organization for the "March" is proceeding with the help of women's clubs, civic groups, etc.

GOVERNOR'S LUNCHEON HELD - Approximately 150 persons attended the Governor's luncheon September 30 at the Kentucky Hotel and heard reports that increased the total of Bookmobiles subscribed for to approximately two-thirds of the goal of 100. Since that time, things have been happening so fast on so many different fronts that it is difficult now to give an up-to-the-minute report on contributions for the Bookmobile purchases. However, progress has been such that consideration now is being given to raising the goal

(more)

"A house without books is like a room without windows." . .
Horace Mann

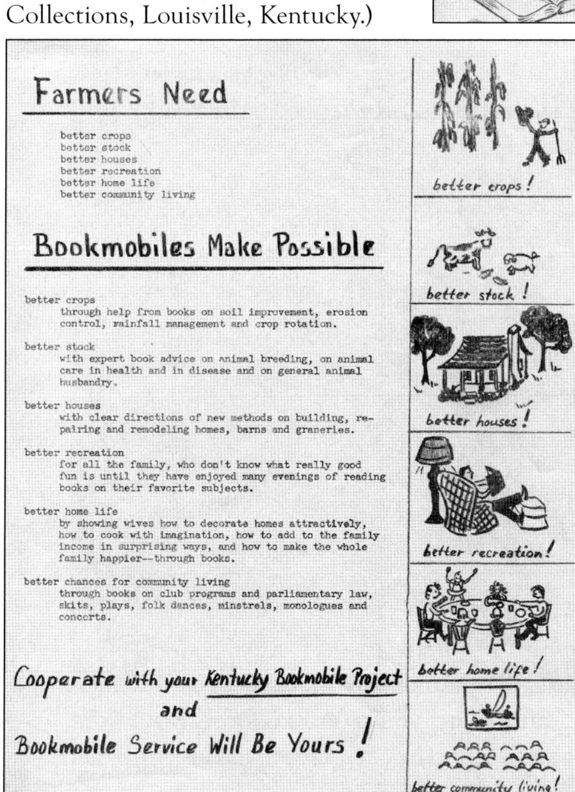

Farmers Need

better crops
better stock
better houses
better recreation
better home life
better community living

Bookmobiles Make Possible

better crops
through help from books on soil improvement, erosion control, rainfall management and crop rotation.

better stock
with expert book advice on animal breeding, on animal care in health and in disease and on general animal husbandry.

better houses
with clear directions of new methods on building, repairing and remodeling homes, barns and graneries.

better recreation
for all the family, who don't know what really good fun is until they have enjoyed many evenings of reading books on their favorite subjects.

better home life
by showing wives how to decorate homes attractively, how to cook with imagination, how to add to the family income in surprising ways, and how to make the whole family happier--through books.

better chances for community living
through books on club programs and parliamentary law, skits, plays, folk dances, minstrels, monologues and concerts.

Cooperate with your Kentucky Bookmobile Project
and
Bookmobile Service Will Be Yours!

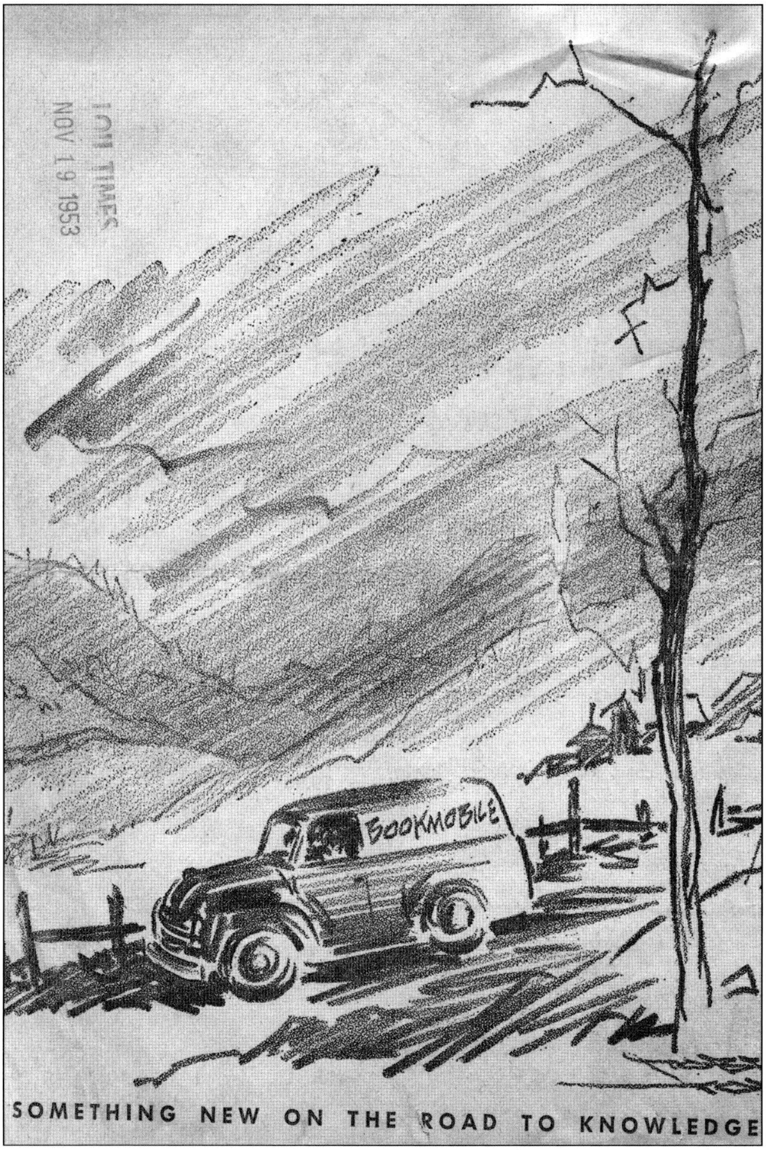

BOOKMOBILE

SOMETHING NEW ON THE ROAD TO KNOWLEDGE

The sketch at left of a Kentucky Bookmobile in the *Louisville Times* newspaper was accompanied by a caption that read, "Something new on the road to knowledge." Below is another sketch of a mobile library bringing books to the Kentucky hills. (Left, courtesy of *Louisville Times*, November 19, 1953, in the Libraries, Bookmobile Project of Friends of Kentucky Libraries, September–December 1953 vertical file, Louisville Free Public Library, Louisville, Kentucky; below, courtesy of Dawkins, O.C. "Books in The Kentucky Hills." *Christian Science Monitor*, November 4, 1953, in the Libraries, Bookmobile Project of Friends of Kentucky Libraries September–December 1953 vertical file, Louisville Free Public Library, Louisville, Kentucky.)

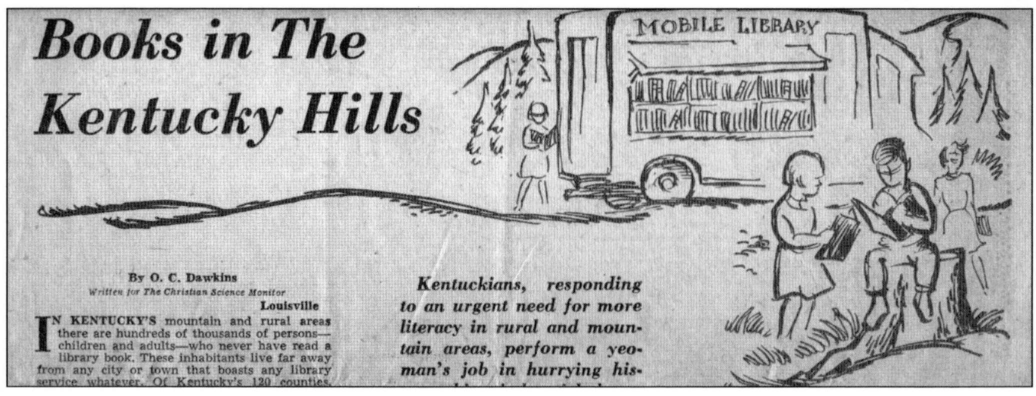

Books in The Kentucky Hills

By O. C. Dawkins
Written for The Christian Science Monitor

Louisville

IN KENTUCKY'S mountain and rural areas there are hundreds of thousands of persons—children and adults—who never have read a library book. These inhabitants live far away from any city or town that boasts any library service whatever. Of Kentucky's 120 counties,

Kentuckians, responding to an urgent need for more literacy in rural and mountain areas, perform a yeoman's job in hurrying his-

Louisville, Kentucky
November 5, 1953

1. I can collect books in the following apartment building November 19. (Mrs. Harold Gordon will contact you if you agree to help.)

Name of Apt.____________________________

Address____________________________

2. I can serve on a committee to cull donated books.

Signed____________________________

Address____________________________

Volunteers were asked to complete the Kentucky Bookmobile volunteer form, dated November 5, 1953, to participate in the program for an apartment collection and to cull donated books. Although not glamorous, volunteer jobs were vital to the bookmobiles running smoothly. (Courtesy of Kentucky Bookmobile Project Newsletter, October 27, 1953, in the Libraries, Bookmobile Project of Friends of Kentucky Libraries [Printed Matter No. 2] vertical file, Louisville Free Public Library, Louisville, Kentucky.)

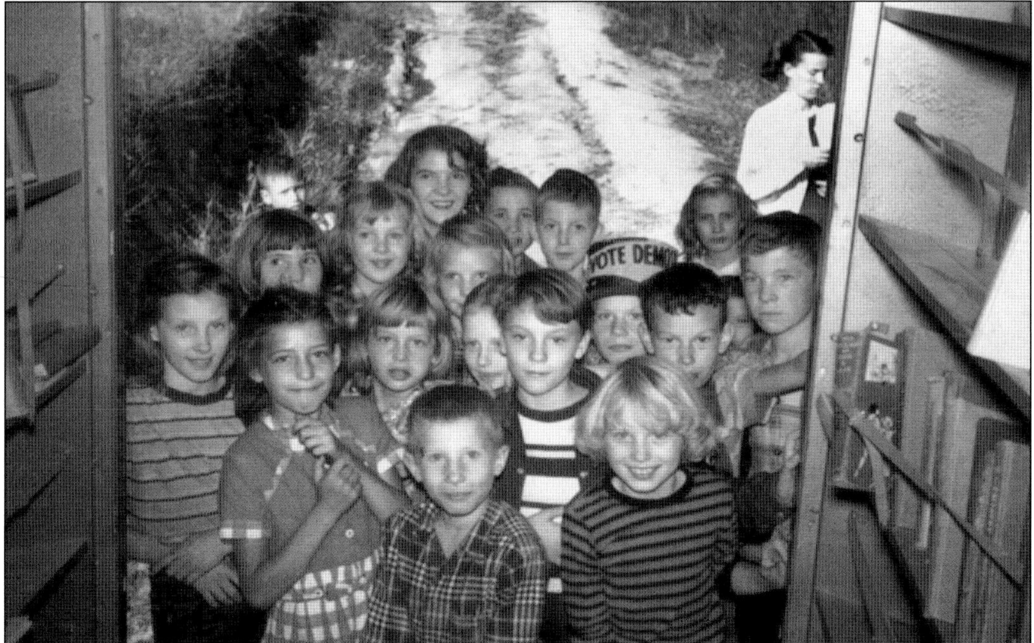

Children peered into the Hindman Settlement School bookmobile eager to check out books. Bookmobiles were a way to connect with patrons outside the physical libraries. Vehicles brought books not only to rural communities, but schools, reservations, and seniors. Bookmobiles helped bring communities together through literacy. (Courtesy of the 1955 Bookmobile Project Collection of the Louisa St. Clair Archive, the Hindman Settlement School.)

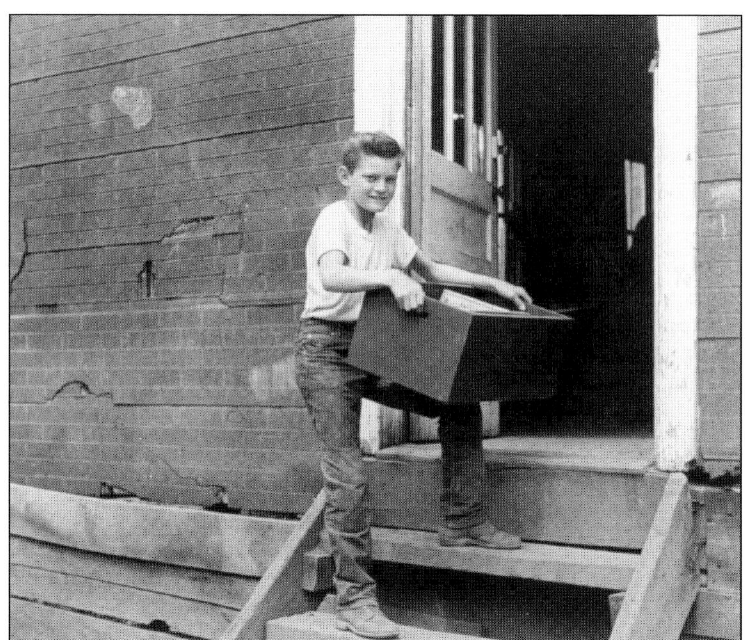

A boy carried a crate full of books inside school in the 1950s. Bookmobiles revived mostly because of the Library Service Act of 1956 and its emphasis on rural library development through federal funding. Prior, public libraries depended on local taxes. The legislation added more than five million reading materials to rural libraries and put 200 new bookmobiles on the road. (Courtesy of Berea College Special Collections and Archives.)

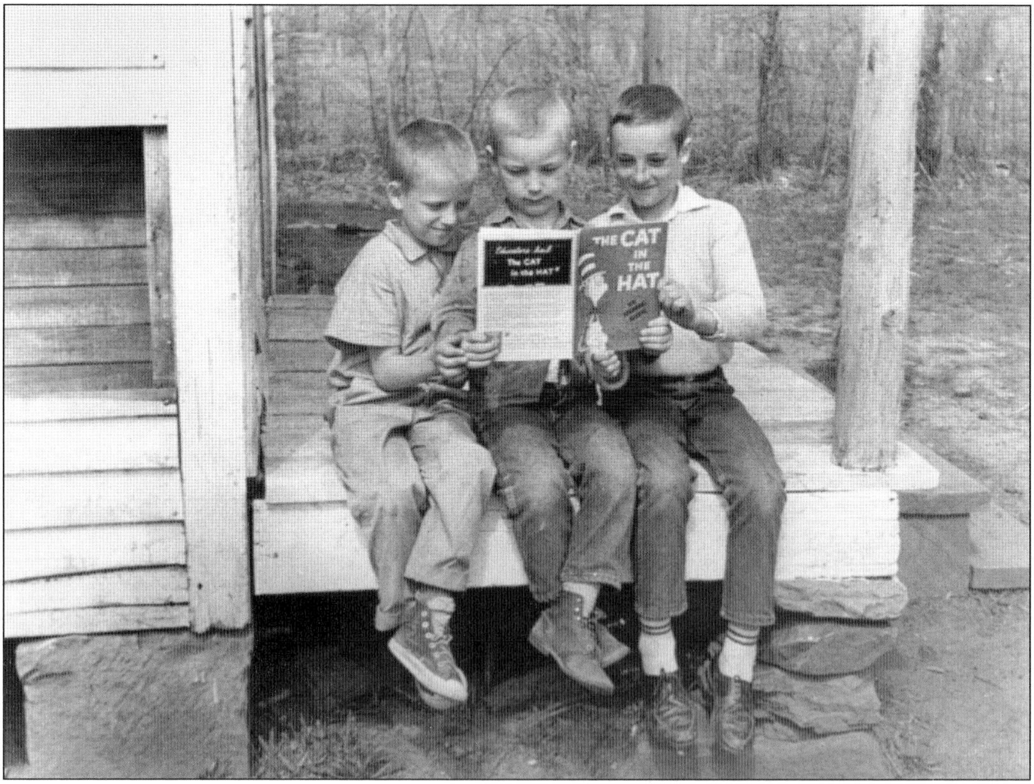

Boys enjoyed *The Cat in the Hat* by Dr. Seuss on a porch in the 1950s. Other children's classics included *Curious George* by H.A. Rey and Margret Rey, *Charlotte's Web* by E.B. White, *Harold and the Purple Crayon* by Crockett Johnson, and *Scruffy the Tugboat* by Gertrude Crampton. (Courtesy of Berea College Special Collections and Archives.)

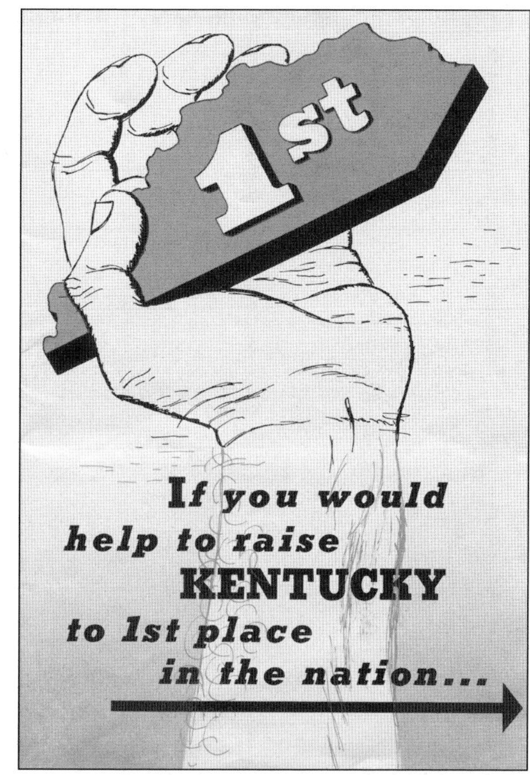

The Kentucky Bookmobile Project newsletter pamphlet cover from the February 1953 issue stated a call to action, "If you would help to raise Kentucky to 1st place in the nation . . . " The solution was through Libraries-On-Wheels Bookmobiles. Bookmobiles were run by librarians and volunteers. (Courtesy of Kentucky Bookmobile Project Newsletter, February 27, 1953, in the Libraries Bookmobile Kentucky Bookmobile Project Information vertical file, Louisville Free Public Library Special Collections, Louisville, Kentucky.)

The Perry County Public Library Bookmobile is committed to making the library collection accessible to their patrons. Residents of Perry County, Kentucky, can be added to the book route by contacting the bookmobile librarian. Many counties in the state provide this service. In 2014, Kentucky public libraries had 75 bookmobiles, which was the largest in the nation. (Courtesy of the Library of Congress.)

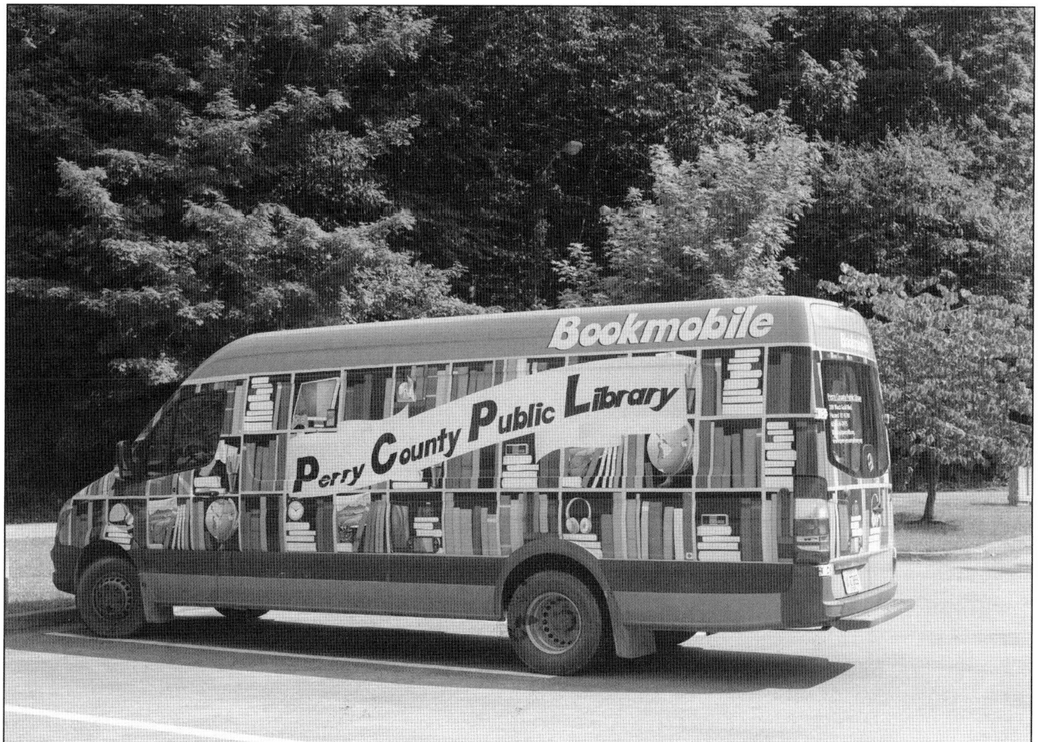

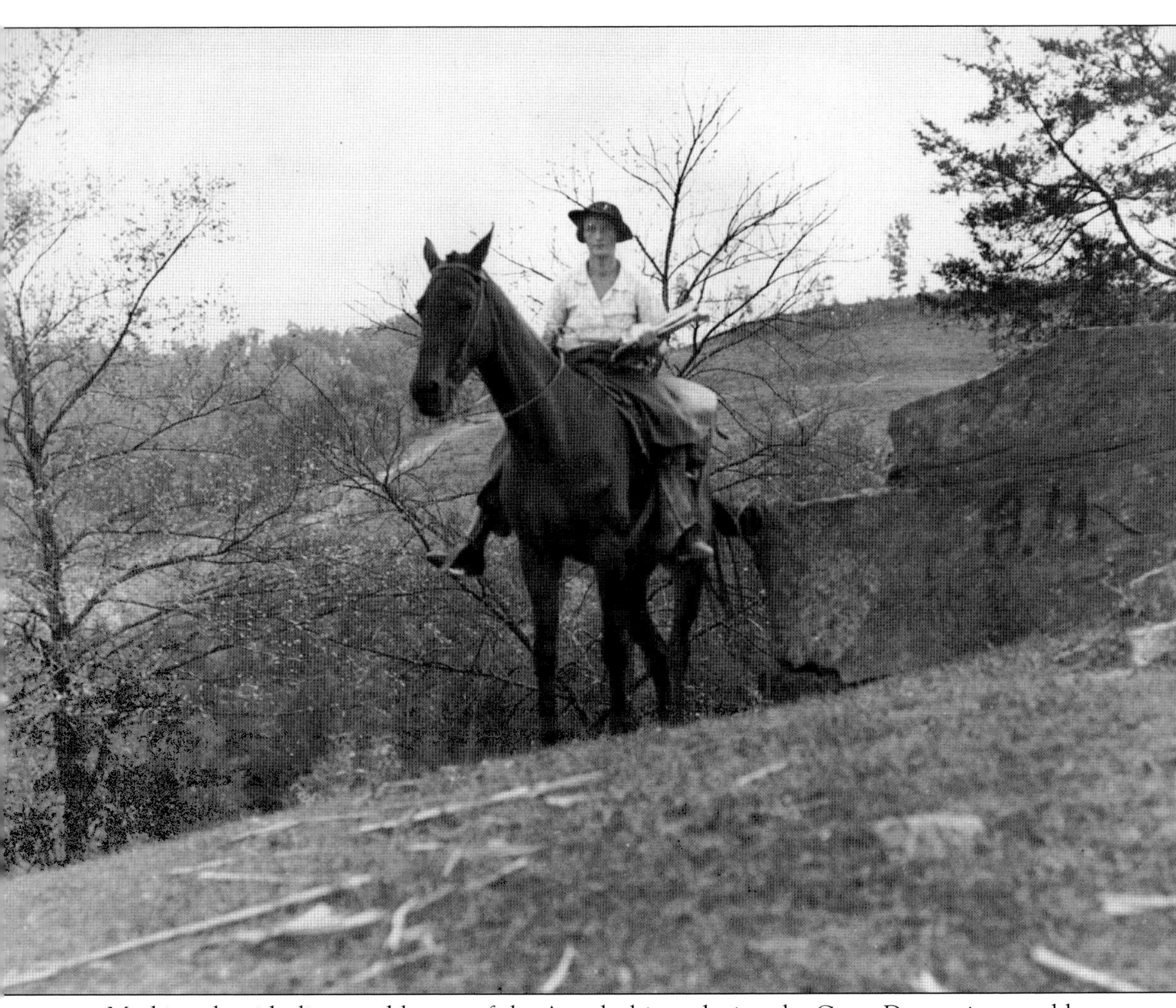

Marking the ridgelines and hearts of the Appalachians during the Great Depression, packhorse librarians delivered hope, one book at a time. The books librarians shared were then and still are windows to the world, giving promise of a brighter future. (Courtesy of WPA collection, Archives and Records Management Division, Kentucky Department for Libraries and Archives.)

Bibliography

Appelt, Kathi, and Jeanne Cannella Schmitzer. *Down Cut Shin Creek.* New York, NY: HarperCollins, 2001.

Archives and Records Management Division. WPA collection. Photograph Caption 005, RG1670. Frankfort, KY: Kentucky Department for Libraries and Archives, 1936–1938.

Bickel, Thomas. *The Pack Horse Librarians of Appalachia.* Lexington, KY: The Kentucky Network, KET, 2022.

Boyd, Donald C. "The Book Women of Kentucky: The WPA Pack Horse Library Project, 1936–1943." *Libraries & the Cultural Record*, Vol. 42, No. 2. 2007: 111–128.

Burgan, Michael. *The Great Depression.* Minneapolis, MN: Compass Point Books, 2002.

Burgess, Anika. "The Women Who Rode Miles on Horseback to Deliver Library Books." *Atlas Obscura.* August 31, 2017.

Maynard, Charles W. *The Appalachians.* New York, NY: Powerkids Press, 2004.

McGraw, Eliza. "Horse-Riding Librarians Were the Great Depression's Bookmobiles." *Smithsonian Magazine.* June 21, 2017.

Mullenbach, Cheryl. *The Great Depression for Kids.* Chicago, IL: Chicago Review Press, 2015.

Ruth, Amy. *Growing Up in the Great Depression.* Minneapolis, MN: Lerner Publishing Company, 2003.

Stoddart, Jess. *Challenge and Change in Appalachia: The Story of Hindman Settlement School.* Lexington, KY: University Press of Kentucky, 2009.

Taylor, Nicki. *American-Made: The Enduring Legacy of the WPA: When FDR Put the Nation to Work.* New York, NY: Bantam Books, Random House, 2008.

Vance, Jason. "Librarians as Authors, Editors, and Self-Publishers: The Information Culture of the Kentucky Pack Horse Library Scrapbooks (1936–1943)." *Library and Information History,* Vol. 28, No. 4. 2012: 289–308.